THE MUSLIM RESOLUTIONS:
BOSNIAK RESPONSES TO WORLD WAR TWO
ATROCITIES IN BOSNIA AND HERZEGOVINA

Publishers:
Center for Islam in the Contemporary World at Shenandoah University
www.contemporaryislam.org
Institute for Islamic Tradition of Bosniaks
www.iitb.ba

Editors:
Hikmet Karčić
Ferid Dautović
Ermin Sinanović

Principal Researcher:
Hikmet Karčić

Researcher:
Emrah Đozić

Translations:
Desmond Maurer
Hikmet Karčić

Copyeditor:
Hikmet Karčić

DTP & Print:
Dobra Knjiga

ISBN:
978-1-955653-01-5

THE MUSLIM RESOLUTIONS: BOSNIAK RESPONSES TO WORLD WAR TWO ATROCITIES IN BOSNIA AND HERZEGOVINA

Edited by

Hikmet Karčić
Ferid Dautović
Ermin Sinanović

Sarajevo / Virginia, 2021

TABLE OF CONTENTS

PREFACE   7

Hikmet Karčić
THE MUSLIM RESOLUTIONS: A NOTE ON
SCHOLARLY INTEREST AND THE ARCHIVES   11

Ferid Dautović
THE BOSNIAK ELITES AS SIGNATORIES
OF THE MUSLIM RESOLUTIONS   19

Ermin Sinanović
STANDING UP FOR JUSTICE
IN THE MUSLIM TRADITION   25

Desmond Maurer
ON READING THE MUSLIM RESOLUTIONS   31

Adnan Jahić
THE MUSLIM RESOLUTIONS OF 1941 EIGHTY YEARS ON   63

Safet Bandžović
THE 1941 MUSLIM RESOLUTIONS AND THEIR ECHO   103

Xavier Bougarel
THE MUSLIM RESOLUTIONS OF 1941:
BETWEEN MORAL COURAGE
AND POLITICAL IMPOTENCE   133

Marko Attila Hoare
MUSLIM BOSNIAK RESISTANCE TO THE USTAŠAS
AND THE MUSLIM RESOLUTIONS OF 1941   139

THE MUSLIM RESOLUTIONS	149
EL-HIDAJE RESOLUTION	151
PRIJEDOR RESOLUTION	155
SARAJEVO RESOLUTION	165
MOSTAR RESOLUTION	179
BANJA LUKA RESOLUTION	183
BIJELJINA RESOLUTION	195
TUZLA RESOLUTION	201
ZENICA RESOLUTION	205
BOSANSKA DUBICA RESOLUTION	211
BUGOJNO RESOLUTION	215
CONTRIBUTORS	219
INDEX	221

PREFACE

The current year of 2021 has seen the 80th anniversary of the start of World War Two in Yugoslavia.

On April 6, 1941, the Axis powers attacked Yugoslavia, bombing all the major towns. Within days, the Yugoslav army had surrendered, and Yugoslavia was officially under occupation.

Serbia was ruled by a puppet government under German occupation. In Croatia, the Ustašas had established a puppet state called "The Independent State of Croatia" (*Nezavisna država Hrvatska* or NDH), led by Ante Pavelić, the *Poglavnik*.

In the NDH, the Ustašas introduced Nazi-style laws against Serbs, Jews, and Roma and established concentration camps, where they incarcerated and murdered members of those peoples. The most infamous of them was Jasenovac. The Ustašas had considerable autonomy and were brutal in their genocidal campaign, the aim of which was to exterminate those considered racially inferior.

Bosniaks (then referred to as Muslims) found themselves between a rock and a hard place. Without proper political representation or institutions, they were split as a nation on all sides. Some joined the Independent State of Croatia, others sided with the Serb royalists (Četniks), and yet others made nice with Nazi Germany, hoping for greater autonomy for Bosnia in return. In reality, large parts of the Bosniak population remained vulnerable and unprotected, subjected to persecution and murder, mainly by the Četniks, who massacred thousands in Eastern Bosnia and in the Sandžak region of Serbia and Montenegro.

While the Ustaša regime did not target Bosniaks (whom they considered to be Croats of Muslim faith) *en masse*, many members of their elites disagreed with the new regime's policies. The persecution of Serbs, Jews, and Roma provoked public condemnation of these crimes.

Under-represented, unprotected, and generally labeled enemies or collaborators, the Bosniak elites were pragmatic in their condemnation of the regime's policies: using it as an opportunity for seeking Bosnia's autonomy, hoping in this way to improve the country's position and the security of their people.

They did so through the resolutions included in this book, which were initiated and signed by members of the Bosniak establishment, which is to say of the clergy and the judicial and economic elites, who sought to distance themselves from the Ustaša regime. In fact, most of the people to actually sign these resolutions were members of *El-Hidaje,* the Association of Muslim Clergy, and so imams.

Reading the resolutions today, it is easy to be critical and downplay their importance. The terminology used and the consistency of certain signatories can be challenged, with some justification. Alliances, loyalties, and even received ideologies shifted often.

The resolutions nonetheless played a large role, not only during the war, but in the post-war era too, as the struggle for Muslim identity and nationhood got underway. They are one of the few cases in the region, perhaps the only, of such atrocities being condemned and criticized by the elite of a "people without a state."

In recent years, interest in the Muslim Resolutions has grown. In 2019, the Bosniak intellectuals Enes Karić and Mustafa Spahić edited a Bosnian-language volume entitled *Nasuprot zlo: Muslimanske rezolucije iz 1941.; Zajednička izjava iz 2015.* (Sarajevo: El-Kalem, 2019), which translates as *Against Evil: The Muslim Resolutions of 1941; A Joint Statement from 2015.* It contained the full texts of the resolutions, along with a number of articles on their importance.

In October, 2021, the Bosniak Institute-Adil Zulfikarpašić Foundation in Sarajevo will hold an international conference to mark the 80th anniversary of the Sarajevo Resolution, entitled *Time and Memory: The Resolutions of the Muslims (1941),* to explore their significance.

Given this growing interest and in recognition of their importance, this publication presents the phenomenon of the Muslim Resolutions to an English-speaking audience. It consists of unredacted translations of the El-Hidaje Resolution and the subsequent resolutions from Prijedor, Sarajevo, Mostar, Banja Luka, Bijeljina, Tuzla, Zenica, Bosanska Dubica, and Bugojno. The final two are in fact newly discovered resolutions and their texts are presented here for the first time. This indicates that archival research in future may well uncover more such examples.

To provide historical context, we have also included articles by leading historians of the topic – Adnan Jahić, Safet Bandžović, Xavier Bougarel, and Marko Attila Hoare. These authors do not necessarily share the same view of these resolutions, and their texts are offered here to promote discussion as to their significance and meaning. Of these, the articles by Bandžović and Jahić were published previously in Bosnian and translated for this volume, while the other two essays, like the other texts included, were commissioned for this volume and written in English.

Given the historical importance of these documents and discrepancies in existing published versions of the texts, the editors have made every effort to locate the originals or faithful transcripts for inclusion in this publication. It is important to note that not all the resolutions are available to us as originals, as most survive only as copies or transcripts, generally those made either by the Ustaša authorities or by the post-war Communist authorities or rather by their *Commission to Investigate the Crimes of the Occupier and the Collaborators*. These copies were not always made with care and some do not include lists of signatories or note to whom the resolutions were addressed. We have selected what seemed to us the most complete and reliable examplars.

Finding documentation on the Muslim Resolutions has been a challenge, especially since research was conducted during the COVID-19 pandemic lockdowns. We would like to thank the staff at the Gazi Husrev-bey Library, Bosniak Institute, Historical Archives of Sarajevo, Historical Museum of Bosnia and Herzegovina, and the Croatian State Archives for their help. We are thankful to Xavier Bougarel who kindly shared his archival documents. Finally, we would like to thank the Center for Islam in the Contemporary World (CICW) at Shenandoah University for financially supporting this important project.

The Editors

Hikmet Karčić

THE MUSLIM RESOLUTIONS: A NOTE ON SCHOLARLY INTEREST AND THE ARCHIVES

When researching significant historical events, it is usual to check the authenticity of the documents and reliability of the informants, especially when there appear to be discrepancies. The Muslim Resolutions are just such an interesting and specific historical datum and one that still requires in-depth research. Since 2000, they have increasingly been the object of mainstream interest in Bosnia and Herzegovina, as well as attracting at least brief mention from a handful of foreign scholars. The aim of this publication is to present this phenomenon to a wider audience, but research on the project started in early 2020, at the height of the COVID-19 pandemic, and has proven more complex than initially anticipated, not least because there appear to be multiple versions of at least some of the resolutions.

One important feature of some of the versions of the Muslim Resolutions published or put into circulation is that they contain textual interventions. This is particularly true of the Prijedor and the Sarajevo Resolutions, whose wording has in some sections been changed and elements omitted, including entire sentences and even paragraphs. There have also been interventions in the list of signatories. While it would be tedious and of limited usefulness to detail all the interventions here, it is worth pointing out that in general they date back to 1950, when the first integral texts were published. During the Communist era, parts of the resolutions that either were or could be interpreted as anti-Communist were omitted or changed, while signatories who were considered *personae non gratae* after 1945 were erased from the lists. This and authorial and editorial negligence in the years that followed gave rise to a certain degree of confusion, as the initial integral texts were reproduced and changed without consulting the archival originals.

In this publication, we have therefore gone back to the original documents, gathered from the archives or the authors themselves (or their heirs), to make our translations directly from them. We are also providing this brief review to assist research and provide insight into the resolutions and their significance.

The first mention of the resolutions appears to be in the first post-war issue of the official *Glasnik Vrhovnog islamskog starješinstva u Federativnoj narodnoj republici Jugoslaviji [Gazette of the Supreme Islamic Authority in the Federative People's Republic of Yugoslavia]* in 1950. It includes a number of articles and sermons that refer to the resolutions, among them a short piece by Murad Šečeragić, deputy Reisu-l-ulema, in which he states:[1]

> As the persecution of Serbs in Bosnia and Herzegovina reached its peak, Muslims in many towns found themselves stirred to issue resolutions and call urgently for an end to the killing and abuse of Serbs. In this case, brotherly love prevailed in the face of the threat entailed by an intervention like the resolution.

Mustafa Sahačić, imam at the Ali-Pasha mosque in Sarajevo, also mentioned the Resolutions in his sermon:[2]

> Given their religious beliefs, Muslims have always sided with the oppressed and the unprotected. During the occupation, Muslims took a strong, risky, public stand against the massacre of innocent Serbs and Jews. The Sarajevo, Mostar, Banja Luka, and the other Muslim Resolutions made during the occupation are the best evidence of this honorable stand.

---

1 Murad Šečeragić, "Bratstvo i jedinstvo jugoslovenskih naroda," *Glasnik Vrhovnog islamskog starješinstva u Federativnoj narodnoj republici Jugoslaviji*, Sarajevo, 1950, 12.

2 Mustafa Sahačić, "Primjer savremene hutbe," *Glasnik Vrhovnog islamskog starješinstva u Federativnoj narodnoj republici Jugoslaviji*, Sarajevo, 1951, 125.

In his response to Viktor Novak's 1948 book *Magnum Crimen*, in which the latter had criticized the Muslim clergy, Husein Brkić wrote:[3]

> It is true that the Muslim masses, because of their low level of political consciousness, fallacies their political leadership had fostered, and injustices they had suffered, tragically failed to understand the nature of the occupation fully. As a result, when the fascist rampage began, they were stunned. Their primal aversion to injustice and violence alarmed their conscience. This helped them start to break free from the framework of feudal-bourgeois political calculus. As a result, the Ustašas' efforts to win them over to their policies, through blandishments, minor concessions, and false vistas, enjoyed little success.

An integral text of the Banja Luka Resolution was published in the *Gazette* in 1950, with a short unsigned commentary that noted that the resolution:[4]

> [...] speaks to the true disposition of the vast majority of Muslims, not only with regard to these unspeakable atrocities and the so-called NDH, but also the occupier, under whose auspices and initiative the crimes and fratricidal massacres were committed. We are not aware of a similar, let alone more forceful public protest made by enslaved citizens under occupation anywhere in Europe.

The text also provides some detail regarding the fate of the signatories:[5]

> [...] some of the signatories of these resolutions confirmed their revolutionary position later by participating personally in the Popular Liberation Struggle, whether directly or through illegal work, while others were deported to the infamous Ustaša camps of Jasenovac, Gradiška, and so on, where some were killed or slaughtered. The resolutions gave Muslims cause to reflect on the events of the time, orient themselves

---

3   Husein Brkić, "Ispravka jednog dokumenta u knjizi „Magnum Crimen" od V. Novaka," *Glasnik Vrhovnog islamskog starješinstva u Federativnoj narodnoj republici Jugoslaviji*, Sarajevo, 1951, 127.

4   NN, "Stav Banjalučkih muslimana u 1941. godini," *Glasnik Vrhovnog islamskog starješinstva u Federativnoj narodnoj republici Jugoslaviji*, Sarajevo, 1950, 335-338.

5   Ibid.

properly, and respond to the call of the leadership of the Popular Liberation Movement and the Communist Party to join the movement *en masse* and fight for its goals.

The text of the Sarajevo Resolution was published in 1951 with an interesting commentary by Šukrija Kurtović. Kurtović's reflections provide some context and justification for its wording:[6]

> The resolution of the Sarajevo Muslims is not as urgent in tone or explanation as the resolutions of the people of Mostar and Banja Luka, but it is very similar in content and in its demands and similarly condemns the criminal acts of the Ustaša authorities overall. To understand it, we must go back in spirit to that terrible time and consider the situation that then prevailed in Sarajevo.

He then attempts to explain why the resolution was not more concretely worded: "it is dangerous to call for religious tolerance and equality for all citizens when the 'state' itself is obviously pursuing and implementing a totally different policy."[7]

In 1955, *Bosanski pogledi*, an émigré publication, produced by Bosniak businessman and former partisan Adil Zulfikarpašić, published the texts of the Sarajevo, Banja Luka, and Mostar Resolutions, along with a brief commentary, in its first issue, which was edited by the well-known Bosniak intellectual Smail Balić.[8] Reviewing these texts, however, makes clear that Balić had simply reprinted the resolutions from the *Gazette* a few years earlier.[9]

The first public academic presentation of the resolutions would take place only some two decades later, when the historian Muhamed Hadžijahić published his academic article on them.[10] The late 1960s were a time of

---

6   Šukrija Kurtović, "Stav sarajevskih muslimana 1941 godine," *Glasnik Vrhovnog islamskog starješinstva u Federativnoj narodnoj republici Jugoslaviji,* Sarajevo, januar-mart, 1951, 23.
7   Ibid.
8   *Bosanski pogledi*, London: 1984, 509-516. In 1984, Adil Zulfikarpašić's Bosniak Institute published a reprint of *Bosanski pogledi*.
9   No reference was made to the *Gazette*.
10 Muhamed Hadžijahić, "Muslimanske rezolucije iz 1941 godine," *Istorija Naroda Bosne i Hercegovine,* Sarajevo: Institut za istoriju radničkog pokreta, (1973), 274–282.

attempts to affirm the Muslims as a nation, spearheaded by Bosnian Muslim Communists. The Muslim Resolutions were used as proof of positive examples and of *revolutionary* activities that it was hoped would strengthen the argument for recognizing Muslim nationhood. Hadžijahić's work remains the most common reference cited.

Three important recent publications to shed light on the resolutions are Nada Kisić Kolanović's *Muslimani i hrvatski nacionalizam 1941.-1945.* (Hrvatski institut za povijest, 2009), Safet Bandžović's *Bošnjaci i antifašizam. Ratni realizam i odjek rezolucija građanske hrabrosti (1941.)* (Sarajevo, 2010), and *Nasuprot zlu: Muslimanske rezolucije iz 1941. – Zajednička izjava iz 2015*, an edition of the resolutions and volume of essays edited by Enes Karić and Mustafa Spahić (El-Kalem, 2019). A critique of these works and the resolutions appeared in 2021 as online articles by Tarik Haverić.[11]

Publications by foreign scholars that have dealt with the resolutions include Marko A. Hoare's *The Bosnian Muslims in the Second World War: A History* (Oxford University Press, 2014), Emily Greble's *Sarajevo, 1941-1945: Muslims, Christians, and Jews in Hitler's Europe* (Cornell University Press, 2011), and David Motadel's *Islam and Nazi Germany's War* (Harvard University Press, 2014).

The goal of the present project is to present the Muslim Resolutions to a wider public, through English translations and by placing them in their historical context, alongside a range of contemporary interpretations. This publication therefore contains the texts of ten Muslim Resolutions, namely the El-Hidaje, Prijedor, Sarajevo, Mostar, Banja Luka, Bijeljina, Tuzla, Zenica, Bosanska Dubica and Bugojno resolutions. The last two are newly discovered and published here for the first time. The El-Hidaje Resolution was the first one issued and is often confused with the Sarajevo Resolution, which was issued just a few months later. The original of the Prijedor Resolution is archived at the Historical Museum in Sarajevo, while there are

---

11 Tarik Haverić, "Muslimanski rezolucionari," https://tarikhaveric.com/muslimanski-rezolucionari-i/. These three articles are part of a publication announced for the end of 2021: *Bošnjaštvo kao promašen projekt. Kako suditi (o) povijesti,* which translates as *The Failed Project of Bosniak National Identity. Judging History.*

early typed copies in the Gazi Husrev-bey Library and the Bosniak Institute, both in Sarajevo.[12] The Sarajevo Resolution, with the original signatures, is in the Gazi Husrev-bey Library.[13] The Mostar Resolution is at the Archive of Bosnia and Herzegovina.[14] Early typed copies of the Banja Luka Resolution are at the Gazi Husrev-bey Library and the Bosniak Institute.[15] There is apparently another original copy at the Military Archive in Serbia, which the editors have not seen.[16] There is an early typed copy of the Bijeljina Resolution at the Historical Museum in Sarajevo and a photocopy of an original Ustaša document at the Bosniak Institute.[17] The Tuzla Resolution is at the Historical Museum in Sarajevo, with a German translation in the Military Archive of Serbia.[18] The Zenica Resolution is at the Gazi Husrev-bey Library.[19] The Bosanska Dubica Resolution is at the Croatian

---

12 Historical Museum of Bosnia and Herzegovina (HMBiH Collection UNS, box 1, doc. 130/3.); Gazi Husrev-Bey Library, Archives of the Islamic Community of Bosnia and Herzegovina (GHB, ZRDA, A-810/B. ONS); Archive of the Bosniak Institute, (Drugi svjetski rat, DSR 3/VIII-2).

13 Gazi Husrev-Bey Library, Archives of the Islamic Community of Bosnia and Herzegovina (GHB, ARIZBIH, A-318/B (A-3200/TO)).

14 Archive of Bosnia and Herzegovina (ABiH, *Zemaljska komisija za utvrđivanje zločina okupatora i njihovih pomagača Sarajevo* (henceforth: ZKURZ), *Referati*, kut. 7, 82. *Rezolucija muslimana grada Mostara.*); Gazi Husrev-Bey Library, Archives of the Islamic Community of Bosnia and Herzegovina (GHB, ZRDA, A-810/B. ONS); Archive of the Bosniak Institute, (Drugi svjetski rat, DSR 3/VIII-2).

15 These documents were kindly provided by Ahmed Zulfikarpašić. Archive of Bosnia and Herzegovina (ABIH, fond Zemaljska komisija za utvrđivanje ratnih zločina okupatora i njihovih pomagača, Referati, kutija 7.); Gazi Husrev-Bey Library, Archives of the Islamic Community of Bosnia and Herzegovina (GHB, ZRDA, A-810/B. ONS, *II knjiga. Banjalučka rezolucija od 12. studenog 1941.*); Archive of the Bosniak Institute, Drugi svjetski rat (DSR 3/VIII-2).

16 We were not able to get a response from the Archive.

17 Archive of the Bosniak Institute, Drugi svjetski rat (DSR 3/VIII-2); Historical Museum in Sarajevo (HMBiH, UNS, Box 1, Document 134). Xavier Bougarel and Ahmet Zulfikarpašić provided these documents.

18 Historical Museum of Bosnia and Herzegovina (HMBiH, UNS, Box 1, Document 177); Military Archives of Serbia (Arhiv oruzanih snaga Srbije, fond Reich, kutija 40 G, fascikl 3, dokument 25). Xavier Bougarel provided these documents.

19 Gazi Husrev-Bey Library, Archives of the Islamic Community of Bosnia and Herzegovina (GHB, ARIZBIH, UM, 1745/42)

State Archives.[20] Finally, the Bugojno Resolution is at the Gazi Husrev-bey Library.[21]

The existence of a Višegrad Resolution was discussed by Samir Beglerović in an article from 2016.[22] Beglerović based his research on two documents located at the Gazi Husrev-bey Library. These two documents from the 1970s are statements by Vejsil Kadić, a former judge from Višegrad, and Abdulah Ploskić, a former official in Višegrad, which refer to the existence of a Višegrad Resolution that condemned Ustaša atrocities. Unfortunately, when a copy of the Resolution did subsequently come to light, it was found that its contents did not match Kadić and Ploskić's statements and it has therefore not been included in this publication.[23]

This research project makes clear that the Muslim Resolutions played a considerable role not just during the Second World War but in the post-war period too. Discovery of the Bugojno Resolution, which calls explicitly for the protection of "White Roma", shows that local archives have not yielded up all their treasures. It is not impossible that there are still resolutions from other towns buried unknown in local archives and still to see the light of day.

---

20 Croatian State Archives (HDA, Zbirka mikrofilmova gradiva iz inozemnih arhiva koje se odnosi na Hrvatsku (ZMGIA-H), HR-HDA-1450, D-2179, MF59, 447. Rezolucija Bos. Dubičkih Muslimana. Prilog dopisu Zapovjedničtva 3. oružničke pukovnije vojnim i redarstvenim vlastima u Zagrebu. Datum: 30. siječanj 1942.). Adnan Jahić provided this document.

21 Gazi Husrev-Bey Library, Archives of the Islamic Community of Bosnia and Herzegovina (GHB, ARIZBIH, UM, 1712/42).

22 Samir Beglerović, "O muslimanskoj rezoluciji protiv progona Srba i Jevreja u Višegradu," *Forum Bosnae*, no. 74-75, 2016, 210-223.

23 Dejan Šegić provided this document.

Ferid Dautović

THE BOSNIAK ELITES AS SIGNATORIES OF THE MUSLIM RESOLUTIONS

The Muslim Resolutions have been a frequent object of interest from historians researching the Muslims of occupied Yugoslavia during World War II. Although not given the attention they deserve, they have been treated as positive examples of solidarity and of the condemnation of Ustaša crimes. This essay is a small contribution to identifying and categorizing the signatories of the resolutions. By considering the background of the various signatories we will be revealing the driving force behind these actions.

Soon after the establishment of the Independent State of Croatia, a majority of Bosnian Muslim clerics realized "that the Pavelić government and the Ustaša puppet state of the NDH would not bring any good to the Muslims or to any other ethnic group in the region."[1] Disappointment with the new authorities' discriminatory policies and genocidal massacres of Bosniaks by Royalist Serb forces in Eastern Bosnia in 1941 motivated the reaction of the Bosniak elites. The driving force was a group of religious figures in Sarajevo gathered around the *El-Hidaje* association of religious scholars and so part of the Islamic Community. The three individuals behind the first *El-Hidaje* Resolution were Mehmed Handžić, Kasim Dobrača, and Muhamed Fočak.

The idea for a resolution came from Handžić. He told Dobrača that,

> This evening, it is just the two of us here. Our task this evening is to put together the text of a statement or resolution to be signed by

---

[1] Hazim Fazlic, "Modern Muslim Thought in the Balkans: The Writings of Mehmed ef. Handžić in the El-Hidaje Periodical in the Context of Discrimination and Genocide," *Journal of Muslim Minority Affairs*, 35:3, (2015), 428-449.

Muslim representatives or a select part of the citizenry. No one has the right to bring about our destruction or impell us down a political path that will lead us to harm. We Muslims have every right to say so publicly and openly.[2]

And it was that evening that the text of the historic resolution was drafted in Sarajevo. According to Dobrača, Handžić had asked him: "Do you think it would be appropriate to include a separate point in the resolution from this year's assembly that makes clear how the *ulema* and Muslims view the turbulent events gathering on the horizon?"[3] The idea was then presented to Fočak, who agreed at once. Dobrača would later write of Muhamed Fočak:

> I cannot forget, or fail to mention, that he immediately agreed and gave his full support when, in the autumn of 1941, he and Handžić and I formed the inner circle of *El-Hidaje* workers and we came up with a proposal to draft and issue an *El-Hidaje* Resolution condemning the atrocities of the fascist regime and warning Muslims not to take part in them and to distance themselves from them, because followers of Islam cannot, indeed must not be the subjects or perpetrators of such crimes.[4]

Once a draft of the resolution had been made, it was put to the vote at the *El-Hidaje* General Assembly on August 14, 1941, where it was unanimously accepted.

One of the points of this resolution would later be cited in the Sarajevo Resolution:

> It is with pain in our hearts and profound condolences that we remember all the innocent Muslim victims struck down through no fault of their own in the unrest that has recently taken place in various places. We condemn any and all individual Muslims who have

---

2 Kasim Dobrača, "Rad Handžića u el-Hidaji i njegov društveni rad uobće," *El-Hidaje* no. 2–3 (VIII/1944), 86.

3 Ibid.

4 Kasim Dobrača, "Muhamed ef. Fočak," *Glasnik Vrhovnog islamskog starješinstva u Federativnoj Narodnoj Republici Jugoslaviji*, no. 4, (1978), 403.

committed any form of attack or violence independently and on their own initiative. We declare that the only people capable of doing such a thing are rogue elements and uncivilized individuals, whose stain we reject both for ourselves and for all Muslims. We call on all Muslims to refrain from such evil acts, in the spirit of the exalted tenets of their religion, Islam, and in the interests of the state. We call on the government authorities to restore law and order as soon as possible to all areas and prevent unauthorized action so that innocent people do not suffer.

Such a reaction to the Ustašas was unprecedented. As Šefkija Kurtović wrote in 1951:

> Crimes against the Communists, Serbs, and Jews were publicly proclaimed government policy and shamelessly justified "theoretically and scientifically" by the highest level Ustaša powers as patriotic acts, and no one was allowed to criticize, intervene, or oppose, as stressed in the press, on pain of being identified with the "leprous enemies."[5]

The Sarajevo Resolution was promulgated a few months later, with 108 signatories. Even though it did not identify the culprits, the Ustaša regime viewed it as an "anti-state act." According to Kurtović,

> the Ustaše considered the resolution a "knife in the back," a "hostile attack on the state," that caused so much resentment and so much upset that, in true fascist fashion, the death penalty was demanded for the signatories. Here, just as in Mostar and Banja Luka and other places, what saved the signatories was the fact that they had expressed the true mood of Muslims on the issue, that they were so numerous and such prominent people, and that it could have raised doubts in the mind of the Occupier about the grounds for having joined Bosnia and Herzegovina to their creature, the NDH.[6]

---

5 Šukrija Kurtović, "Dokumenti iz perioda narodnooslobodilačke borbe. Stav sarajevskih muslimana 1941 godine," *Glasnik Vrhovnog islamskog starješinstva u Federativnoj Narodnoj Republici Jugoslaviji* br. 1–3 (1951), 24–25.

6 Ibid.

The resolutions subsequently passed in several towns in Bosnia and Herzegovina shook the new state to its foundations. According to Nada Kisić-Kolanović, "one might say that the Muslims, especially sensitive to religious and ethnic differences, had, with their resolutions of 1941, provoked a crisis of legitimacy in the NDH."[7]

The initiators and signatories of the resolutions came primarily from the circle of religious scholars, who enjoyed the confidence of the leading citizens, landowners, beys, cultural workers, academics, and the ordinary people. The Sarajevo Resolution was signed by 108 individuals, members of the Sarajevo Bosniak elite. This included members of the *Ulema-medžlis*,[8] the governing body of the Islamic Community, directors and representatives of Islamic educational institutions,[9] representatives of Muslim cultural organizations,[10] Sharia justices,[11] court and administrative officials,[12] and professors at Islamic educational institutions.[13]

The Banja Luka Resolution was initiated and signed by religious figures like Mustafa Nurkić, former Mufti of Banja Luka. Its signatories

---

7   Nada Kisić-Kolanović, *Muslimanski i hrvatski nacionalizam 1941.-1945.*, Školska knjiga and Hrvatski institut za povijest, 2009, 214.

8   The council of scholars (*majlis al-'Ulama*), which administered Islamic affairs. E.g. Mehmed-Ali Ćerimović, Šaćir Mesihović, Muhamed Bahtijarević, Muhamed Pandža and Alija Aganović.

9   E.g. Muhamed Pašić, director of the Sharia High School, Ahmed Burek, director of the Gazi Husrev-bey madrasah, and Dr Šaćir Sikirić, Rector of the Higher Islamic Sharia and Theological School.

10 Including religious, national, and humanitarian organizations, like *El-Hidaje, Merhamet, Narodna uzdanica, Hurijet, Trezvenost, El-Kamer,* etc.

11 E.g. hfz. Sulejman Kulenović, Osman Omerhodžić, Ahmed Selimović, Osman Forta, and h. hfz. Ibrahim Redžić.

12 Both retired and serving judicial officials, like Dr Behaudin Salihagić, Dr Husein Mašić, Nasib Repovac, Dr Muhamed Kulenović, President of the Sarajevo Court, Muhamed Fidahić, Council Member of the Supreme Court in Sarajevo, Osman Sikirić, Council Member of the Supreme Court in Sarajevo, and Bekir Omersoftić, Assistant Attorney General.

13 E.g. Muhamed Hazim Tulić, Hamdija Kapidžić, Mustafa Drljević, Ćazim Nožić, Mahmud Bajraktarević, Ahmed Kasumović, and Besim Korkut.

included many non-religious former and serving officials, and representatives of local organizations like *Sloga, Fadilet, Bratstvo,* and *Islahijet*.

The first five signatories of the Bijeljina Resolution were imams. The rest included the Mayor, Murat-beg Pašić, and a number of businessmen and professors or teachers. The Mostar Resolution was also initiated and signed by a former Mufti of Mostar, Omer ef. Džabić, and several of the signatories were Muslim religious figures, while the first signatory to the Zenica Resolution was Šaćir Konjhodžić, President of the District Court. Other leading figures included Abdulah Serdarević, Director of the Madrasah and President of the Waqf and Educational Board, and Ragib Hadžiabdić, Governor of the Zenica Prison.

With the end of the war and the establishment of the new Communist regime, the fate of the signatories varied. Those who had initiated the Sarajevo Resolution, like Kasim Dobrača, were sent to prison by the new authorities. In other cases, some were given new positions by the postwar Islamic Community. For example, Ibrahim Fejić, one of the signatories of the Mostar Resolution, was later appointed Grand Mufti. Half a century later, a handful of the surviving signatories faced a new war and new persecution. Muhamed Zahirović, then the only still living signatory of the Banja Luka Resolution, spent the 1992-1995 war in Banja Luka, where he was subjected to maltreatment and provocations. In 1992, Abdulah Budimlija, the only surviving signatory of the Bijeljina Resolution, was expelled from Bijeljina.

To sum up, the signatories of the Muslim Resolutions were people of very different backgrounds, most of whom however had some religious education and affiliation. In the post-World War II period, they suffered different fates under the Communist regime and most of them remain virtually unknown in Bosnia and Herzegovina.

Ermin Sinanović

STANDING UP FOR JUSTICE IN THE MUSLIM TRADITION

In his essay for this volume, Xavier Bougarel correctly states that the Resolutions were "a moral condemnation, in the name of Islam," of the violence instigated by a fascist regime. While the motivations for the Resolutions were multi-dimensional, as established in this book, it is important to highlight the role Islamic teachings and Muslim sensibilities played in their formation. This short essay is an overview of basic Islamic teachings on justice and equitable dealings. It frames the basic shared understandings Muslims have held since Islam's inception on the issues of establishing and standing up for justice.

Justice as a central tenet of Islam

Justice is one of the central categories in Islamic teachings. There are numerous verses in the Qur'an and sayings from the Prophet Muhammad (PBUH)[1] that stress the importance and centrality of justice. Even as a young man, the Prophet showed great sensitivity toward issues of social justice, oppression, and inequality in society. This is one of the reasons why he chose to seclude himself in the hills around Mecca and contemplate, among other things, the Meccans' inequitable dealing with the poor, orphans, women, and other disadvantaged categories at the time. It was during this phase in his life that, according to Muslim belief, the Angel Gabriel came to him and delivered the first revelation.

In the Qur'an, God commanded the Prophet to set up an example of righteousness, fortitude, and just behavior. He was also instructed – and all

---

1   PBUH – Peace be upon him, a pious phrase Muslims use when mentioning the Prophet.

Muslims are expected to adhere to this pattern of behavior – to be just and equitable in adjudicating between people:

> Behold, God bids you to deliver all that you have been entrusted with unto those who are entitled thereto, and whenever you judge between people, to judge with justice. Verily, most excellent is what God exhorts you to do: verily, God is all-hearing, all-seeing![2]

The imperative of justice is so paramount that no other consideration can or should take precedence over it. Indeed, one is expected to establish justice even if that meant harming one's own interests or the interests of those one loves and is close to.

> O you who have attained to faith! Be ever steadfast in upholding equity, bearing witness to the truth for the sake of God, even though it be against your own selves or your parents and kinsfolk. Whether the person concerned be rich or poor, God's claim takes precedence over [the claims of] either of them. Do not, then, follow your own desires, lest you swerve from justice: for if you distort [the truth], behold, God is indeed aware of all that you do![3]

Furthermore, the Qur'an teaches Muslims that even in cases in which enmity exists between their community and other groups of people, Muslims should remain faithful to the ideal of just conduct. In short, there is no excuse for injustice. This is because justice is qualitatively next to piety. In other words, one cannot achieve true piety and God-consciousness without adhering to justice:

> O you who have attained to faith! Be ever steadfast in your devotion to God, bearing witness to the truth in all equity; and never let hatred of anyone lead you into the sin of deviating from justice. Be just: this is closest to being God-conscious. And remain conscious of God: verily, God is aware of all that you do.[4]

---

2   The Qur'an, 4:58, in Muhammad Asad's translation, "The Message of the Qur'an," available online on various portals. This is the translation used throughout.

3   The Qur'an, 4:135.

4   The Qur'an, 5:8.

On the other hand, injustice and corruption are seen as vice, sin, and indecency and so as to be corrected. Justice is often contrasted with its opposite in the Qur'an:

> Behold, God enjoins justice, and the doing of good, and generosity towards [one's] fellow-men; and He forbids all that is shameful and all that runs counter to reason, as well as envy; [and] He exhorts you [repeatedly] so that you might bear [all this] in mind.[5]

In the same vein as God loves those who are just and equitable, so too "He does not love those who are unjust,"[6] who deliberately harm others and make them suffer.

Speaking up and acting against injustice

The plight of those who are oppressed and against whom injustice has been committed should not be ignored. Instead, righteous people are expected to mobilize their forces to rescue the oppressed and remove injustice. Establishing justice is a religious imperative of the highest order:

> And how could you refuse to fight in the cause of God and of the utterly helpless men and women and children who are crying, "O our Sustainer! Lead us forth [to freedom] out of this land whose people are oppressors, and raise for us, out of Thy grace, a protector, and raise for us, out of Thy grace, one who will bring us succor!"[7]

Motivated in part by this verse, a famous Muslim theologian, Ibn Taymiyah (d.1328), sent a letter to the Mongol invaders of Baghdad, asking them to release all Jewish and Christian prisoners who had, prior to that, been subjects of the Muslim state. He vowed that Muslims would liberate as many Christian prisoners as they could.[8] Commenting on the verse, a modern Muslim scholar, Sayyid Qutb (d.1966), has stated that "one should

---

5   The Qur'an, 16:90. This verse is usually recited after the sermon during Friday prayers.
6   The Qur'an, 3:57 and 3:140.
7   The Qur'an, 4:75.
8   Ermin Sinanovic, "Humanitarian Intervention in Islamic and International Law," *American Journal of Islamic Social Sciences* 20:1 (2003), 99.

not sit idle while people are enduring ongoing abuse."[9] This is even more important in cases of religious persecution, for it touches the innermost core of what constitutes a human being.

Social justice

Building on the notion of general and universal justice, the Qur'an also contains many teachings in support of social justice. Like other religions in general, and the Abrahamic religions in particular, Islam teaches Muslims to be aware of the injustices present in their environment and – more importantly – to do something about fixing them. It further exhorts Muslims to be generous, to help and feed the needy and the orphan. A Muslim needs to spend "his substance - however much he himself may cherish it - upon his near of kin, and the orphans, and the needy, and the wayfarer, and the beggars, and for the freeing of human beings from bondage."[10]

In the classical age of Islam, these injunctions regarding social justice were discussed in scholarly works. They were often incorporated, with various degrees of success, into the actual policies of diverse Muslim polities. Issues such as just taxation, protection of private property, care for the poor and the elderly, spending on education, and distribution of wealth, in general, were seen as hallmarks of good governance. For example, Ibn Khaldun has a chapter entitled "Injustice brings about the ruin of civilization," in his famous *al-Muqaddimah* (Introduction to History). After narrating a Persian story of an unjust king who was admonished for his corruption and eventually returned to the way of justice, Ibn Khaldun writes,

> The lesson this (story) teaches is that injustice ruins civilization... Thus, the dynasty which committed the infringements (of justice) may be replaced before the city is ruined... Injustice should not be understood to imply only the confiscation of money or other property from the owners, without compensation and without cause. It is commonly understood in that way, but it is something more general

---

9   Ibid, 100.
10 The Qur'an, 2:177.

than that. Whoever takes someone's property, or uses him for forced labor, or presses an unjustified claim against him, or imposes upon him a duty not required by the religious law, does an injustice to that particular person. People who collect unjustified taxes commit an injustice. Those who infringe upon property (rights) commit an injustice. Those who take away property commit an injustice. Those who deny people their rights commit an injustice. Those who, in general, take property by force, commit an injustice… Since, as we have seen, injustice calls for the eradication of the (human) species by leading to the ruin of civilization, it contains in itself a good reason for being prohibited. Consequently, it is important that it be forbidden. There is ample evidence for that in the Qur'an and the Sunnah.[11]

Among the Muslim rulers of India, the Persian-Arabic genre of literature known as "advice to kings/rulers" [nasihat al-muluk] assumed a high level of importance. One such author, Shah Muhibbullah (d.1250), wrote, "justice requires that the thought of the welfare of men should be uppermost in the minds of the rulers, so that the people might be protected from the tyranny of officials."[12]

Fazlur Rahman (d.1988), a Pakistani-American scholar, wrote in 1970, "the supreme value in the Islamic social message is adequate social justice."[13] And again,

> The vehement passages which denounce those who are busy counting their money while there are some who cannot afford the necessities of life, rank among the most volcanic expressions of the early Suras of the Qur'an. …the Qur'an called upon the rich to pay out a portion of their

---

11 Ibn Khaldun, *The Muqaddimah: An Introduction to History*, trans. Franz Rosenthal, 3 vols (Princeton: Princeton University Press, 2nd ed. 1967), vol. 2, 106-7.
12 Quoted in Linda T. Darling, ""Do Justice, Do Justice, For That is Paradise": Middle Eastern Advice for Indian Muslim Rulers," *Comparative Studies of South Asia, Africa and the Middle East* 22.1-2 (2002), 3-19; the quote is from 6.
13 Fazlur Rahman, "Islam and Social Justice," *Pakistan Forum* (Oct-Nov 1970), 4-9. The quote is from 5.

wealth and told them that they had no right over their portion, even if they may have earned it.[14]

It is entirely plausible to conclude, from these sections, that many Muslim scholars have believed that cultural and civilizational progress is closely interlinked with the degree of justice established in a given society.

This concise overview, as rudimentary as it may seem, sums up basic Muslim teachings on public justice. While one has to be careful in ascribing religious motivation to political action, it is not an unrealistic leap of the imagination to conclude that these teachings probably played an important role in motivating the Bosniak elites to write the Resolutions and to raise their voices against the unspeakable horrors unleashed by the fascist regime and the inter-ethnic violence it instigated.

---

14   Ibid.

Desmond Maurer

ON READING THE MUSLIM RESOLUTIONS

This book presents, in translation, ten resolutions, drafted and signed by groups of Bosnian Muslim clerics, intellectuals, and social worthies in 1941 and, to a lesser degree, in 1942, after the invasion of Yugoslavia in April 1941 by German Nazi and Italian Fascist forces and the establishment of a new state, referred to as the Independent State of Croatia, that incorporated all of Bosnia and Herzegovina within a new pro-fascist order. They represent only a subsection of the total number of such petitions signed, some of which are lost to history or remain in archives. They were prompted by the fact that the new authorities had, instead of simply establishing themselves and public order, embarked almost immediately upon campaigns targeting particular categories of the population with violence and, ultimately, for extermination. The categories in question were Serbs, Jews, and Roma, in that order.[1] While with time this violence would be channeled through a system of murder camps, in its initial phases it involved discriminatory measures, work bans, confiscations of property and homes, expulsions, and mass killings in their communities, especially of the Serbs, provoking many to flee to the woods and take up arms in response, carrying out reprisals, which were for various reasons often aimed at their neighbors, rather than directly at the new authorities. This created

---

1   Extermination of the Jews was the priority of the German occupiers and taken on board as a goal by the collaborating administrations largely for that reason, though not with much reluctance in either Zagreb or Belgrade. The same is true of the anti-Roma campaign. The anti-Serb campaign, which included activities ranging from forced conversion and assimilation, through expulsion and ethnic cleansing, all the way to extermination, was by contrast a priority of the Ustaša regime, and accepted by the Germans largely on those grounds, as a pet project of their pets.

an escalating cycle of violence, in which many Muslims were caught up as victims. The situation not merely threatened to get out of hand. It did.

The resolutions are documents of varying length that thus share a common concern, namely to address officials and express worries regarding the security situation in the state, with an emphasis on the status of ordinary Muslims and threats to their well-being under the new order, and then, generally as a secondary issue, unhappiness regarding the attacks on Serb citizens by the new authorities and their minions. The initial focus of the signatories' remarks regarding these attacks was to point out that although some individual Muslims may have been involved, they were not carried out by or on behalf of the local Muslim communities, who generally did not approve of them, but who appeared to be being blamed for them and bearing the brunt of the Serb response, not least because the government-organized and sponsored perpetrators were disguising themselves as Muslims and doing their best to leave the impression that Muslims had carried them out. This primary complaint thus relates to the impact on Muslims and the Muslim community of the violence against Serbs rather than its impact on its direct victims. While the signatories clearly also found the situation unacceptable in human terms and out of fellow feeling for their Serb fellow citizens, they expressed themselves and their concerns in terms of the impact on public safety, the potential in the situation for escalation and further destabilization, and the status of and threat to their own group.

Essentially, however, what they wanted was a state that did its job, which is to say ensured public order, and it was normally at this point that they included the most important recommendations, on which the moral authority of the letters rests, namely the call for a disbanding of all the formal and informal groups carrying out such criminal activities, a guarantee of personal safety and religious freedom for all citizens, regardless of ethnic or religious background, for everyone to be treated equally, and finally a call for those who had carried out or ordered the attacks to be held criminally responsible. In other words, rather than condemn explicitly the abuses and attacks as inherently immoral, they asked for them to be discontinued on grounds of public safety and stabilization of the situation and then included amongst the remedial actions the restoration of full civic status to the targeted groups, along with a restoration of the rule of law for all, and the disciplining and punishment of those who had violated it. Universal considerations were introduced under cover of practical recommendations and dealing with the situation pragmatically rather than on moral grounds. These limited goals are reflected in the absence of any call in the resolutions for a repealing of discriminatory provisions or a restoration of property or jobs and status.

While the treatment of Serbs is explicitly mentioned and there is an explicit call for an end to all forms of mistreatment of them, the same cannot be said with regard to the treatment of their Jewish fellow citizens or of Roma as a group overall. Two of the later resolutions do make explicit calls for an end to the targeting of "white" Roma and are largely dedicated to that topic, but the grounds invoked for doing so operate from within the logic of the new racial laws, namely that these groups had been "declared" Aryan and that they were Muslim by religion, meaning that they were not subject to the racial laws, and that there was an explicit ordinance to this effect.

Some of the resolutions also note that while Islam was formally equal to Catholicism under the new state, it was not so treated. Muslims were treated as second class citizens when it came to the allocation of office or benefices, including specifically those made available by the firing and expulsion of their previous occupants. Moreover, while conversion to a recognized religion was one way for the Orthodox Serbs and others to save themselves, in practice conversion to Islam was discouraged in favor of conversion to Catholicism. This is a complicated issue, insofar as such conversion, whether to Islam or Catholicism, was often used as a mechanism for creating a formal, if temporary, change in status and so staving off persecution, and it was subject to contradictory attitudes on the part of religious authorities, government officials, and potential converts. Again, the Muslim concern seems to have been more about the implications for the standing of their religion than for that of the converts themselves. They feared, with good reason, that these differences in how Catholicism and Islam were viewed and between Catholics and Muslims in terms of how they were treated by the new state presaged a long-term game plan, whereby Muslims would be the next target of a machinery of violence and persecution in constant need of new categories of victim. From this perspective they viewed the Serbs as a sort of canary in the coalmine. Some, at least, of the signatories were also farsighted enough to doubt that the Ustaša program of violence and extermination of the Serbs could succeed and to worry about its long-term implications for inter-ethnic relations in the state. In the end, they suspected that the viability of their historically plural society and of their own place in it would be the major casualties.

The officials addressed in the resolutions were in some cases actually representatives of the Muslim community themselves, but generally speaking they were Muslims who held high office of some sort within the government that took power as a result of the Nazi and Fascist invasion in April 1941. In the case of the first or *El-Hidaje* Resolution, the document took the form of a resolution passed by the assembly of the *El-Hidaje* Association of Muslim Clergy and was published in the organization's journal, rather than a petition directed through official channels. It may be considered a type of open letter and the topic of the violence and the call for it to be stopped were expressed in only one of its several numbered paragraphs. Most of the remainder expressed solidarity with the new regime, albeit in less effusive terms than is sometimes suggested - the resolution is reprinted in this volume precisely because it has become the subject of debate over the motives of the signatories and is often cited as proof that they were avid pro-fascists, just as the other resolutions are cited to prove the anti-fascist disposition of their signatories. As will become clear from the following, the present author does not share either view.

The initiators of the relevant paragraph in the *El-Hidaje* Resolution were also behind at least some of the subsequent resolutions, which did focus more or less solely on the topic of violence but were not generally produced under the formal aegis of an institution, even if the signatories did not hesitate to identify themselves or the institutions with which they were affiliated, thus intimating some degree of moral, if not formal backing. Overall, the other letters are probably best considered intra-Muslim communications and to have been at most semi-public in character, circulated as copies rather than published, though there is evidence that some of them did make their way to high-level Ustaša officials in Zagreb.

Most of the resolutions called upon representatives of the community close to or in power to advocate for the positions set out within them, and in many cases they bear a striking resemblance to the type of petitions that would always have been sent by groups with a grievance to monarchical authorities like the Sultan, the Austrian Emperor, and the Russian Tsar, which is to say they assume the legitimacy and benevolence of the ultimate authority and a desire on its part to correct any wrongs or injustices at lower levels within the system, which are clearly the result of abuses by corrupt or wicked lower-level authorities, and which will equally obviously be corrected once brought to the attention of those ultimate authorities by honest and high-minded intermediaries, because it is in everybody's interest to promote right relations within society and a just social order under a sovereign dedicated to the common good of the people. Whether or not the signatories believed this to be the case is irrelevant. This was the idiom within which such petitions had previously been written and within which they would continue to be written, even after World War II, to Stalin and Tito, by their respective subjects.

There is a logic to this approach that applies even when one knows full well that the sovereign is not even-handedly benevolent towards all the people. This is that tyrants are to be addressed in the terms of a rhetoric that assumes their benevolence and attempts to "persuade" them to act as just rulers, not by confronting them with their crimes, but by assuming their interest in justice and their ability to see that their interest lies with the common interest.[2] It also more or less assumes that every ruler is a tyrant

---

2 For a discussion of this approach, see Leo Strauss, *On Tyranny*, Corrected and Expanded Edition, Chicago University Press, 2013. Cf. the review by Eric Voegelin in the *Review of Politics*, Apr. 1949, vol. 11, no. 2, 241-4, who points out the importance of the historical moment of the degradation of democracy, combined with the obliteration of the distinction between king and tyrant. One may compare the fact that

and should not be told so directly to his face, because one has little choice but to live under the rule of tyranny, given that absolute justice is impossible in a world that is not the kingdom of heaven. It is easy to misunderstand this if one has lived under an order that supposes the ultimate justification of politics through the people's will and that the people is a non-problematic concept. The Bosnian Muslims, like most peoples in most places in most of history did not find themselves under such circumstances. Any response to local problems within such a context, necessarily, involves arguing from within the central authority's point of view, rather than confronting it, and so attempting to bring about an internal transformation of a bad situation. This approach is often taken by groups who do not identify fully with the regime or sovereign, but see no better alternatives on the horizon, and who value the establishment and maintenance of public order and a governmental framework, however imperfect, as a brake against anarchy. That there are limits to the effectiveness of such an approach is clear, but so too is the fact that it is not inherently immoral.

It is important to appreciate this mindset, because it helps one understand how various groups across Europe and within both Croatia and Bosnia and Herzegovina could have accepted and even welcomed the establishment of fascist regimes without necessarily being pro-fascist themselves in their ideology or approach. The new regimes promised the establishment of order and stability and, for many groups that had felt disadvantaged or dissatisfied under interwar regimes, a chance for improved status. There would be new opportunities based upon the new balance of power. It is not necessarily simply opportunism. It may be grounded in quite hard-nosed pragmatism and realism. The new opportunities may even give rise to a certain degree of enthusiasm for the situation, if not for the regime, before a fuller understanding of all the implications of the changes introduced is gained.

---

the German representatives in Zagreb were on record as holding the view that the Ustašas had overestimated their capacities and underestimated the magnitude of the task of eliminating the Serbs and would be forced to abandon the attempt, so that their interest lay in finding a *modus vivendi* with them before things went too far.

Moreover, the response to these new regimes must always be judged in terms of an understanding of what the available alternatives were or seemed to be. The prospects for resistance were few, at least in the short-term, and attachment to and viability of the old regime and old system limited or even non-existent. It would take a considerable period of time for a viable order of resistance and the prospect of an alternative new order to emerge. What is more, for many the idea that this new order should be based upon Soviet-sponsored Communism was anathema, not just for political but for religious reasons. Fascism and Nazism had initially emerged as forms of resistance to Communism and despair at liberal democracy and were openly supported by the various Christian churches and some Islamic authorities. Communism had, moreover, been a factor of at best minor significance in Yugoslavia before the outbreak of the war, especially in Bosnia and Herzegovina. And the Nazi-Soviet pact had rather ham-strung the immediate Communist response to the invasion. For many, under the circumstances that prevailed in the first years of the Second World War, there quite simply seemed to be no alternative to accommodation with the new regimes and their Nazi and Fascist sponsors. To consider the resolutions as anti-fascist is therefore to judge them in terms of a position that few had yet fully embraced and those who had more often rejected fascism in favor of another totalitarian ideology than out of deep-rooted liberal democratic convictions. To consider the resolutions a protest against how the fascist regime of the NDH was treating some of its citizens and putting public order at risk is more justified, as is viewing them as a step on the path for some but not all of their signatories towards more determined anti-fascist positions down the line. If they came to be presented after the end of the war as proof of anti-fascist convictions and action on the part of their signatories, this was more a reflection of the political situation and justificatory discourses under the new Communist regime and the need of Bosnian Muslims to distance themselves from the Ustaša regime and provide proofs of their affiliation with the resistance to it from the very beginning.

The remainder of this essay provides a brief historical sketch that some readers may find helpful in understanding the position the Bosnian Muslims found themselves in and their reasons for drafting their resolutions.

The Bosnian Muslims: From elite to minority

The Muslims were a declining elite, whose status and even survival under any given order in the post-Congress of Berlin Balkans was permanently in doubt and who saw their only medium to long-term prospects in terms of a policy of tactical accommodation with whatever powers happened to be dominant at any given time. Their preferred option was the preservation of their ancestral homeland, Bosnia and Herzegovina, as an administrative and political entity, but their bottom line was the preservation of a minimum of religious, social, and cultural autonomy under whatever political order was in the ascendent, so that they could maintain their identity. This meant that their politics was always essentially tactical and from a place of relative weakness, which is not the same as to say that it was immoral and opportunistic.[3] After all, as Bismarck said, politics is the art of the possible.

Bosnia and Herzegovina was the last of the mediaeval states of the Western Balkans to experience its flowering and it did so partly thanks to a relative decline on the part of its neighbors. Mediaeval Croatia and Slavonia were incorporated into Hungary, while mediaeval Dalmatia was sold to Venice. Mediaeval Serbia quickly reached its apogee, and as quickly declined from it, devolving into a number of rival claimants to a non-existent hegemony. By the late 14th century, it was securely within the Ottoman ambit. Bosnia thrived, but its time would come soon enough, as it was conquered in turn by the Ottomans over a period of approximately 80 years, from the mid-15th through to the early 16th centuries. Unlike its neighbors, however, Bosnia retained a strong degree of administrative and political identity for the entire period of Ottoman rule.

When Bosnia finally passed into Habsburg hands, in 1878, it was as a *corpus separatum*, within its existing borders. It did so, however, as an

---

3   The events of the 1990s and since have made clear that this situation was not fundamentally altered by the defeat of fascism. The problem for the Muslims of the Balkans and of Bosnia more particularly is structural in nature and consequently comes to the fore whenever major shifts in the broader geopolitical context encourage local and regional power-factors to pursue programs of change within the region.

internally divided society, insofar as the Muslims represented a very numerous aristocratic, landowning, military, and urban class, as well as part of the free peasantry, while the Orthodox and the considerably less numerous Catholics made up the bulk of the tied peasantry, sometimes wrongly referred to as serfs, though they also formed part of the merchant class and such specialized groups as stonemasons and miners. Class (essentially agrarian) tensions were thus reinforced by religious and, with the spread of national ideologies, what came to be experienced as ethnic differences. This provided powerful symbolic resources for the narrativization of *ressentiment* on the part of all three socio-religious communities.

It is important that Bosnia and Herzegovina has always been a multi-faith society, based upon the coexistence of religious communities. During the Ottoman period this was in a clear and fairly strictly imposed hierarchy, known as the Millet system. It was changing even before the withdrawal of the Ottomans from the Balkans, under the Tanzimat reforms that began in 1839 and introduced formal religious equality to the Empire, but it was not a particularly smooth or rapid process. 19th-century Bosnian society was thus characterized by a strong degree of inequality based upon religious affiliation, which overlapped with class and occupational categories and ultimately ethnic or national identities, and was interpreted and so experienced in terms of differential historical trajectories and destinies. These distinctions and the antagonisms that went with them would remain engrained in the popular mentality after the replacement of the Ottomans by the Austro-Hungarians and then incorporation within first one and then a second Serb-dominated Yugoslavia.

Croatia and Serbia and the origins of ethnic cleansing

Both Croatia and Serbia were strongly influenced during the 19th century by Western and essentially Franco-German ideologies of folkish nationalism and of macro- or pan-nationalism. These grew into rival visions of a pan-southern-Slavic union, referred to at different times as Illyrianism and Yugoslavism, on the one hand, and mutually incompatible

Greater Serbian and Greater Croatian projects, on the other. Common to all these visions was the absorption of Bosnia and Herzegovina and so the dissolution of its separate administrative and political identity. The Muslims were conceived of as a surplus to be absorbed and assimilated into the Greater Croat or Greater Serb identity, to be encouraged to emigrate, or simply eliminated as a factor. As a result, the Bosnian Muslims and their country were a large part of what made these ideologies incompatible and conflict over their ultimate destiny was always on the horizon. Croat and Serb aspirations with regard to Bosnia and Herzegovina were simultaneously fostered and restrained by the geopolitical situation and the interests of the great powers, Austria-Hungary, Russia, Germany, and Great Britain, in what is normally referred to as the Eastern Question – how to manage and profit from the gradual dissolution of the declining Ottoman Empire.

In this regard, the Croat and Serb ideologies represented a continuation of what had already been the practice of the Habsburgs and the Venetians when they "liberated" the former Crown lands of St Stephen (Hungary, Slavonia, and Transylvania) and the Dalmatian littoral after the failed siege of Vienna in 1683 – a policy of faith-based ethnic cleansing and the transfer of populations. This Habsburg "Reconquista" had also played an important role in Serbian history, insofar as it saw the permanent establishment of the Vojvodina in what is now northern Serbia and prompted the mass emigration of Serbs from Ottoman territory into the Habsburg Empire, both in the Vojvodina and along the Military Frontier.[4] It also

---

4   The militarized zone that ran all along the border between the Habsburgs and the Ottomans, more or less from the Dalmatian littoral to Romania. It refers particularly, however, to the border areas between Croatia and Bosnia and Slavonia and Bosnia, where the term used is the Krajina or the Vojna Krajina. The word translates more or less as borderland. The authors of the resolutions refer at various points to the Hrvatska Krajina and the Bosanska Krajina, or the Croatian and Bosnian borderlands. The areas within Croatia and Slavonia were settled by colonists, who received landholdings in exchange for military service. They tended to be Orthodox and thanks to Habsburg activities in Serbia during the 17th and 18th centuries included many Serbs who had migrated there from southern Serbia. This process fostered, over time, the identification of pre-existing Orthodox communities in these areas, historically called Vlachs, as Serbs as well. Again, it was this process that created the particular distribution of Orthodox or Serb communities in Croatia and Slavonia, particularly

saw Belgrade and the surrounding territory come under Habsburg control for several decades, leading to the destruction of the town's mosques and provoking yet more demographic change in the northern part of Serbia (including the areas south of the Danube). The Ottomans recovered Belgrade in 1739, but it was back in Habsburg hands for a short period in the 1780s. This transformation of northern Serbia into a frontier region, subject to cultural and political influences from a Vojvodina that was itself undergoing rapid and thorough processes of militarization and colonization, was crucial in creating the conditions for the first and second Serbian uprisings, against the background of the Napoleonic wars. This led ultimately to the establishment of a dependent principality of Serbia under the suzerainty of the Porte, which was homogenously Serb by design, and from which all Muslims were encouraged by various means, including atrocities, to withdraw over the subsequent 50 or so years.

Serbia's context was also undergoing major changes. Greece gained its independence during the 1820s, Romania its in a long-drawn-out process from the Crimean War of the 1850s through to the 1870s, and Bulgaria its in the 1870s, which was also when Serbia consolidated the gradual gains it had seen over the intervening 50 years and was recognized as an independent kingdom. The 1870s were thus the crucial decade in consolidating the rise of the new Christian kingdoms of the Balkans. All these processes saw atrocities and the mass emigration and expulsion of Muslims from areas that had previously been under Ottoman control. This was a demographic revolution, which is largely passed over in silence by the national historiographies of the region in favor of a rhetoric of "national liberation," and it left the remaining Balkan Muslim populations of Bosnia, Albania, and the strip of territory linking them to each other and to Istanbul in a precarious situation.

---

around the border with Bosnia and Herzegovina, that determined both the focus of Ustaša anti-Serb violence and the loci of practical resistance to it. The Bosnian side of the border had also historically been militarized, with the Orthodox there largely serving as a tied peasantry.

The middle decades of the 19th century also saw a concerted effort on the part of Serbia, and to a lesser extent Montenegro, to raise Serbian national consciousness amongst the Orthodox population of Bosnia and Herzegovina and to provoke agrarian unrest, which culminated in the Herzegovinian uprising of 1875, which they hoped would lead to a Serbian annexation of the province.

The Austro-Hungarian interlude as breathing space

Aware of the combustible nature of the situation, the European Great Powers convened the Congress of Berlin in 1878 to settle the situation, at least *pro tem*. The aspirations of the emergent Christian kingdoms of the Balkans were simultaneously confirmed and reined in, within a clear context of Great Power sponsorship. This was particularly true of Serbia, whose aspirations towards Bosnia and Herzegovina were thwarted by international approval of an Austro-Hungarian occupation and colonial administration, under nominal Ottoman suzerainty, while the Sandžak and Albania and Kosovo and Macedonia and Thrace remained under more direct Ottoman rule, albeit with the presence of Austro-Hungarian garrisons in the Sandžak. The nature of the Austro-Hungarian occupation of Bosnia and Herzegovina also represented a frustration of Croat aspirations, insofar as the province was treated as a *corpus separatum*, under the direct rule of the joint ministries in Vienna, rather than joined to Croatia and Slavonia under the Hungarian crown.

In 1908, Austria-Hungary formally annexed the province but retained its anomalous status within its own structures. This reflected the fact that Austria-Hungary viewed Bosnia and Herzegovina less as a "recovered Crown land" than as a "proximate colony", after the model of the former Ottoman possessions in North Africa that had been taken over by the French and the British under what they explicitly considered a "civilizing mission."[5] The presence of Muslims was a necessary precondition for such

---

5   The term was introduced with respect to Bosnia and Herzegovina by the American historian Robert Donia in an article entitled "The Proximate Colony, Bosnia-Herzegovina under Austro-Hungarian Rule," published in *WechselWirkungen,*

an approach to Bosnia and Herzegovina, and the Austro-Hungarian policy was to promote their continued residence within the province. Given that Catholics were by far the least numerous of the three major confessional groups in Bosnia and Herzegovina, Croat aspirations also depended on the Muslims identifying as Croats and so forging a form of ethnic alliance with them and *keeping them in situ*. Without them, Bosnia and Herzegovina would clearly have been an Orthodox and so, under the ethnic-nationalist logic of the day, a Serb land.

During the decades of Austro-Hungarian occupation, the Muslims of Bosnia and Herzegovina developed a new *modus vivendi*. While many did emigrate to territories still in Ottoman hands, unable to accept life under an infidel regime, most opted for forms of accommodation with the new regime and adaptation to the new conditions, as no longer the dominant class. They developed a program of religious, social, and cultural autonomy (including the retention of sharia law, Muslim educational establishments, and Muslim *waqf* or administered trusts and endowments, which played a major role both in the management of inheritance and of religious and public foundations), on the one hand, and the deferral of agrarian reform, on the other. This would be pursued through the representative institutions established by the Austro-Hungarians and so began the political organization of the Bosnian Muslims as a religious-ethnic-class fraction within a wider Bosnian society that lacked a broader political identity that transcended the society's internal religious, ethnic, and class divides. The Bosnian Muslims did not assume the form of a *national* movement, precisely because they never envisaged the possibility of once again being the dominant class within a state of their own and so being able to identify themselves with the state. They accepted the reality of minority status within a broader state or structure of governance with which they could not fully identify. This would be formalized after the First World War under the arrangements governing minority rights included in the various treaties.

Austria-Hungary, Bosnia-Herzegovina, and the Western Balkans, 1878–1918, eds. Clemens Ruthner et al., Peter Lang, 2015.

Croatia and Serbia's predatory ideologies

By contrast, there were simultaneous and largely successful processes of nationalizing the Catholic and Orthodox populations of Bosnia and Herzegovina as, respectively, Croats and Serbs and so as adjunct to the greater Croat and greater Serb national projects. While both the Croats and the Serbs were willing to regard the Muslims as essentially members of their ethnic group, who had, thanks to the vagaries of history, lost their way and required national re-education, the Serbs tended to insist that it be on the basis of full assimilation and renunciation of their Muslim identity, while the Croats, who had, as we have noted, more need of the Muslims to make up the numbers within Bosnia and Herzegovina, were inclined to accept Muslim identity as a subspecies of Croat identity. This was, however, largely a matter of mathematics rather than of an inherently gentler or less exclusionary ideology.

During the decades between the occupation of Bosnia and Herzegovina and the outbreak of World War I, Serbia and Montenegro were busy consolidating their national territories and preparing for further expansion into the Sandžak, Northern Albania, Kosovo, and Macedonia. The chance came with the first and second Balkan wars, which saw both of them radically increase their territories at the expense of what had been predominantly Muslim-populated areas. This action had been precipitated by the annexation of Bosnia and Herzegovina and the withdrawal of Austro-Hungarian troops from the Sandžak. Again, the result was mass violence against Muslims, forced conversions, and mass Muslim emigration, both towards the Ottomans and towards Bosnia and Herzegovina.

Nor did the slaking of Serbia's appetites to its south and east mean that it had given up on its aspirations with regard to Bosnia and Herzegovina. The Serbian state, or rogue elements within it, continued to support Serb nationalists within Bosnia and Herzegovina and it was some of these who organized the surprisingly successful assassination of Archduke Franz Ferdinand and his wife in Sarajevo and thus triggered the First World War. The result was strongly elevated anti-Serb sentiment within Austria-Hungary, the persecution of Serbs both in Bosnia and Herzegovina and in other parts of the Empire, and a hard fought and punitive occupation of Serbia and Montenegro. Serbia, already exhausted from the two Balkan wars, suffered highly disproportionate casualties during the First World War, not least because of a decision to evacuate the army via Corfu. The experience became known as Serbia's Golgotha.[6]

Making...

When the war was over, Serbia was not merely on the winning side. It was also burdened by an enormous sense of victimhood and grievance and many saw the establishment of a vastly expanded kingdom to be a homeland for all Serbs, incorporating Bosnia and Herzegovina, much of Dalmatia, the Vojvodina, and anywhere else Serbs lived, as its deserved reward. There was less appetite for the establishment of a southern Slav kingdom that would also incorporate Croats and Slovenes, but the dynasty was open to it and it seemed like the path of least resistance towards the incorporation of all Serbs within a single state. For the Croats and Slovenes, it represented their best hope of not being swallowed up by Italy and possibly Hungary in whatever post-war order emerged.[7] And so, the new kingdom of Serbs, Croats, and Slovenes was born out of the dissolution of Austria-Hungary, a certain lukewarm Yugoslavism, a fear of Italian

---

6   This reflects the traditional view of the Serbian experience during the First World War. Recent scholarship has put the Austro-Hungarian occupation of Serbia in somewhat different light. See, e.g. Jonathan E. Gumz, *The Resurrection and Collapse of Empire in Habsburg Serbia, 1914-1918*, Cambridge, 2009. Serbian suffering was developed into a legitimating myth, which, while not entirely unfounded in reality, nonetheless took on a life of its own, merging with other mythologemes to inform the Serbian reading of history and so of relations with other ethnic groups and countries.

7   Italy had entered the war late on the Allied side and been promised, in the secret Treaty of London of 1915, extensive Adriatic territories. The allies also promised Serbia various additional territories, and these promises were not always fully compatible. The Croats and Slovenes had no desire to swap one non-Slav master for another, but their leaders realized that they would have little prospect of facing down the Italians on their own, particularly given that they had been on the wrong side themselves. So, they headed off like "geese into the fog", as the Croat nationalist leader Stjepan Radić famously put it.

irredentism, and *faute-de-mieux* opportunism. On the Serb side, greater Serbian aspirations and assumptions of hegemony coexisted uneasily with integral Yugoslavism and dynastic centralism, while on the Croat side there was a constant desire for some form of federalism and Croat autonomy based upon the integration of the so-called "Croat lands", namely Slavonia, Croatia, Dalmatia, and, to the extent possible, Bosnia and Herzegovina.

The Bosnian Muslims thus found themselves once again positioned as a minority within a framework with which they could not fully identify and so condemned to a politics of tactical accommodation, aiming at survival as a distinct community, with as great a degree of religious, legal, educational, and cultural autonomy as possible, and preserving the historical, administrative, and political continuity of Bosnia and Herzegovina, albeit within the context of the new state. This task was rendered more urgent by the fact that it took some time for order to be fully restored after the end of the war, given that the Habsburg state had essentially disappeared and the Karađorđević (Serbian) state was not immediately able to take its place as effective sovereign and guarantor of order in all regards and all areas. The Muslims of Bosnia found themselves on the receiving end of considerable violence from non-state actors during this period, as did the Muslims of the Sandžak, whose position was even more precarious, not least because of what was, to all intents and purposes, a low-grade civil war in Montenegro, between those who supported and those who were against abolition of the native dynasty there and assimilation of the country into the new more or less Serbian state and so the reduction of Montenegrin identity to a form of Serbhood. The situation was partially resolved by promoting the colonization of the Sandžak and later of Kosovo and parts of Bosnia and Herzegovina by veterans and other deserving Serbs and Montenegrins, a process often carried out with threats or with actual violence. Government-sponsored internal colonization of Serb and Montenegrin veterans would remain a feature of the next two decades, as would pressure on Muslim populations.

Still, in the years that followed, the Bosnian Muslims did manage to secure for themselves not just a continuation but an expansion of the system of sharia law and the preservation of their system of educational institutions and *waqfs* or religious and charitable endowments and trusts, which played a prominent role in the management of Muslim inheritance and the administration of which was closely tied up with the role and status of the Muslim clergy.

...and breaking the first Yugoslavia

Unfortunately, worsening tensions between the federalist and in some cases even secessionist Croats and the integrationist and centralizing Serbs rendered attempts to establish a functioning democracy during the first decade of the new state's existence fruitless, culminating in the assassination in parliament of the Croat leader Stjepan Radić in 1928. This provoked a suspension of parliament and a declaration of personal dictatorship by King Aleksandar who ultimately imposed a new constitution and embarked on a radical reorganization of the state that was designed to promote a new Yugoslav identity and consequently did away with the inherited administrative and political structures in favor of new ones that cut across existing identities and boundaries. Aleksandar established nine administrative regions called banovinas, one of which was predominantly Slovene, two of which were predominantly Croat, and the remaining six of which were predominantly Serb. Bosnia and Herzegovina was being erased from the map and as an administrative or political reality, with the Bosnian Muslims parceled out under the new gerrymandered order as so much ballast. This sent both the Croats and Muslims into opposition, but their opposition was rendered rather ineffectual by the outlawing of political parties in favor of regime-sponsored organizations. The Muslims were able to maintain a sense of cohesion and common political purpose for a while but became increasingly disaffected from the new Yugoslav order, which seemed determined to deny them.

Croat resistance was more effective, with the mobilization of most of the Croat population through the mass political and cultural movement associated with the banned Croat Peasants' Party (Hrvatska Seljačka Stranka), which had been led by Stjepan Radić until his assassination and was afterwards led by his successor Vladko Maček. By 1938/9, Maček's tactics had borne fruit in the Maček-Cvetković *Sporazum*, a political agreement with the Prime Minister of the Yugoslav government that was approved by the Regent, Prince Paul, who had been appointed after King Aleksandar's assassination in Marseille in 1934, and which established a new semi-autonomous super-Banovina of Croatia within what was now a quasi-federalized Yugoslavia that had all the hallmarks of a Serb-Croat condominium. This new agreement confirmed the erasure of Bosnia and Herzegovina, parts of which were incorporated into the new Banovina, and the rest of which were left within the Serb-dominated remnant. As such, it also confirmed the alienation of the Bosnian Muslims and their leadership, some of whom continued to hold ministries and serve in the government, but with increasingly bad grace and bad blood. A second important consequence of the new agreement was that it provoked strong resentment in Serbia proper, where many considered it an unacceptable concession to disloyal Croats and felt that it should at the very least be counterbalanced by the creation of a properly Serb unit. The situation was not improved by Maček's clearly expressed view that what he had achieved via the *Sporazum* represented at best a provisional arrangement and that additional territories would have to be included within his Croat Banovina under any final settlement.

When it came to the Yugoslav Muslims, the situation could not but appear a logical development of political and governmental initiatives present through the 1930s aimed at exploring possibilities of mass population exchange (or rather sponsored emigration, as there would be no influx in exchange) between Yugoslavia and Turkey.[8] Mehmed Spaho, the veteran

---

8 There was a finalized but ultimately unsigned agreement between the kingdom of Yugoslavia and Turkey from 1938 to regulate the already existing practice of Muslim emigration, whereby Yugoslavia paid Turkey to receive her surplus Muslim citizens. An English translation of it is available, along with various other relevant documents and extensive bibliographical resources, on the website of the late Dr Robert Elsie, http://www.albanianhistory.net/1938_Convention/index.html. Other documents also available there in Dr Elsie's translations include Ivo Andrić's *Draft on Albania* and a number of Yugoslav memoranda on how to deal with the Albanian and Hungarian questions within Yugoslavia by leading Yugoslav historian, Vaso Čubrilović. Andrić was, in addition to being a poet and novelist, also a very successful Yugoslav

leader of the main Muslim political party, the Yugoslav Muslim Organization or JMO, died in 1939, possibly as a result of a regime-backed assassination, and the new leadership, under Džafer-beg Kulenović, was less inclined to cooperate with the Belgrade-based and Serb-dominated regime, and more oriented towards Zagreb, not least because of the feeling that the latter offered a potentially more welcoming environment for Muslims than the former.

Hitler's new disorder

By now, of course, the international situation was also undergoing a major transformation. Yugoslavia had maintained its neutrality for a while, but by early 1941 it was central to Hitler's plans, as he needed to send his troops through it to clean up Mussolini's mess in Greece, before embarking on his planned invasion of Russia. A certain effort was therefore invested in enticing/pressuring Yugoslavia into joining the Tripartite Pact and becoming a fully-fledged ally of the Axis. The terms were negotiated by Ivo Andrić, who was a Yugoslav career diplomat, had been to all intents and purposes the head of the foreign office during the later 1930s, and was at this point the Yugoslav minister in Berlin. The response in Belgrade was fatal. The army and much of the political establishment refused to accept the shift in alliances and a coup was executed, with British encouragement and moral support, which removed the regent and his prime minister, elevated the minor king to an

---

diplomat and de facto head of the Yugoslav foreign office in the late 1930s. It will not surprise the reader to learn that his and Čubrilović's recommendations involved annexing Northern Albania and utilising the agreement with Turkey to deal with the Albanian Muslims, while integrating Catholic Albanians into Yugoslav society. Čubrilović's second, post-war memorandum, addressed to Tito and his inner circle, recommended taking a similar approach to the Hungarians and Volksdeutsch inhabitants of the Vojvodina. The degree to which any of these plans were implemented is disputed, but the fact of population movements is not. Not merely were around 500,000 Volksdeutsch expelled after WWII, Tito also agreed the transfer of 160,000 Yugoslav Muslims to Turkey between 1946-8, and as many as a further 250,000 seem to have emigrated there, with government encouragement, in the subsequent 20 years. These were primarily Muslims from the Sandžak and Macedonia, ethnic Albanians, or ethnic Turks, rather than Bosnian Muslims.

early majority, and put in place a new government that repudiated the treaty in what must surely rank as one of history's most bizarrely self-destructive acts. Hitler, enraged at the insult and the implications for both his Balkan strategy and his plans for Russia, ordered the invasion of Yugoslavia and its obliteration from the map. This was coordinated with Mussolini's Italy and on April 6, 1941, the Axis powers attacked Yugoslavia, bombing all the major towns. Within days, the Yugoslav army had surrendered, the government and the king gone into exile, and Yugoslavia was officially under occupation and broken up into its constituent elements.

Under the new dispensation, a rump Serbia was ruled by a puppet government led by General Nedić under German occupation, while Southern Serbia (now Northern Macedonia), and various parts to the north and east of Belgrade were given to the Axis allies, Bulgaria, Romania, and Hungary. Kosovo, Montenegro, and much of the Sandžak were, like Albania, incorporated into or administered by the Kingdom of Italy, whose king was in any case married to the daughter of the former king of Montenegro (deposed in the aftermath of World War I), and the area consequently passed under direct Italian rule. Slovenia was divided up between Hitler's Reich and Mussolini's Italy and destined for ethnic re-engineering, with the native Slovenes to be deported into eastern Bosnia to make room for Germans in Slovenia.

In Croatia, the Nazis and the Italian Fascists first offered Maček and his HSS a role in government, but when he refused, they established a puppet state called "The Independent State of Croatia" (*Nezavisna država Hrvatska* or NDH) as technically a kingdom with a monarch from the Italian royal house, the Duke of Spoleto, but in reality a dictatorship ruled by the *Ustašas*,[9] a pre-war fascist movement that had been in Italian exile for much of the 20s and 30s, and led by Ante Pavelić, the Bosnian-born *Poglavnik*, a term which meant much the same as *Duce* or *Fuehrer*. Its borders extended to

---

9   This term means Insurgents or Rebels, those who engage in an uprising or *Ustanak*, which was confusingly also the name given to the initial resistance to the Occupiers and the collaborating regimes. *Ustaša* is the singular noun, while the nominative plural would be *Ustaše*. An anglicized plural *Ustašas* is common.

include both some of the Vojvodina (so that the border between the NDH and Serbia was at Belgrade) and all of Bosnia and Herzegovina. It was split into a northern German-occupied and a southern Italian-occupied half. The Italian half had three zones, the first of which included parts of Dalmatia and Istria which were under direct Italian rule. The second zone was under direct Italian military occupation, with the Ustašas essentially excluded, while only the third and innermost zone was under Ustaša military control. While the Ustašas themselves were relatively few in number, their ranks were swelled by the transfer of many, if not most, of the adherents of the now disbanded HSS and the JMO and their supporters. Many of them joined ancillary organizations and militias, like the Home Guard, rather than enrolling directly as Ustašas. There were also bands of "wild" or irregular Ustašas.

In both Serbia and the NDH, the new administrations took swift action to introduce Nazi-style laws against Jews and Roma and establish concentration camps, where they incarcerated and ultimately murdered members of those peoples. The most infamous of them, located straddling the northern border of Bosnia with Croatia, was called Jasenovac and has become shorthand for a system that spread throughout the NDH and operated at a level of brutality that reflected both the nature of the regime and the crude resources at their disposal. This would lead to the extermination during the war of at least three quarters of the Jewish population of the areas under their control, which was estimated to be approximately 40,000. The German occupiers and their collaborationist puppet government did much the same for Serbia and its 30,000 Jews, rounding them up and then shooting them in retaliatory executions or sending them to the death camp at Sajmište in Semlin (Zemun) on the NDH side of the Belgrade-based border. Belgrade itself served as the testing ground for mobile gas units that would provide the technical model for the gas chambers at Auschwitz, helping the Banat and Serbia become two of the first *Judenrein* territories in Nazi-occupied Europe, alongside the NDH itself.[10]

---

10 Estonia was the first. The grisly figure for Serbia's 33,000 Jews was about 90%, which includes the numbers for the Hungarian and Bulgarian occupied territories. The major difference was that in Serbia the Germans did the killing, while in the NDH it was Croats.

The new *Ustaša* regime also targeted, in even greater numbers and with even greater brutality, the Serb populations on their newly-consolidated territories, with a view to exterminating those they did not manage to drive out to Serbia or subject to mass conversions to Catholicism. This was tolerated and even to some degree supported, with reservations over the practicality, by the Germans, and the Ustaša had considerable autonomy in their genocidal campaign. There were approximately 1.9 million Serbs or Orthodox Christians on what would become the territory of the NDH, accounting for a little less than one third of the overall population of around 6.5 million. By contrast, there were approximately 750,000 Muslims. Catholic Croats were a bit more than half the total population, leaving around a couple of hundred thousand made up of one form of minority or another (ethnic Italians, Slovenes, Hungarians, ethnic Germans or Volksdeutsch, Jews and Roma, et cetera).

Cleansing the realm was clearly going to take some doing, and the Ustašas set to it with a will. As noted above, the Serbs of the NDH were subjected to a campaign of terror, forced expulsion to Serbia, and massacre that began very shortly after the establishment of the new regime and was concentrated in areas with higher levels of Serb population, especially the old Military Frontier between western Bosnia and Croatia, northern and western Bosnia, and central and eastern Herzegovina. This provoked resistance and a spontaneous uprising by these Serb populations during the Summer of 1941, which in turn elicited harsh and even more brutal Ustaša responses, in an escalation of violence that would last through 1941 and 1942. The emerging dynamic thus followed a non-symmetrical pattern, whereby predominantly Croat Ustaša units, many of them roving or mobile and so-called wild Ustašas, would target Serb communities, often recruiting militias or groups from the local Croat and Muslim populations. This provoked a Serb-dominated insurgency, that took its revenge primarily on local Muslim groups, and not just those individuals who had assisted the Ustaša units. Naturally enough, this response was not in itself particularly unwelcome to the Croat Ustašas and it was certainly little deterrent to further escalation.

The Ustaša activities targeting Serbs started as early as May 1941 in Mostar, moving on the eastern Herzegovinian town of Trebinje and then on to other heavily Serb municipalities in the region. Ustaša units came in from elsewhere, fabricated allegations, and started rounding up prominent local Serbs on that basis. The situation very quickly moved to killing and the rounding up of ever-increasing numbers of predominantly men, but also boys and women. Locals were recruited to assist in the process, which involved making use of convenient features of the local karst landscape, namely natural pits and dykes, which offered a ready-made disposal mechanism for the bodies. Individual massacres involved hundreds of victims each. The Ustašas made special efforts to engage the local Muslims and played on existing tensions between the Muslims and the Serbs, which were deeply-rooted in agrarian issues. The process lasted a couple of weeks, during which the Serbs naturally began to organize their resistance, partly on the basis of existing sectarian athletics, youth, and veterans' organizations. The insurgents began retaliating on Muslim villages, including women and children. They also turned for protection to the Italians, who proved sympathetic. The Ustaša massacres thus laid the groundwork for an insurgency that increasingly turned to Četnik leaders and ideology and sought alliance with the Italian occupiers.

This phase in Herzegovina culminated with the St Vitus' Day massacres on or around June 28. The Ustaša killings then petered out in the first days of July to pause and be followed by aggressively promoted conversion for the "assimilable", under cover of which many of the "unassimilable" were arrested and sent to the newly established camps, where most of them ultimately died. This was also the period that saw the active rounding up of Jews begin in earnest. In August, around Elijah's Day, a second wave of more indiscriminate mass killings, including larger numbers of women and children, began, but it was hampered by the gathering insurgency, which itself also involved increasingly frequent and brutal reprisals against local villagers, again predominantly Muslims. The processes were at this stage in full schismogenetic mode. The situation in Herzegovina was already affecting tens of thousands of all ethnic and religious backgrounds, with thousands already murdered by both sides. This provided an opportunity for the Italians to re-occupy the third zone, effectively halting Ustaša operations, while offering the Četniks an opportunity to regroup and ushering in a period of more cordial relations and ultimately collaboration.

As this summary suggests, the type and level of violence, and the directionality, depended on the role being played by the occupier and the freedom of action enjoyed by either the Ustašas or the Insurgents. Where the occupier cared to exercise control, there was real scope for tamping down the escalating cycle of violence. Where the occupier was either not present or not concerned, the local (i.e. Ustašas or Četniks) factors had an incentive to make the most of their freedom.

Thus, in eastern Bosnia, where the Ustašas had far less of an effective presence and were not able to organize anything like the same level of violence against the local Serb populations, those taken off to be dealt with numbered in the dozens rather than the thousands. For a variety of reasons, including the relatively weak presence of either the Ustašas or the occupiers, the Insurgents, and more particularly Četnik groups, started making inroads from out of Serbia and Montenegro as early as August. At first, the Četniks indulged mostly in intimidation, looting, and burning. The mass killings began in October and intensified in November and December, when the Četniks reached an agreement with the Italians that the occupier would withdraw fully and leave them in possession of the field, as the Ustašas were further to the West. At that point, they embarked on a series of extremely bloody killing sprees that lasted through the winter and would only be halted as the Partisans took control of areas. Such respite proved temporary, however, and once the Četniks were in control of areas again, the killing resumed.

A further important element of background for understanding all this was the joint Communist-Četnik insurgency in Serbia, declared on July 4 and followed by similar uprisings in Montenegro, Slovenia, and in Western Bosnia over the following month. Initially hampered in their anti-fascism by the existence of the Nazi-Soviet pact, once Hitler actually attacked the Soviet Union, the Communists were free to organize themselves as a proto-resistance movement in Serbia, as did what remained of the Royal

Yugoslav Army, which joined up in a loose alliance with irregular bands of Serbian militia based on pre-war Četnik veterans' organizations with a history of paramilitary and partisan-style activity that went back to the Balkan Wars and World War I. Together they set up the Republic of Užice, just over the Drina, which held through August and September. When the Republic fell in November, so did the pact between the Communists and the Četniks. During this time both groups had been passing over into eastern Bosnia and setting up rival operations.

These two movements would become the focal points of resistance to and, paradoxically, collaboration with the Axis Occupiers over the following four years. In the case of the Communists this collaboration would be tactical, limited, and resorted to only *in extremis*. They developed into a multi-ethnic resistance that functioned as the hegemon to a Popular Front and National Liberation Movement (generally known by its acronym, the NOP), and would eventually become the preferred ally of the Allies. As their position evolved over the war, they committed to the creation of a federal Yugoslavia, comprising national republics, with the abolition of the monarchy as a core principle.

By contrast, the Royal Yugoslav Army in the Homeland was the official military resistance arm of the Yugoslav government-in-exile, based in London, and the young king Petar II. It quickly came to be dominated by a group derived from the pre-war *Serb Cultural Club* that promoted a greater Serbian ideology and envisaged a break-up of Yugoslavia, with by far the lion's share falling to Serbia, once it had been cleansed of non-Serbs. This "homogenized Serbia", as it was called, was to stretch across Bosnia and Herzegovina and incorporate the old Military Frontier, most of Slavonia, and most of Dalmatia. With time this led to the identification of the king's cause and his army with the Četnik movement, cemented the break with the Communists, and saw the emergence of a strategy of tactical collaboration with a view to outlasting the Communists and putting themselves in a position to consolidate as much cleansed territory as possible within a Serb state under whatever order emerged post-war. As a result, the Četniks both worked with the Allies and collaborated openly with the Italians and, increasingly over time, with the Germans.

It was at least partly in response to the Ustaša terror waged against the Serb populations of the NDH that the Četniks conducted their own campaigns of mass violence, killing, and cleansing in the areas under their control or within their sphere of action, but it was also partly inspired by their own ideology, which helps explain why they very often targeted areas in which Serbs had not themselves been targeted but which offered a longer-term or strategic prospect with regard to their plan for a greater Serb state. This was true particularly of the areas along the Drina and eastern Bosnia, where, as we have seen, the populations affected were largely Muslim and had generally played no role whatsoever in Ustaša activities against Serb civilians. Tens of thousands were killed or forced from their homes during the period from 1941 through 1942 by this Četnik violence and then once more in 1943. While much of this took place after the first resolutions had been signed, it provides context as to the state of mind and expectations of Muslim worthies in the latter part of 1941 and early 1942. The terrain was being prepared and the Muslims had every reason to fear a spreading of the flames already burning in Herzegovina. In the end, it would be in these regions that Muslims would suffer most, ironically where the Ustašas had been least active.

The situation in northern and western Bosnia was somewhat different, insofar as the Serb communities there were attacked first and Četnik atrocities generally took the form of retaliation or revenge, rather than pre-emptive strikes or ethnic cleansing with a tendency to tip over into genocide, as was the case along the Drina. Here too the initial Ustaša attacks began as early as in May, as did the first signs of resistance from the local Serbs. The insurgency in the borderlands was thus spontaneous initially but subsequently coopted and developed by both the Četniks and the Communists. The way in which the two movements worked together to begin with, with rank-and-file members crossing over between them with some fluidity, was a further complicating factor, as the line between Communist resistance and Četnik atrocities was often blurred. This affected the willingness of Muslims and Croats to engage with either resistance movement, particularly in the early stages of the war. With time, however, the differences between them became clearer and the Communist-led anti-Fascist Popular Front became a more truly multi-ethnic movement, with significant Muslim and Croat participation. This Popular Front would establish its first effective base in Bihać and then Jajce, followed by Drvar, all in western and central Bosnia, the heartlands of the insurgency. This is also where the foundations of the post-war order of a federal Yugoslavia with six national republics were laid, at the constitutional assemblies known as the Anti-Fascist Councils for the National Liberation of Yugoslavia and of Bosnia and Herzegovina. Not merely did many Bosnian Muslims play an active role at these assemblies, it was at them that they finally achieved the promise of what had always been their goal, a constitutional order based upon recognition of Bosnia and Herzegovina's historical continuity and a guarantee of their own identity as a group constitutive of that historical continuity (this part it would take them some time to realize in practice, as it would not be until the 1970s that their status as a people or nation was fully recognized).

Finally, we may turn our attention to the cost in lives of the war. Even during it, all sides exaggerated casualty numbers or numbers that they had themselves killed, but the real problem with numbers came afterwards, when victim estimates were required for the calculation of reparations' claims. What appears to have been a more or less back-of-the-envelope calculation by a junior official, intended to represent not merely casualties but all deaths associated with the war and demographic losses incurred as a result of it (i.e. lost population growth, rather than just actual mortality), was taken for and represented as an actual death toll. It was around 800,000 too high, but so long as the Communist regime lasted, so did lip service to the number of 1.7 million war dead. Overall, the total number of war dead in Yugoslavia (not including the occupier) was probably somewhere around a million, 100,000 of them at least, and probably many more, killed within the Jasenovac system, and tens of thousands more at Sajmište. The genocidal activity of the Ustašas against the Serbs played a great role in this high death toll, as did that of the Četniks against the Muslims in their high death toll. How much of this pointless suffering might have been avoided had the resolutions fallen on less deaf ears is not an entirely comfortable question. Not much perhaps, as it would not have affected the sufferings of the Jews or Roma being targeted by the regime or have had much impact on the activities of the Četniks in eastern Bosnia. At best, the resolutions appear a flawed response to an impossible situation, but one that deserves our understanding and respect.

A bibliographical note or recommended reading

Those interested in pursuing the issues raised by the Muslim Resolutions or by the overview provided in this short essay may find the following bibliographical suggestions useful. All are works were either originally composed or are at least available in English.

For the history of the Balkans, a first port of call is Mark Mazower, *The Balkans: A Short History*, Modern Library, 2000. For those desirous of a more in-depth treatment, the standard textbook is L. S. Stavrianos, *The Balkans since 1453*, originally published in 1958, but reissued with a new introduction by Traian Stoianovich by NYU Press, 2000. For the Balkans under the Ottomans, see Peter Sugar, *Southeastern Europe under Ottoman Rule, 1354-1804*, University of Washington Press, 1977. For the history of the 19th-century Balkans and of Yugoslavia, see Barbara and Charles Jelavich, *The Establishment of the Balkan National States, 1804-1920*, University of Washington Press, 1984. A good, more recent treatment is Mark Biondich, *The Balkans: Revolution, War, and Political Violence since 1878*, Oxford University Press, 2011.

For the history of Bosnia, the standard, indeed magisterial English account is Noel Malcolm, *Bosnia: A Short History*, NYU press, 1996 (updated edition). There is a shorter introduction by Cathie Carmichael, an expert on genocide, particularly in the Balkans, entitled *A Concise History of Bosnia*, and published by Cambridge University Press, 2015. More expansive and engaged is Marko Attila Hoare, *The History of Bosnia, from the Middle Ages to the present day*, Saqi books, 2007, which, despite its title, concentrates rather considerably on the 19th and 20th centuries, but provides for those periods an unparalleled narrative account, based upon an enviable mastery of the sources and the literature.

For the Bosnian Muslims or Bosniaks, the best overall volume in English remains Mark Pinson, ed., *The Muslims of Bosnia-Herzegovina: Their historic development from the Middle Ages to the dissolution of Yugoslavia*, Harvard University Press, 1994. On national ideologies and their development over the centuries, culminating in the formation of Yugoslavia, the key work remains Ivo Banac, *The National Question in Yugoslavia*, Cornell University press, 1984. If there is one single work that makes clear the context within which the Bosnian Muslims were operating, this is it. For the situation in Yugoslavia during the 1930s, a well-received treatment is Dejan Djokić, *Elusive Compromise: a History of Interwar Yugoslavia*, Oxford University Press, 2007, a book whose treatment of the Maček-Cvetković *Sporazum* and the understanding of Yugoslavia as essentially a Serb-Croat condominium is symptomatic of the continued denial of Bosnia. For an alternative, interesting, and in many ways more satisfactory treatment, see Christian Axboe Nielsen, *Making Yugoslavs: Identity in King Aleksander's Yugoslavia*, University of Toronto Press, 2014. A classic study, recently translated into English, that sheds light on the position and preoccupations of the Bosnian Muslims under the first Yugoslavia is Fikret Karčić, *Shari'a Courts in Yugoslavia, 1918-1941*, Center for Advanced Studies, 2019.

For the wartime movements of the Partisans, Četniks, and Ustaša, the best introductions in English remain the works of Jozo Tomasevich, and particularly his *War and Revolution in Yugoslavia, 1941-1945: The Chetniks,* Stanford University Press, 1975, and posthumous *War and Revolution in Yugoslavia, 1941-1945: Occupation and Collaboration*, Stanford University Press, 2002. For the war in Bosnia and Herzegovina itself, the standard treatment is Enver Redžić, *Bosnia and Herzegovina and the Second World War*, Frank Cass, 2005. This is a classic, essentially pro partisan, and therefore traditional narrative. For an alternative, rather more pro-Serbian, but not particularly pro-Partisan view, see Stevan Pavlowitch, *Hitler's New Disorder*, Hurst, 2nd edition, with an afterword by Dejan Djokić, 2021. For the nature of the Italian occupation and their relationship to the Četniks, see Davide Rodogno, *Fascism's European Empire, Italian Occupation during the Second World War*, Cambridge, 2006. For the nature of the Jasenovac system and the fate of Croatia's Jews, see Ivo and Slavko

Goldstein, *The Holocaust in Croatia*, University of Pittsburgh Press, 2016. For Sajmište and the Jews of Serbia, see Jovan Byford, "The Collaborationist Administration and the Treatment of the Jews in Nazi-Occupied Serbia", in *Serbia and the Serbs in World War Two*, ed. Sabrina Ramet and Ola Listhaug, Palgrave MacMillan, 2011.

For the events of 1941 through 1943 in Bosnia and Herzegovina and in particular the escalation of violence, see first Marko Attila Hoare, *Genocide and Resistance in Hitler's Bosnia: the Partisans and the Chetniks, 1941-1943*, the British Academy, 2007, and idem, *The Bosnian Muslims in the Second World War, A History*, Oxford University Press, 2014. While the detail of these treatments can be overwhelming for those who do not understand the history of the region and the Second World War well, they are immensely rewarding for those who do. Also important, but comparatively difficult to come by, is the treatment by Tomislav Dulić, *Utopias of Nation: Local Mass Killing in Bosnia-Herzegovina, 1941-1942*, Studia Historica Upsaliensia, 2005. Least satisfactory, but perhaps more accessible, is Max Bergholz, *Violence as a Generative Force: Identity, Nationalism, and Memory in a Balkan Community*, Cornell University Press, 2016. Hoare's treatment is holistic, while Dulić focuses upon the processes in particular locales in eastern Herzegovina and Bosnia and north and north-western Bosnia. Bergholz's study is the most narrowly focused, geographically, but takes the longest temporal view. Another useful book that deals with the resolutions and the situation that generated them is Emily Greble, *Sarajevo 1941-1945 Muslims, Christians, and Jews in Hitler's Europe,* Cornell, 2011.

For the broader question of what Safet Bandžović calls the de-ottomanisation of the Balkans, the classic starting point remains Justin McCarthy, *Death and Exile: The Ethnic Cleansing of Ottoman Muslims, 1821-1922*, Darwin Press, 1996. There is a good overview of Balkan demography for the same period in Michael Palairet, *The Balkan Economies c.1800-1914, Evolution without Development,* Cambridge, 1997. Otherwise, see the essays in Kemal Karpat, *Studies on Ottoman Social and Political History*, Brill, 2002, esp. "Ottoman Migration, Ethnopolitics, and the Formation of Nation States in South East Europe and Israel". Other relevant works include Cathie Carmichael, *Ethnic Cleansing in the Balkans: Nationalism and the Destruction of Tradition,* Routledge, 2003, and Paul Mojzes, *Balkan Genocides: Holocaust and Ethnic Cleansing in the 20th Century*, Rowman and Littlefield, 2011.

Adnan Jahić

THE MUSLIM RESOLUTIONS OF 1941 EIGHTY YEARS ON*

Some 10 years after the end of the Second World War, one of the only two Muslim members of the prewar Ustaša émigré movement, Muhamed Pilav, offered in the *American Croatian Herald* his assessment of attitudes of the leading members of the former Yugoslav Muslim Organization (JMO) during the first few months of the *Independent State of Croatia* (NDH). A critic of the prewar politics of Spaho's party, Pilav rebuked the leadership of the former JMO, led by Dr Džafer-beg Kulenović, for not finding it appropriate to go to the people when the occupation began and inform them of the international situation and prepare them for coming events. The result, he wrote, was that the Muslims of Bosnia and Herzegovina ended up suffering more than anyone else, "thanks in large part to Dr Džafer." As part of his negative assessment of the Ustaša state, Pilav pointed out that Kulenović, when asked by a majority of the Central Committee of the JMO why he had joined the Ustaša government without consulting them, had responded, "I did it on my own and in my own name." According to Pilav, Kulenović's behavior and declaration meant he had cut himself off finally from the Muslim people, whose attitude towards Ustaša politics was clearly expressed in the series of resolutions presented by assemblies of clerics (*ulema*) and leading Muslims of Bosnia and Herzegovina.[1]

---

*   This paper is a supplemented translation of "Muslimanske rezolucije 1941. U povodu 80 godina od njihovog potpisivanja," *Prilozi* no.49, 2020, 167-210.

1   See Croatian National Archives (henceforth: HDA), Zagreb, *Služba državne sigurnosti Republičkog sekretarijata unutarnjih poslova Socijalističke Republike Hrvatske* (henceforth: SDS RSUP SRH), HR-HDA-1561, 010.0.7. *Uprava državne bezbjednosti NR Hrvatske Upravi državne bezbjednosti Državnog sekretarijata za unutrašnje poslove FNRJ Beograd.* Date: 18. 7. 1956.

Similar observations were made by Pilav's contemporary Muhamed Hadžijahić. In a wartime writing, dated 1944, he noted that Kulenović's transition from having been a member of the pre-war Simović cabinet to joining the Pavelić government on 7 November, 1941, struck the Bosnian Muslims (Bosniaks) a "terrible blow", both domestically and internationally. Kulenović had done so despite the leading Muslim politicians having decided, at a meeting in Doboj, that he had no place joining the Croatian government, regardless of pressure from the Ustaša side.[2]

Although some of the details of these allegations are difficult to verify, these assessments and views were given by well-informed observers of wartime events and political realities in the NDH. Dr Mehmed Alajbegović, twice minister in the NDH government, stated in a post-war prison manuscript that once Pavelić had succeeded in drawing Džafer Kulenović into government, "with an eye to bringing in the Muslims," he had then "sidelined him," and that it had been Hakija Hadžić, Alija Šuljak, and their fellow-travellers who had harangued the Muslim population and worked actively for the Ustaša movement. Kulenović had an office "without reputation or work," and therefore without influence, and the real Deputy Prime Minister had been Vjekoslav Vrančić. Kulenović did nothing to respond to the numerous initiatives directed towards Zagreb and intended to halt the disastrous Ustaša policy in Bosnia; responding to his critics that he represented "only himself" in the government, he did not deviate from his position, "even as the *dance macabre* continued to make its way through Bosnia and Herzegovina."[3]

One consequence of Kulenović's entry into the government was to compromise what had once been the strongest political party of the Bosnian Muslims in the eyes of ordinary people and many of the victims. Just a day after Kulenović was appointed Deputy Prime Minister, the Bulgarian Ambassador to the NDH Jordan Mečkarov reported a noticeable cooling

---

2   Muhamed Hadžijahić, *Posebnost Bosne i Hercegovine i stradanja Muslimana. Rukopis dostavljen savezničkim snagama 1944.* (Sarajevo: Centar za bosansko-muslimanske studije, 1991), 37–38.

3   HDA, SDS RSUP SRH, HR-HDA-1561, 004.2. *O bosansko-hercegovačkim muslimanima* – a report by Dr Mehmed Alajbegović, 7.

on the part of Muslims towards Zagreb,[4] the combined result of several causes and circumstances, from the favoring of Catholics over Muslims to dragging Muslims into the deadly campaign against "the Greek-Easterners." From the end of 1941, Kulenović personified the opportunistic and unproductive current within the Bosnian Muslim elite, which was attacked by both opponents and supporters of the NDH, for their respective reasons. One critic, who considered it baneful to insist on Muslim particularism in the Croatian state, attacked "our most prominent people" for not taking even one step away from the "methods of prewar politics." They were still driven by the thought that it was best to "hold some vague position, so that in any case there is access to both groups." He warned Muslims, and more especially those responsible for their fate, "that current developments are not parliamentary wrangling over the composition of government and political combinations and coalitions," but "historic and fateful events" that require Muslims to opt clearly for one side or another. Apparently, the author considered the majority of Muslims in positions of authority in the Independent State of Croatia "half-hearted Croats" and mere profiteers who were not interested in the fate of the ordinary Muslim people, but only in "religious measures and quotas" through which they sought to snatch "richer positions" and security in the lee of wartime uncertainty.[5]

Although one could hardly have said that Kulenović held "some vague position," neither he nor his party associates were particularly visible in the public life of the Ustaša state after taking positions in the NDH authorities. Kulenović left no trace of any activity to protect the rights of his ethnic fellows. On the other hand, his presence in the NDH government nevertheless served the Yugoslav government-in-exile when making

---

4   Nada Kisić Kolanović, *Muslimani i hrvatski nacionalizam 1941. – 1945.* (Zagreb: Školska knjiga, Hrvatski institut za povijest, 2009), 158.
5   Gazi Husrev-bey Library (henceforth: GHB), Sarajevo, *Zbirka rasutih dokumenata i arhivalija na bosanskom jeziku* (henceforth: ZRDA), A-810/B-3. The author is hidden behind the pseudonym *Mujezin*. He popped up a few times during 1943 with extended analyses of the military and political situation. He seems to have been a member of a shrinking Bosniak circle advocating unconditional loyalty to the Third Reich and the NDH.

negative assessments of the attitude of the Bosnian Muslims in the occupied Yugoslavia. When Kulenović entered the NDH government, Minister Branko Čubrilović declared on Radio London that, once the war was over, the question would have to be raised as to "whether Muslims would be able to cooperate as brothers in a renewed, great and free state," since they were, even if only as peaceful observers, "culprits and accomplices in torturing the Serb people."[6] Stjepan Gaži, a confidant of Dr Juraj Krnjević, employed at the Yugoslav consulate in Geneva, wrote, in a report of 4 December, 1941, that immediately after the April war the Muslims had "declared themselves Croats" and launched atrocities against both the Serbs in Bosnia and Croat Communists in Croatia, "without asking anyone for permission." Final consolidation of this trend came when Džafer Kulenović took up the position of deputy head of the Ustaša government, "which one may well describe as the only actually existing political force supporting Pavelić, since we all know the number of real Ustašas."[7] While Yugoslav émigré circles used Kulenović's joining of the NDH government to spread among the public of the Allied countries a highly negative image of Bosnian Muslims, those responsible in the country faced chaotic circumstances in society and called upon their political leader to use his position to rein the violence and end the suffering of ordinary people. "My dear Džafer," Reisu-l-ulema Spaho wrote to Kulenović, "by joining the government during these fateful days you have taken on a great responsibility towards the people, and it is your duty to find a way out of this unbearable situation. I beseech you, therefore, to address the most relevant authorities and to ask them to correct immediately the mistakes made [by the Croatian civil and military authorities] and to take whatever steps are required to ensure they

---

6   In Zlatko Hasanbegović, *Jugoslavenska muslimanska organizacija 1929. – 1941. (u ratu i revoluciji 1941. – 1945.)* (Zagreb: Bošnjačka nacionalna zajednica za Grad Zagreb i Zagrebačku županiju, Institut društvenih znanosti Ivo Pilar, Medžlis Islamske zajednice Zagreb, 2012), 759–760.

7   Ljubo Boban, *Hrvatska u arhivima izbjegličke vlade 1941–1943. Izvještaji informatora o prilikama u Hrvatskoj* (Zagreb: Globus, 1985), 41.

do not happen again."⁸ Kulenović took no action,⁹ and it was clear to many that indirect paths would have to be found to halt the violence and prevent further public suffering.

On 14 August, 1941, the very same day Džafer-beg Kulenović announced in Zagreb that the former JMO had in fact been merged with the Ustaša movement from the first day of the NDH,¹⁰ the assembly of the *El-Hidaje Association of Muslim Clerics of the NDH* approved a resolution in Sarajevo that called, in carefully chosen words, on the Ustaša government to secure the full legal safety of all inhabitants of the NDH. This proclamation by senior clergy who had also played an active social role in the Kingdom of Yugoslavia was reminiscent of petitions written by Reis Džemaludin Čaušević and his muftis, who complained to the new authorities after the Great War about the looting and killing of Muslims – filling the political vacuum that had arisen with the wartime disintegration of Muslim party organizations. Although the resolution was published only in its official gazette, the leadership of *El-Hidaje*, headed by Mehmed ef. Handžić, probably considered that the moment had come when it was necessary to stand up for the Muslim population, given the fact that their political leaders remained silent and passive, and some even actively supported the regime in its policy of terror and repression.

---

8   The Sarajevo Historical Archive (henceforth: HAS), Sarajevo, *Zbirka Fehim Spaho* (henceforth: FS), SF-800. A letter from Fehim Spaho to Džafer Kulenović dated 5 May, 1942.

9   In September 1944, an informant from Zagreb noted in a report, "Dr Džaferbeg Kulenović has practically no supporters amongst the Muslims of Bosnia and Herzegovina. This is attributed to his inertness in office as vice-president of the government and the circumstance that he has, according to the Muslims, always suceeded to date in preventing any benevolent attempt on the part of the national government to even attempt to sort out matters in Bosnia and Herzegovina. Dr Džaferbeg Kulenović is particularly despised by Muslims for preventing implementation of the constitution of the Islamic Religious Community, which was drawn up by recognized experts from the clergy and the sharia judiciary." See Military Archive (henceforth: VA), Belgrade, *Nezavisna Država Hrvatska* (henceforth: NDH), kut. 153c, fasc. 4, dok. 14.

10 *Hrvatski narod*, 15. August, 1941, 1.

But the *El-Hidaje* clerics were hardly the only factor in Bosniak society in 1941 to take a critical view of internal realities in the NDH. Disturbing circumstances in local communities pushed concerned leaders to react and seek remedies to existing problems, often pointing fingers at specific culprits. Thus, at the end of May 1941, the Imamate of the Jamaat (*Imamat džemata*) in Gornji Vakuf complained of the liberties being taken by local Ustaša Catholics, who had first usurped all the official positions in the town and then turned on the Muslims much, as they might have on the Orthodox "were there any here."[11] In June 1941, the imam of Prijedor, Derviš ef. Bibić, traveled to Sarajevo to deliver a letter to Reis Spaho from a group of prominent Prijedor citizens calling on their religious leadership to call "in the Muslim interest" for a cessation to forced conversions to Catholicism and to ensure religious freedom for the Orthodox population.[12] In September 1941, the local imam in Ljubuški informed the Reis that the full-time employees at the local tobacco station Abdulah Orman, Mustafa Kadragić, Hazim Ćerić, Hasan Osmić, and Reško Hrnjičević had been fired without any procedure.[13] Even supporters of the new regime expressed dissatisfaction, disappointed at how Ustaša officers and officials had behaved at critical moments for local security. Three "Croatian citizens of Gračanica" informed the *Poglavnik*, on 17 September, 1941, of how top officials of the town and district had conducted themselves during a Četnik attack on the town on 23 August, 1941.[14] They alleged that by fleeing the town and other forms of cowardly behavior they had hung out to dry "the peaceful and loyal people of Gračanica," who had been abandoned by

---

11   GHB, *Arhiv Islamske zajednice* (henceforth: AIZ), *Ulema-medžlis* (henceforth: UM), 1-2864/1941. In: UM, 2-304-1941.

12   Tomislav Dulić, *Utopias of Nation. Local Mass Killing in Bosnia and Herzegovina, 1941–42* (Uppsala, Sweden: Uppsala University Library, 2005), 229.

13   Adnan Jahić, *Vrijeme izazova. Bošnjaci u prvoj polovini XX stoljeća* (Zagreb – Sarajevo: Bošnjačka nacionalna zajednica za Grad Zagreb i Zagrebačku županiju, Bošnjački institut – Fondacija Adila Zulfikarpašića, 2014), 338.

14   For more on the insurgents and their attack on Gračanica, see Esad Tihić, Omer Hamzić, *Gračanica i okolina u NOB-u i revoluciji* (Gračanica: Komisija za istoriju Opštinskog komiteta SK BiH and Opštinski odbor SUBNOR-a Gračanica, 1988), 136–139.

their leaders to welcome the Četniks on their own. Fortunately, the Četniks were quickly repulsed – thanks to the energetic intervention of "our beloved army."[15]

A disappointed supporter of Hakija Hadžić and Alija Šuljak wrote to the *Vojskovođa*, Slavko Kvaternik, on 15 October, 1941, outlining the scale of the sabotage that had preceded the destruction of the Muslim villages in Bileća district and strongly condemning the political and military authorities there for having betrayed the people and the state and allowed "Četniks" to slaughter innocent local Muslims. He claimed that the Muslim leaders in Bileća had requested the local commander, Captain Branko Nališ, to assign a detail to patrol the surrounding area by night, but that he had replied he would not send soldiers, saying that "if Poland hadn't rushed to the border, it wouldn't have lost the war." During the Četnik attack on Bileća, Major Jagić had removed his officer's insignia and hid in a basement, while he had had his wife removed from the barracks to the house of a known local Četnik, Lučić. When the district chief Marko Šakić was leaving for Sarajevo, the farewell evening was prepared for him by mostly Serbs, "and next to him sat the wife of an outlaw Četnik teacher, Kokolj, who commanded a Četnik gang and was carrying out these massacres." The author of the report, who had been officially authorized by the Minister of Social Affairs to go to Trebinje and Bileća and organize the transfer of victims to Tuzla, concluded that the military and civil officials in Bileća should be asked why, given the attacks that had already been made on Berkovići and Divin, they had not evacuated the women and children from Plana municipality to the fortified camp at Bileća and instead had calmly watched the Četnik gangs conduct their slaughter and occupy other municipalities, "and why they had issued only 500 bullets per 1,000 peasant

---

15   HDA, *Ministarstvo unutarnjih poslova Nezavisne Države Hrvatske* (henceforth: MUP NDH), HR-HDA-223, kut. 141, 47565. The following individuals are indited in the report: the Gračanica district Ustaša commander Franjo Taborski, the district magistrate and deputy district chief Franjo Šajkaš, the mayor of Gračanica Hifzo Hifziefendić, the chief of the tax office in Gračanica Josip Trkman, and the district supervisor of schools Anto Zidarić. The report was signed by a railway official, Ratimir I. Gadžo, a businessman, Ibrahim Širbegović, and a notary, Salih Džaferović.

rifles in Plana municipality." He complained that the Četniks had carried out their most bestial crimes in Bileća district, "They stripped the women naked and massacred them in the street, killing any children that fell into their hands and throwing many of them alive into the deepest pits."[16]

Reisu-l-ulema Fehim Spaho was particularly prominent in expressing dissatisfaction and condemning the actions of Croatian military and political officials. Contrary to later stereotypes that he was insensitive to other peoples' troubles,[17] numerous reports unequivocally show that the Muslim religious leader spared no effort in trying to protect his compatriots or reduce the suffering of ordinary people, not only Muslims but also members of other faiths.[18] Of course, his main concern was for Muslims, especially once he had been made aware of the pointlessness of advocating for Orthodox and Jewish people in the NDH and been faced with the scale of Muslim suffering during the first months of the uprising. He expressed the most open criticism of the chaotic situation in the Independent State of Croatia in a letter to an unknown government official, probably from mid-September 1941, which, due to its indicative allegations, deserves to be presented in more detail. In it, Spaho refers to a letter he had sent to Slavko Kvaternik on June 8, 1941, but to which the Vojskovođa did not reply. In the letter the Reis conveyed complaints about the following: the dismemberment of Bosnia by demarcation of the new great counties (*velika župa*), the appointment of exclusively Catholic commissioners to the Sarajevo

---

16   The Historical Institute in Sarajevo (HIS), Sarajevo, *Arhivska grada* (AG), kut. 65/1941-45, 14. A copy of a letter to the military commander. Tuzla, 15. X 1941. For more on insurgent crimes in Bileća district, see "Izvještaj Uglješe Danilovića Tempu," *Vojnoistorijski glasnik* br. 4 (avgust 1951): 179–182. See also *Spomenica poginulim Bilećanima u NOR i revoluciji* (Bileća: Opštinski odbor SUBNOR-a Bileće, 1983), XXIV; Branko Popadić, "Na prostoru Stoca i Bileće," in *Hercegovina u NOB*, 2, ed. Sveto Kovačević (Belgrade: Vojnoizdavački i novinski centar – Belgrade, Istorijski arhiv Hercegovine – Mostar, 1986), 631–650; Tahir Pervan, *Nad jamom* (Sarajevo: Safe House, 2010), 72–81. Cf. GHB, ZRDA, A-810/B. Odbor narodnog spasa (henceforth: ONS), III knjiga. Chapter on "Četnički zulumi" [Bileća].

17   Enver Redžić, *Bosna i Hercegovina u Drugom svjetskom ratu* (Sarajevo: OKO, 1998), 320.

18   For an illustration, see HAS, FS, SF-694; HAS, FS, SF-698; HAS, FS, SF-745.

courts and government legal services, the filling of prominent positions in the municipalities of Sarajevo and Mostar districts only by Catholics, and the admitting of 41 Catholics and only nine Muslims to the railway school in Sarajevo. He stated that Muslims were better represented at the "Belgrade traffic school." He added a number of other objections, from Muslim children in Trebinje being forced to attend a private kindergarten run by nuns – the incompatibility of which with Sharia he had mentioned to the Poglavnik – to swearing at and insulting of Muslims by Ustaša Catholics. He cited searches of Muslim houses at various locations, including Gornja Tuzla, Gračanica, and Sarajevo, that were conducted without due consideration for Muslim religious customs. The Ustaša commission for Bosnia and Herzegovina, he said, had denied that Ustašas had been targeting Muslims,[19] although in all cases only Muslims and their womenfolk had been harrassed. He reiterated allegations of unequal treatment of Jews who converted to Islam and Jews who converted to Catholicism, adding that in Budoželj near Visoko, the Jamaat imam (*džematski imam*) had been threatened with being killed "if he continued to convert Greek-Easterners to Islam."[20]

The Reis's main complaints related to how military officials conducted themselves when insurgents attacked villages and towns. The military authorities had investigated the killings of Muslims at Avtovac and Mulje, near Gacko, and confirmed the truth of the Avtovac imam's report, informing the Reis of the results of their investigation, without, however, making

---

[19] After Reis Spaho had sent him a number of complaints about Ustaša conduct towards Muslims, the Ustaša Commissar for Bosnia and Herzegovina, Jure Francetić, reminded the Reis of the Poglavnik's well known position on Muslims: "It is simply not true that there have been any cases, not even one, of abuses towards Muslims by Ustašas. In fact the opposite is true, that, in spite of having been supporters of various previous regimes, Muslims have nonetheless been placed in positions of leadership by Ustaša officials wherever possible." See GHB, AIZ, UM, 1-2864/1941. in UM, 2-304-1941. Francetić's letter to Spaho of 26 June, 1941.

[20] For the Croat authorities' attitude towards Spaho's complaints, see HDA, MUP NDH, HR-HDA-223, kut. 32, 921. *Izvještaj Velikog župana Velike župe Lašva i Glaž dr. Nikole Tusuna Ministarstvu unutarnjih poslova NDH od 5. rujna 1941. godine.* His complaints were considered made-up.

any recommendations on how to protect the local population in future. A delegation of Gacko locals had visited Spaho on 30 August, 1941, afraid of new massacres, and informed him that "Četnik activity had resumed." The Reis sent a new letter to the Vojskovođa requesting the locals be armed and provided ammunition for self-defence, as well as reinforcement of the garrisons at and around Gacko, including soldiers from hilly areas, who were used to the sort of terrain involved, "because those stationed there up till now have come from the Slavonian plains and are un-used to the terrain and find it difficult to engage with the Četniks." He also requested the government authorities to assist with or themselves carry out the evacuation of women, children, and the elderly to some other region, as well as saving the summer harvest, which had just been gathered, "as there is a great danger that the Četniks are attacking precisely because of the harvest, to commandeer it for themselves and so secure provisions." Again the Vojskovođa did not respond, "nor do I have any further report on what has been done." The Reis also made accusations of treason against the commander of the local unit entrusted with protecting Berkovići, on the road between Stolac and Bileća. While many civilians, some of them certainly innocent, had been court-martialed for considerably lesser offences, this officer was handed over to the regular military court in Mostar, where word was he would be acquitted and released. The only official answer the Reis got to his complaint about this officer was that he was a "Yugoslav officer." The following quote is illustrative of the information available to the Muslim religious leader regarding the fatal events afflicting the population displaced from Bileća and its environs:

> All Muslims from Bileća district, who have not been killed, some 3500 of them, have fled. All their houses have been set on fire and all their property looted. They have nowhere to return to and no intention of going back. A delegation has gone to Zagreb to request a location for them in Bosnia to move to. Around 700 of these refugees were to be escorted to Stolac but never arrived there, and their whereabouts are now unknown.[21]

---

21   GHB, ZRDA, A-814/B. The transcription of the Reis' letter is unfortunately incomplete. The first page, which would have made clear who the official it was sent to was,

Had the Reis given his presentation a more general tone and had it adopted by a competent religious assembly or some other forum, historians would no doubt refer to it today as *the Spaho Resolution*. It brought together in one place a number of the characteristic complaints subscribed to by the Muslim elite and sent to various addresses in the autumn of 1941. Although he emphasized individual responsibility, Spaho indirectly attacked the whole system – that it was building an order to suit only Croat Catholics, showing extreme insensitivity to the needs, rights, and feelings of Muslims. There is, however, a key difference between Spaho and the signatories of the various resolutions. Spaho nowhere mentions violence against Serbs. As a religious leader, he clearly considered it his duty to try to stop or at least alleviate the suffering of his fellow believers under attack by anti-Muslim Serb insurgents, something he most likely felt he could achieve only by remaining within the framework of regular communication with the official authorities of the Ustaša state, no matter how imbued that communication might be with undertones of anger, criticism, and condemnation. One may safely assume that he considered it likely to be unproductive to provoke NDH officials in such communication by finger-pointing at injustices and crimes against the Orthodox and so to reduce any potential impact in terms of the relief being sought for Muslims. Spaho did not believe in the effectiveness of signing resolutions,[22] remaining committed to individual advocacy as, in his opinion, the only productive means of fighting for the people's interest. He did not change this approach, regardless of the warning he gave in a letter to the NDH Secretary of State, Asim Ugljen, that the appearance of resolutions as the NDH was sinking into the chaos of war was quite understandable and that the behavior of the relevant ministry towards the person of the Reisu-l-ulema could drive even him to join the "resolutionaries."[23]

---

is missing. The final page lacks a signature, date, or any other sigil. It may have been sent to deputy president of the NDH government, Osman-beg Kulenović, whom the Reis had contacted previously in relation to other problems and issues.

22 Hasanbegović, *Jugoslavenska muslimanska organizacija*, 754–755.
23 Kisić Kolanović, *Muslimani i hrvatski nacionalizam*, 196.

In fact, some of Spaho's remonstrations were more pointed and concrete than the *El-Hidaje* assembly's resolution of August 14, 1941. This is understandable, given that the latter was a public document and the *El-Hidaje* leadership had been caught up in the first months of the NDH by an enthusiasm over the adoption of a new constitution for the Islamic Religious Community that reflected the Association's goals. Under these circumstances, the *El-Hidaje* Resolution looked more like a new declaration of loyalty and support to the NDH than one directed against its policy. It included several expressions of loyalty to the Croatian state and national idea, to the point of calling on "the relevant authorities to promote the inclusion of the Sandžak within the framework of the Independent State of Croatia." Closer reading, however, makes clear the three major motives and reasons its authors had for writing it: ensuring that the new state pass into law as soon as possible a new Islamic Religious Community constitution that would reflect the wishes of senior ulema, the evident unequal treatment of Catholics and Muslims within the NDH, and the worrying security situation in the country. The Croatian state was not blamed for the situation, with government authorities simply called upon "to restore law and order as soon as possible to all areas and prevent unauthorized action so that innocent people do not suffer." This could be understood as an admittedly unrealistic and unfounded aspiration for the regular authorities to suppress the malign influence of the Ustaša movement, whose destructive activities were surely well-known to *El-Hidaje*. The resolution authors, however, make no mention of the savage and lawless treatment of the Serbs, but only of innocent Muslim victims, "struck down through no fault of their own in the unrest that has recently taken place in various places." They also thought it best to condemn only those individual Muslims "who have committed any form of attack or violence independently and at their own initiative." This reduced the many crimes of the Ustašas to sporadic unrest and outbursts produced by "rogue elements and uncivilized individuals," independently of and outside the system, which was thus carefully amnestied of all responsibility. *El-Hidaje* did not refer to these individuals as "wild Ustašas," (*divlje ustaše*) but did make it clear that it repudiated their stain both personally and on behalf of all Muslims. Like

Reis Čaušević after the Sarajevo assassination in 1914, the resolution authors called on all Muslims in Bosnia and Herzegovina to refrain from evil acts, both in the spirit of the sublime tenets of Islam and "in the interests of the state."[24]

While the resolution's connection with the Muslim Resolutions to follow is barely visible, Muhammed Hadžijahić seems to have been right in considering it their point of inspiration, particularly for the Sarajevo Resolution,[25] which was again supported by prominent members of *El-Hidaje*. But this status did not derive from the condemnation of crimes so much as from demands for law and order and for equal treatment of Catholics and Muslims in public life in the NDH. It is quite understandable that *El-Hidaje* should have been primarily concerned with the Bosnian Muslim population. While any call for the rule of law and justice has universal implications, theirs was largely motivated by the presumptive consequences of seeing it applied consistently, namely the safety and protection of Muslims. According to Kasim ef. Dobrača, Mehmed ef. Handžić, the intellectual father of the Sarajevo Resolution, had told him, as a close friend invited for an intimate evening at home, that, "This evening, it's just the two of us here. Our task this evening is to put together the text of a statement or resolution to be signed by Muslim representatives or a select part of the citizenry. No one has the right to destroy us or impell us down a political path that will result in our suffering. We Muslims have every right to say it publicly and openly."[26] "[...] to destroy us" is quite clearly a reference to the Serb insurgents, as "impell us down a political path" is to the Croat Ustašas – Handžić appears to have realized very quickly that the Muslims found themselves between hammer and anvil, incorporated into a perfect system of manipulation, victimhood, and destruction. The two months following the *El-Hidaje* Resolution had seen massacres at Berkovići, Trusina, and Kulen Vakuf and the Ustašas prosecute merciless "cleansing" of

---

24   *El-Hidaje* br. 1 (V/1941-2): 27–29.

25   Muhamed Hadžijahić, "Muslimanske rezolucije iz 1941. godine," in *1941. u istoriji naroda Bosne i Hercegovine* (Sarajevo: Veselin Masleša, 1973), 275.

26   Kasim Dobrača, "Rad Handžića u el-Hidaji i njegov društveni rad uobće," *El-Hidaje* br. 2–3 (VIII/1944): 86.

villages associated with insurgent activities, and the initiators of the Sarajevo Resolution – known also as the Ramadan resolution – felt they had to be much more specific in listing those responsible for the ongoing chaos and the measures to be taken to protect the lives and rights of ordinary people. They therefore designated the perpetrators of crimes against innocent Muslim civilians "rogue elements and insurgent Serbs" instead of the term preferred by officials and journalists, namely "Četniks" or "Četnik-Communist gangs." One post-war statement suggests that circles close to the Communist Party of Yugoslavia (KPJ) in Sarajevo may have had some influence on the formulation used in the resolution.[27] By contrast to the *El-Hidaje* assembly resolution of August, the Sarajevo one placed responsibility for insurgent action indirectly with the regime and directly with "individual authorities" in the NDH that, it was alleged, had been and were continuing to take action that was increasingly provoking "harsh reaction from the insurgents," resulting in even more suffering on the part of the wretched and unprotected populace. This repeated a critique already presented by many home guard and gendarmerie commanders (*domobranstvo i oružništvo*), appalled by the uncontrolled violence of the Ustašas.

---

27 Dr Zaim Šarac, an influential anti-fascist and the Chair of the underground National Liberation Committee in occupied Sarajevo and, after WWII, a prominent minister, national deputy, and member of the Constitutional Court, signed a statement on May 10, 1964, in Sarajevo, vouching for the moral and political correctness of Kasim ef. Dobrača, a former member of the *El-Hidaje* board and post-war political prisoner. In his statement, he admitted to having tried to exert influence through Dobrača on the content of the Sarajevo Resolution before it was finally signed. "While the resolution was still being drafted, I pointed out to you [Dobrača] that certain phrases or views in it, which could have had unfortunate consequences for the Partisans, should be removed or corrected. You agreed with me personally, but later informed me that you had not been able *fully* [italics: A. J.] to do so because of the resistance of others, who also had to sign the Resolution, – as those phrases referred to elements that were not under the command or authority of the Partisans." Šarac added that the motivation behind the resolution had been "to condemn the crimes of the fascists" and that in their conversations Dobrača had always condemned the recruitment or involvement of "our people" in the various fascist organizations and military formations, particularly the 13th Highland SS Division. See further Adnan Jahić, "Bilješke o djelovanju bosanskohercegovačke uleme u Drugom svjetskom ratu," *Historijska misao* br. 1 (2015): 181–184.

"Instead of engaging in open combat against the insurgents, i.e. those individuals who have actually risen in an uprising," we read in a report on conditions in eastern Bosnia and Herzegovina by the commander of the fourth gendarmerie regiment, "the approach has been to destroy their villages and kill their families, to loot, and so on, so that the resistance has become even more determined, as people who previously had no thought of doing so are now joining the insurgency."[28] The many human victims, their property seized or destroyed and their villages burned, a stop put to peaceful village life, as all headed *en masse* for the towns and orphans fought over scraps of food or for protection – this is what prompted the authors of the resolution to underscore "these are not sacrifices the patriotic must bear for their native land," but rather "a general and widening disturbance that threatens the Muslims of Bosnia and Herzegovina with ruin." The key observation was still to come:

> All this is undermining confidence in public safety and adding fuel to attempts, grounded in the course of events themselves and, to some degree, in Communist propaganda, to convince the uninformed masses that there is a systematic plan behind it all that is being consciously prosecuted.

Part of this "system" was recognized in the claims by "many Catholics" that Muslims were to blame for all the misdeeds and that "these events" were to be interpreted "exclusively" as a mutual settling of accounts between Muslims and Orthodox. The resolution's signatories made no bones about the participation of pro-Ustaša Muslim elite groups in "provoking" the Orthodox and characterized all Muslim perpetrators of such criminal acts as "rabble and habitual criminals" of the sort found in every community. They did, however, also point out that "they did not take such action independently, but only once they had been given weapons, uniforms, authorization, and frequently even orders." Similar points were, we may note, made by the signatories of the other resolutions and even by some military authorities writing about the mobilization of Muslims in

---

28 *Zbornik dokumenata i podataka o narodnooslobodilačkom ratu jugoslovenskih naroda*, tom IV, knjiga 1 (Belgrade: Vojnoistorijski institut JNA, 1951), dokument br. 245, 546–547.

"anti-Greek-Easterner" raids. When the commander of the gendarmerie station at Žirovac prevented a new assault by an armed Muslim mob and new atrocities against the peaceful Orthodox villagers of the area around Dvor na Uni in August 1941, who were being "cleansed" even though the district had not been declared an insurgent region, he faced unpleasant questions from the Grand Prefect in Bihać as to whose orders he had been following in halting the Muslims' attack on the area covered by his station and was even threatened with being thrown out of government service as a "non-Croat."[29] Still, while these crimes certainly required arms, authoriza-

---

29   An account given by the commander of the gendarmerie station at Žirovac was taken over in full in a report of the command of the 3rd Croat Gendarmerie Regiment, dated August 25, 1941. It states that at around 8 a.m. on the 22nd of August some 2000 Muslims led by the commander of the Ravnica gendarmerie station (north of Bosanska Krupa) had attacked the territory of the neighboring station at Žirovac and begun rounding up people, regardless of sex, and killing them and looting everything they came across. After the slaughter and mayhem, the crowd had rounded up some 300 women and young children and killed them all on the territory of Ravnica. The district chief at Dvor na Uni had immediately ordered the commander of the Žirovac station to do everything in his power to stop the violence of the rampant crowd, resulting in a several-hour-long armed stand-off between the gendarmes and the civilians from either side of the Una, at the end of which the Bosnians were finally repulsed. The next day, the Muslim mob, now without the leadership of the gendarmes, broke through to Žirovac again, but the district chief had in the meantime requested help from the Grand Prefect in Petrinja and the Muslim civilians were completely routed; some 50 of the attackers were disarmed, relieved of their booty, and then removed to Glina. "On this occasion, the army in question also arrested the commander of the gendarmerie station in Ravnica, Sergeant Marin Pilinger, disarmed him, and took him away to Glina to explain on whose orders he had raised the mob and allowed them free rein." See Archive of BiH (henceforth: ABiH), Sarajevo, *Zbirka NOR-a* (henceforth: NOR), *Neprijateljska dokumenta* (henceforth: ND) *1941. Kompilacija izvještaja Zapovjedničtva 3. hrvatske oružničke pukovnije, 6–7.* That this was not 2000 but just 200 armed Bosnian Muslims is clear from the report of the Gendarmerie Station in Dvor na Uni of August 24, 1941. Cf Slavko Vukčević, ed., *Zločini na jugoslovenskim prostorima u Prvom i Drugom svetskom ratu. Zbornik dokumenata, tom I, Zločini Nezavisne Države Hrvatske 1941.–1945.* (Belgrade: Vojnoistorijski institut, 1993), dok. 244, 585–586; Ljuban Đurić, *Banijski partizanski odredi 41–45* (Belgrade: Vojnoizdavački i novinski centar, 1988), 50–51. According to Đurić, the armed Muslims led by Pilinger were Ustašas from Cazin and Bužim, who had, alongside Muslim Ustašas from Vrnograč, already committed several crimes against the Serb population of the Cazin frontier. Đuro Zatezalo noted that on August 22, 1941, Ustašas, Gendarmes,

tion, and orders, which could only have come from the holders of political power in the NDH, who were generally Croat Catholics, the signatories of the resolution could hardly themselves have been in possession of the information required to back up the claim they so boldly made – namely that "in no given case" could Muslims be responsible for these crimes or have initiated them, unless by *Muslims* they meant the people or community as a whole. A claim often made by contemporaries, which could hardly have been fabricated, was once again repeated, namely that various atrocities in Bosnia were being committed by people wearing the fes and referring to each other with Muslim names, from which the resolution's signatories concluded that the hidden intention of those orchestrating it all from the shadows was to ensure the crimes were indelibly associated with the Muslim element. As proof that Muslims had neither intended nor planned any harm to anyone they pointed to the nature of life under Turkish rule, when the Muslims had been the only masters and had tolerated all religions and left everyone in peace, as well as to the fact that Muslims who had been serving as Yugoslav soldiers had handed over their weapons to the new authorities immediately after the April War of 1941.

While their main goal may have been to stop the violence threatening Muslims with new losses, in the demands they sent to all the relevant instances and levels of government and to all Muslim religious and political leaders the signatories of the resolution gave the broadest civic meaning to their call for the restoration of security and justice and the punishment of the perpetrators of any atrocities – explicitly stressing "without distinction of any kind" and insisting on absolute religious tolerance, albeit within a state that was destroying religious buildings, promoted conversions to Catholicism, and was still carrying out persecution and killings on religious grounds. They did not limit their demand for judicial prosecution just to

---

Home Guards, and "Muslim Ustaša civilians" had attacked Serb villages along Suva međa from the direction of Bosanska Otoka and Vrnograč and others in the districts of Dvor and Glina. They had rounded up the men, women, and children. "They killed 700 of them brutally with knives and mallets in the woods at Rastovača, not far from Suva međa, near Gornji Žirovac." See Đuro Zatezalo, "Razvoj i rad KPJ i organa narodne vlasti. Čerkezovački partizanski odred," in *Dvor na Uni. Od prijeslavenskog doba do naših dana*, knj. 1, ed. Mile Joka (Dvor na Uni: Skupština Općine Dvor na Uni, 1991), 301.

the perpetrators of such crimes. They also included anyone who had ordered or in any way facilitated them. The key demand was for the law to be enforced in future exclusively by the regular authorities and the regular army, which was a direct attack on the Ustaša movement – not just the rogue or wild Ustašas but the regular sworn-in Ustašas involved in the campaign against "the Greek-Easterners." The signatories and supporters of the resolution included the leading figures of Sarajevo Muslim religious and social life: prominent members of *El-Hidaje*, members of the *Ulema-medžlis*, except for Mehmedalija ef. Ćerimović, *Waqf* director Dr Hazim Muftić, the administrators of Islamic educational institutions, the presidents and secretaries of the various Muslim societies, including a leading member of the pro-Croat *Narodna uzdanica*, Edhem Mulabdić, political personalities like Uzeir-aga Hadžihasanović, Hasan-aga Nezirhodžić and Edhem Bičakčić, qadis, imams, businessmen, teachers, teacher trainees and students, and a number of individuals of a particularly Croat national orientation, like hafiz Akif Handžić, Hazim Šabanović, and Halid Čaušević.[30]

While basically very similar to the Sarajevo Resolution, the petition of the Prijedor District Waqf and Educational Committee (*Kotarsko vakufsko-mearifsko povjerenstvo*) dated September 22, 1941, and supported by prominent citizens of Prijedor, was characterized in the accompanying note of the Commander of the Military Border to the Ministry of the Croat Home Guard of November 6, 1941, as especially directed against Catholic Croats, unlike the Sarajevo, Foča[31] and other declarations. The intention was to draw attention to the favoring of Catholics over Muslims, "and the initiators were in any case the so-called Yugo-Muslims."[32] In the judgement

---

30 GHB, ZRDA, A-810/B. ONS, *II knjiga. Sarajevska rezolucija od 12. listopada 1941.*

31 Unfortunately, we do not know the contents of the Foča resolution, which has remained inaccessible to historiography. It would no doubt contribute to clarifying, at least from the perspective of the historical sciences, the still rather murky relations in Foča during the first months of the NDH, particularly given the unfounded claims that the crimes of the insurgents and Četniks were always and everywhere in response to Ustašas running amok and slaughtering of the Serb population. For conditions in Foča between April and December 1941, see VA, NDH, kut. 258, fasc. 3, dok. 13; Adil Zulfikarpašić, "Put u Foču. 25. I. 1942. Godine," *Godišnjak* br. 4 (1957), 44–55; Vladimir Dedijer, Anton Miletić, *Proterivanje Srba sa ognjišta 1941–1944. Svedočanstva* (Belgrade: Prosveta, 1989), 282–284.

32 ABiH, NOR, ND 1941, 174/7774.

of one Ustaša official, however, these "Yugo-Muslims" were certainly not an insignificant minority in Prijedor. The Muslims of Prijedor were far from so loyal an element as is often held. "The Muslims of the town are given to complaining about the authorities and the state and are increasingly defecting to the Četniks and Communists, particularly the young, students [...]"[33] After the war, an Ustaša émigré linked the agile local imam Derviš ef. Bibić with the local branch of the Communist Party of Yugoslavia. Bibić had declared publicly in the mosque "that Islam and the Koran are very close to communism."[34] These claims cast some light on the fact that the Prijedor Muslims' resolution makes no mention at all of Partisans or Četniks and instead focuses exclusively on the Croatian authorities and Catholic Ustašas, who are accused of conducting a policy of discrimination against Muslims and stirring up conflict between them and the Orthodox. The signatories to the resolution, however, presented the local Muslims as a loyal Croat group that only wanted equal treatment in local public and political life, by which they also meant inclusion in local governance and the local Ustaša headquarters (*logor*) – which they were being denied by the local Catholic minority on the grounds of unreliability. As a result, Catholics had monopolized all positions of authority in Prijedor so that not a single local Muslim was employed in any official position after the establishment of the NDH, "even though plenty of situations have become available since the Serbs were expelled." This policy led to the cultural and social marginalization of Muslims, including baseless accusations against Muslim youth that they were infected by communism, as well as pressure on converts to Islam to convert to Catholicism. The signatories reserved their most serious complaints for the local Ustaša headquarters, which they claimed had mobilized local Muslim residents and got them involved in bloody campaigns against the Orthodox:

---

33 Cited after Izudin Čaušević, "Ustaška vlast i teror na Kozari 1941–1942 godine," in *Kozara u Narodnooslobodilačkoj borbi i socijalističkoj revoluciji (1941–1945). Radovi sa naučnog skupa održanog na Kozari (Mrakovica) 27. i 28. oktobra 1977. godine u okviru proslave Titovih jubileja i 35-godišnjice kozarske epopeje*, ur. Nikola Babić (Prijedor: Nacionalni park „Kozara", 1980), 115.

34 Safet Jaskić, *Srbokomunistički zločin nad Bosnom*, reprint, (Tuzla: Izdavačko prometno preduzeće „Hamidović", 2003), 74.

During the insurrection, without consulting any of the Muslims, the *Logor* included amongst those it armed the worst rabble, and even gypsies, and deployed these types alongside the Ustaša irregulars to kill perfectly peaceable civilians of the Greek-Eastern rite. This was later worked up to suggest that only Muslims had committed atrocities and that the Catholic Church consequently offered the only safe haven from Muslim terror.

Showing Muslims in an ugly light like this has gone so far that some mobile Catholic Ustašas have hauled the women of captured rebels before the courts to get them to testify that their husbands did not flee into the forests to escape "the perfectly correct behavior of the Ustaša irregulars but because of terror imposed by local Muslims, who joined the Ustašas in order to loot and kill without mercy."

In a nearby branch office in Kozarac, some Ustaša irregulars who have since gone to ground forced some Muslims at gunpoint to hack some Greek-Eastern rite villagers to death and later presented it as a settling of long-standing accounts between the Muslims and the villagers. With the *Logor's* complicity, the Ustaša irregulars put on the fes, creating the misapprehension that all this havoc was being carried out by Muslims. Even the name of the Ustaša officer who gave the first order for killing in the locality, one Tomislav Dizdar, has been used to prove that the commander was a Muslim.

Indigent local Muslims have been court-martialed, condemned to death, and executed for allegedly extracting a few gold crowns from the jaws of the already dead, but no attention has been paid to the disappearance of property worth millions, carried off in broad daylight during the insurrection, though a complaint has been forwarded to the relevant authorities.[35]

The available historical sources support many of the claims made in the Prijedor Resolution. One German source states that in early June, 1941, Ustašas from Ljubuški killed a large number of Orthodox, including women and children, in Sanski Most, Ključ, Bosanski Petrovac, and

---

35   ABiH, NOR, ND 1941, 174/7774. *Deklaracija Muslimana iz Prijedora*.

Prijedor, on orders from the Grand Prefect Ljubomir Kvaternik.³⁶ A report by Colonel Dolanjski states that some "mobile Ustašas" from Herzegovina had joined the local Ustašas in Prijedor in carrying out atrocities and that they had come up from Herzegovina to the territory of Sanski Most, Ključ, Bosanski Petrovac, and Prijedor on government orders. According to Dolanjski, there were also some Zagreb Ustašas in Prijedor, but it is not clear on whose orders they had come.³⁷ In July and August 1941, the Ustaša Pinto, a converted Jew who had become a Catholic seminarian, had joined with local and Zagreb Ustašas to slaughter some 1500 people in Prijedor over a period of 13 days.³⁸ However, how credible is the claim that all Muslim criminals committed crimes against the Orthodox population of Prijedor and the surrounding areas only by order and under the pressure of the leading Ustašas? The signatories to the resolution did not distance themselves from the behavior during the atrocities of summer 1941 of their ethnic fellows, like Husejn Mujagić, who led a group of

---

36 Vukčević, ed., *Zločini*, dok. 372, 971.
37 According to the account given in her book by Vedrana Adamović, these were members of the so-called Kvaternik Guard, which took an oath on University Square in Zagreb during the first days of the NDH and then set off for Bosnia under the command of Colonel Mate Čanić. It was stationed in part in Banja Luka and in part in the Prijedor region. The Prijedor commander was Ustaša captain Slavko Dasović. According to the sources the author cites, the members of the so-called Kvaternik Guard, some 120 youths aged between 16 and 20, reached Prijedor on July 29, 1941, just before a mass slaughter of Serbs. They had red Hussar caps on their heads, marked with the letter U, and their commander was Vjekoslav Dizdar from Makarska. Dizdar was in direct command during the killing of Serbs in Prijedor on August 1, 1941. See Vedrana Adamović, *Godine stradanja 1941/42. NDH i njeni zločini nad srpskim narodom u Prijedoru i okolini 1941/42. (Prilog proučavanju zločina genocida nad srpskim narodom u Potkozarju)* (Prijedor: Muzej Kozare, 2018), 29–31, 81, 84, 96. As we have seen, the commander was named in the Prijedor Resolution as Tomislav Dizdar. The so-called Kvaternik Guard appears to have been a component of the Bosnian and Herzegovinian section of the Croat Army, formed with a view to taking control and forming military units in Bosnia and Herzegovina. See Milan Vukmanović, "Okupacija i uspostavljanje ustaške vlasti na području Bosanske krajine i Srednje Bosne u prvim mjesecima 1941. Godine," in *Oblasna partijska savjetovanja na Šehitlucima u junu i julu 1941. u razvoju ustanka u Bosanskoj krajini* (Banja Luka: Institut za istoriju u Banjaluci, 1981), 71–72.
38 HDA, *Odjeljenje zaštite naroda za Hrvatsku (OZNA)*, HR-HDA-1491, 4.1.9.

wild Ustašas near Kozarac, where several hundred "Greek-Easterners" were axed to death.[39] Nor did they mention the freedom-of-movement ribbons worn by Muslims and Catholics in Prijedor to distinguish them from the Orthodox during the Ilindan (mid-Summer) massacres.[40] There, as elsewhere, the Ustaša order-givers drew on local rabble and involved them in the massacres with promises of looting and riches, as is made clear by a detail from the *Memorandum of the Serbian Orthodox Church* to the military commander of occupied Serbia, Heinrich Dankelmann, which alleges the formation of special units "of Muslims and gypsies" to remove the corpses of killed Serbs and with licence to loot the victims. "They stripped them naked, even removing gold teeth, piling them 7 to 8 corpses high on the wagons, and driving them off to enormous ditches created by aerial bombs close to the graveyard, into which they tossed and buried some, while others they threw into the Sana."[41] After the war, the former district chief at Dvor na Uni, Dr Marin Bučan, testified that mass killings of Serbs had taken place in the Bosnian border districts, including Prijedor, on orders received from the NDH Ministry of Internal Affairs and that the immediate perpetrators had shared the possessions of those they had murdered and looted between themselves as a type of reward.[42] While it is very difficult to ascertain the degree to which a particular community was involved in the crimes committed and practically impossible to penetrate their primary reasons or motivation, it seems reasonable to suppose that the same social and psychological circumstances were at work in Prijedor as elsewhere throughout the NDH, giving rise to an atmosphere of insecurity, fear, and the avoidance of public activity, and fostering the mobilization of the dregs of society, people living hand-to-mouth and often in trouble with the law, with primitive views of life and society and ready to take advantage of any opportunity and make themselves available to the new power-factors, who in return afforded them copious satisfaction of their "needs."

---

39   Čaušević, "Ustaška vlast i teror na Kozari," 107.
40   Adamović, *Godine stradanja*, 90–92.
41   Vukčević, ed., *Zločini*, dok. 249, 612–613.
42   Milan Bulajić, *Ustaški zločini genocida i suđenje Andriji Artukoviću 1986. godine*, I (Belgrade: Izdavačka radna organizacija „Rad," 1988), 736–737.

The signatories of the Prijedor Resolution offered no concrete suggestions as to what, if anything, might be done to change the situation, beyond calling upon leading Muslims to intervene with the *Poglavnik* and other senior officials in order to have a stop put "from the highest level" to the events they were describing. The signatories of the Muslim resolution from Bosanska Dubica were more concrete in their demands, due no doubt to the insupportable reign of terror and anarchy being conducted against the peaceful existence of the local population in this Bosnian border district. Again, in contrast to their fellows from Prijedor, this petition's authors found it necessary to condemn openly the crimes being committed against local Serbs, whom they said had no connection at all with any disturbances or rebellion. They placed the main responsibility for the crimes squarely with the Ustaša headquarters in Bosanska Dubica, which had entirely ignored the orders and intentions of national and district authorities, not to mention the desires and wishes of the distressed locals of Bosanska Dubica. The very first steps taken by these self-declared Ustašas, who were the yes-men of every conceivable political current in the former Yugoslavia, indicated quite clearly how the miserable situation in and around Dubica was likely to develop:

> The persecution, looting, and killing of innocent and peaceful townsfolk and villagers of the Orthodox faith started immediately, and in the face of this violence the latter started to take to the woods and take up arms.
>
> This is how the current insupportable and desperate situation arose, in which thousands of our sons, wives, and children are losing their lives, and villages and towns and the fruits of hard labor, sacrifice, and work are being destroyed in barbarous ways across our blood-stained Herceg-Bosna.
>
> Even if the *Poglavnik's* Ordinance has restored normal conditions in the Independent State of Croatia, the members of the Ustaša *Logor* in our town are continuing with their violent methods and are in constant conflict with the district authorities, which, in accordance with the wishes of the majority of the honest, peace-loving, and industrious

local citizenry, are attempting to restore order and peace and create trust in the regular authorities of the state.

The signatories to the Bosanska Dubica resolution stressed that "conscious and honest citizens" wanted the persecution, burning, slaughter, and looting to stop and an end to all and any violence against Orthodox people minding their own business at home, even if Ustaša officials in Bosanska Dubica declared them enemies of the state. In addition to their wishes for peace, prosperity, and a secure tomorrow, the notables of Dubica set out four specific demands – in line with the demands from the resolution presented by the Sarajevo elite: for all Ustaša officials and all armed members of the Ustaša *logor* to be removed from office and appropriately sanctioned, for the Ustaša troops stationed in Bosanska Dubica to be replaced by the home guard, for the truth of the resolution authors' claims to be subjected to strict and thorough checking, and for the demands in the petition to be dealt with to prevent the locality from suffering the same fate as Kulen Vakuf or other similar places. The signatories also stressed their moral right to present the petition: "Our sons and brothers are fighting on the Eastern Front, serving and fighting in the Home Guard, or working in the mines and factories of Germany, while our villages are burning, and our labors and suffering go unseen. We have a moral right to demand our voice be heard."[43]

The signatories to the Muslim Resolutions placed their principal emphasis on the establishment of law and order and ending the violence against innocent locals, regardless of origin or confessional status. Yet in their background, in addition to dissatisfaction with the repressive measures that had led to the suffering of Muslims, there was undoubtedly a growing clash of interests between the Muslim and Catholic elites, fostered by the increasingly

---

43 HDA, *Zbirka mikrofilmova gradiva iz inozemnih arhiva koje se odnosi na Hrvatsku* (ZMGIA-H), HR-HDA-1450, D-2179, MF59, 447. *Rezolucija Bos. Dubičkih Muslimana. Prilog dopisu Zapovjedničtva 3. oružničke pukovnije vojnim i redarstvenim vlastima u Zagrebu. Datum: 30. siječanj 1942.* The attached document does not show a date or indicate the address or the circumstances under which the resolution was made.

obvious Catholic domination, to which urban Muslim groups reacted with characteristic sensitivity and expressions of grievance. The reason for reacting was at least as much concern at being denied their "due" benefits and privileges as concern over their religious fellows' equality. In the beginning of November 1941, 78 leading Muslims of Konjic signed a petition that was delivered personally to the *Poglavnik*, pointing out that the town and its environs were largely inhabited by Muslims and that it was their "desire that this circumstance be respected and that the administration of certain official bodies be entrusted to Muslims." They provided examples to support the claim that "our brothers of the Catholic faith are forcing out Muslims with the intention of appointing only Catholics in their place."[44] A complaint of "delegates of the Banja Luka Muslims," sent to the Grand Prefect of the Great County of Sana and Luka, Ladislav Ritter Aleman, on August 9, 1941, lists allegations against the new mayor of Banja Luka, Rudolf Ertl, which are very similar to those made by the signatories of the Prijedor declaration, but with added emphasis on the dissatisfaction of Muslims over "being stiffed" when divvying up Jewish and Orthodox businesses, "as Muslims received only two, with the rest all going to Catholics." As in other petitions and resolutions, the seizure of Jewish and Serb property was not condemned, nor was the dismissal of Jewish and Serb officials. What was condemned was the firing of 48 Muslims and the pensioning off of another five, "most of whom were still capable of working and being of service to the municipality."[45] Still, a month after the Sarajevo Resolution, the Banja Luka Muslim community leaders came out with their own resolution directed exclusively against the Ustaša policy of discrimination, terror, and crimes against undesirable individuals and groups, leaving to one side the question of Muslim equality and rights within the communal framework. The Banja Luka Resolution of 12 November, 1941, which Catholic critics termed a pamphlet and a ruse to deflect blame from the Muslims for the disturbances and crimes, was the richest in

---

44 GHB, AIZ, UM, 1-85/1941. In UM, 2-304-1941. *Imamat džemata u Konjicu Ulema-medžlisu u Sarajevu*. Br. 594/41. Datum: 8. studeni 1941; GHB, AIZ, UM, 1-31/1943. In UM, 2-304-1941. *Želja Muslimana Hrvata kotara konjičkog župe Humske. Njegovoj ekselenciji dr. Anti Paveliću*.

45 Vukčević, ed., *Zločini*, dok. 191, 462.

terms of content and the most comprehensive in terms of the claims and allegations made. It left absolutely no room for doubt that it was accusing not just a group of wild Ustašas but the entire system of the Ustaša state, with the sole exception, of course, of the *Poglavnik* himself, who was to be "informed" by the Muslim members of the government as to what was happening in the wretched districts of the "Croatian borderlands" (*Hrvatska krajina*).

Some of the most appalling crimes to occur in occupied Yugoslavia took place in the Bosnian borderlands, and the authors of the resolution felt a need to take a stand and explain the role of Muslims involved in them. The cumulative cruelty of the Ustaša regime towards the defenceless Orthodox population and their leaders is described quite openly. "The slaughter of priests and other leading individuals, without trial or verdict, and the mass shooting and abuse of all too often entirely innocent people, women, even children, and the driving of entire families *en masse* from their homes and their beds with but an hour or two to prepare for deportation to an unknown destination; the alienation and looting of property, forced conversions to Catholicism, all these are facts that cannot but leave any sincere human being aghast and have had a most unsettling effect on us, the local Muslims." They stressed that Muslims had never expected, far less wanted the application of "such operational and administrative methods" in these regions. With some reservations, the authors described the activities as a policy with catastrophic results; religious toleration, which had previously been high, had been undermined, while the brotherhood of the two segments of the people, the Catholic and the Muslim, was "now well on the way to absolute collapse." Military officials from Banja Luka had made similar observations, though denying the exclusive responsibility of Catholics for the situation. The break between the Muslims and Catholics was "practically complete." Impressed by the "Četnik" efforts and successes, the Muslims were beginning to be concerned over their own situation, which led them to extend their protection to "the Greek-Easterners." They were putting distance between themselves and Croats in conversation, by saying, for example: "we Muslims..., and you Croats." Poor economic circumstances found some Muslims expressing sympathy for "the Communists and the Greek-Easterners," while refugee circles in Belgrade included Muslims distributing leaflets blaming the Croats for all the troubles in Bosnia and claiming that it was Croats in the fes who were committing the violence against Serbs.[46] The authors of the Banja Luka Resolution blamed this estrangement primarily on "some Ustašas and other regular units and rogue elements," as well as on some Catholic clergy, who, they stressed, had been taking unscrupulous advantage of the new political situation. Their actions clearly showed that the followers of Islam did not enjoy equal rights on the ground in the NDH:

> Propaganda for conversion has reached heights that recall the Spanish Inquisition. Under this pressure, and with the tacit approval of the public authorities, there have been mass Catholic conversions of the Orthodox. Those who up till recently were denied even a scrap of citizenship or national kinship are thus at a stroke made full and equal citizens and national Croats, purely on the basis of having formally received the Catholic faith. The equal standing of Islam, emphasized so often in writing and by frequent statements from the highest levels, is now all too often put in question, in daily life and practical terms. Conversion to Islam, which we have never pushed, has also never afforded the protection that conversion to the Catholic faith does. Many intellectuals have paid for the attempt with their lives – as was the case in Travnik. Insulting songs are often to be heard from some Catholics – insulting the religious feelings of Muslims and predicting the same destiny for them as for the Orthodox.[47]

---

46   Tuzla Canton Archive (henceforth: ATKT), Tuzla, *Radnički pokret i NOB u sjeveroistočnoj Bosni 1920. – 1945.* [digital archives] (RP-NOB), 3-OJ66-41. *Doglasno izvješće Zapovjedničtva II. Domobranskog zbora za vrieme od 16.-31. prosinca 1941. godine.*

47   The Travnik Case relates to the killing of a civil engineer, Stanko Turudija, from Travnik. According to Mustafa Mulalić, the Ustašas killed him because he converted to Islam instead of Catholicism, claiming that Islam was also a state religion of the NDH. See Adnan Jahić, "Zbivanja u Bosni i Hercegovini 1941. godine prema Hronici Mustafe Mulalića," in *Bosna i Herzegovina 1941: novi pogledi*, ed. Husnija Kamberović (Sarajevo: Institut za istoriju, 2012), 177–178. Reis Spaho made the same claim in a letter to Dr Osman-beg Kulenović of September 22, 1941. See GHB, AIZ, *Povjerljiva arhivska grada*, POV-5, 1193/1941. *Dragi Osman-beže!*

Some Ustaša military units, and not just wild ones, did carry out serious assaults and attacks on Orthodox Christians and individual Muslims. For example, in Banja Luka, the Ustaša Josip Babić killed an innocent village imam, Edhem ef. Hodžić, in plain daylight, in the courtyard of the hospital. "Most regrettably of all, we still do not know today whether the perpetrator has even been arrested, something all the Banja Luka Muslims, in fact the entire Muslim population, have demanded and still demand." The case of the murdered imam offers a vivid image of the social and psychological reality in the NDH and how cheap human life was. What had happened? The 28-year-old imam from Kozarac had been brought to the Banja Luka hospital for treatment on 30 September, 1941, suffering from an acute mental condition. He soon made his way out into the hospital courtyard and started shouting at the top of his voice: "Long live King Peter!" At which point, an Ustaša "pulled out his revolver and shot two rounds at Hadžić [sic], hitting him in the head and killing him on the spot."[48] A day later, a leading Banja Luka politician and public official Suljaga Salihagić made a short speech at the murdered imam's funeral, declaring to the gathered crowd that Hodžić's "mind had darkened in fear" after having witnessed a terrible crime. He added that the very people who should "take us under their protection and defend us from attack are the ones who killed this wretched man in a truly beastly way." At this, shouts of protest broke forth from the gathered citizens against the killer and the Ustašas.[49] According to the signatories, other types of attack on Muslims were laid at the feet of communism; because of the occasional Communist with a Muslim name, people who had never been Communists were harassed and arrested, while many Catholics who had been notorious Communists were not just protected but often even rewarded with sinecures or jobs. Again, the signatories were particularly disturbed that the very individuals "who had provoked the uprising" had then drawn a certain portion of the Muslim

---

48   ABiH, NOR, ND 1941. *Kompilacija izvještaja Zapovjedničtva 3. hrvatske oružničke pukovnije, 10. Izvještaj zapovjednika redarstvene straže u Banjoj Luci Stjepana Tereta od 1. listopada 1941.*

49   GHB, ZRDA, A-810/B. ONS, II knjiga. Suljaga Salihagić made this speech, "prompted by the people," at the funeral of Edhem ef. Hodžić on October 1, 1941.

underclass into their anti-Serb activities. This was something they both regretted and condemned:

> We are aware of many examples of Ustašas donning the *fes* when going out to kill and slaughter. That was the case in Bos[anski] Novi, where four lorries arrived from Prijeko full of Ustašas with *feses* on their heads and joined up with the Muslim rabble to carry out a mass killing of the Orthodox. The same happened at Bos[anska] Kostajnica, where 862 of the Orthodox were killed the same way in a single day. And they did the same in Kulen Vakuf, where the Ustaša Miroslav Matijević, from Vrtoč, played a particularly prominent role. Around 950 Orthodox Christians were slaughtered on that occasion, prompting revenge on the part of the Četniks on August 6, when Kulen Vakuf was set alight and 1365 Muslim men, women, and children paid with their lives. We also know of cases when Catholic Ustašas have attacked Orthodox Christians with cries of "Hit him Mujo, hold him Huso, don't let him get away Meho!" and so forth. We are also aware of cases of whispering in the ears of the Orthodox that we Balije have been killing and slaughtering them in the hope of exterminating them entirely. Had we wanted to exterminate, kill, or convert the Serbs or anyone else, surely we could have done so rather more easily a couple of centuries ago, when our power in the land was greater than today and such behavior easier to justify.

Once conflict had broken out between the Muslims and the Orthodox Christians, Muslim soldiers were called on to put down the conflict and so to continue killing and being killed by Serbs, "so that we end up slaughtering and exterminating each other, with no idea when it'll stop or what the consequences will be." Again, innocent Muslim civilians would pay the highest price, while the instigators of chaos could withdraw, parade around in uniforms, and amuse themselves looting Serb and Jewish properties. At the end, the signatories to the resolution expressed their support for the goals and demands of the Sarajevo Muslims, published on October 12, 1941, and called on the Muslim representatives in the NDH government to ensure the *Poglavnik* was fully informed and to exert all their influence "to put an end to this awful situation."[50] The resolution was

---

50   Our citation follows the text of the resolution in GHB, ZRDA, A-810/B. ONS, *II*

signed by leading religious figures, former mayors, sharia judges, teachers, officials, businessmen, craftsmen, and other prominent members of Banja Luka society, including the serving mayor and the brother of a minister in the NDH government, Hilmija Bešlagić, Hakija, as well as by Suljaga Salihagić, who had spoken at the funeral of the murdered imam.

The remaining three available resolutions, from Mostar, Bijeljina, and Tuzla, largely contained the same or similar claims and complaints, though there was a significant difference between the Bijeljina text and the other resolutions: it refers to all the inhabitants of Bosnia and Herzegovina as Bosnians who had undergone a process of historical formation that distinguished them from the Croats and Serbs. The Mostar Resolution contained six concise statements condemning all crimes committed in the NDH and expressing a wish for absolute equality of status and legality to be introduced for everyone in the NDH, regardless of religious or ethnic/national identity – with explicit reference to "Orthodox Serbs" and not "Greek-Easterners" (which is how they were referred to in the Bijeljina Resolution). This may be related to some of the more prominent signatories to the Mostar Resolution having been supporters of the Serb or Yugoslav national ideas before the war.[51] No mention was made of the Ustašas, the insurgents, or other Communists, while "Muslim brothers" were cautioned to think carefully about the hidden intentions of individuals involved in criminal acts "against our fellow citizens," whether as their intellectual initiators or the executive agents, and who had indicated, within their own circles, "that they have something similar in mind for Muslims too."[52] The

---

knjiga. Banjalučka rezolucija od 12. studenog 1941. We have corrected a number of obvious transcription mistakes and other errors after the version in HDA, *Velika župa Posavje* (henceforth: VŽP), HR-HDA-254, kut. 3, 148/1942. *Kotarski predstojnik u Brčkom velikom županu Velike župe Posavje dr. Vladimiru Saboliću. Rezolucija Muslimana Banje Luke.*

51 Zlatko Hasanbegović, "Muslimanske rezolucije iz 1941. godine. Problem interpretacije," *Bošnjačka pismohrana, Zbornik radova XIX simpozija „Bošnjačko iskustvo antifašizma"* 12 (br. 36–37, 2013): 170.

52 ABiH, *Zemaljska komisija za utvrđivanje zločina okupatora i njihovih pomagača Sarajevo* (henceforth: ZKURZ), *Referati*, kut. 7, 82. *Rezolucija muslimana grada Mostara.*

declaration of the Muslims of the town and district of Bijeljina of December 2, 1941, like the Tuzla Resolution of 11 December, 1941, was made in response to the massacre of innocent people in Koraj on November 27, 1941.[53] They were the most direct expression of concern by the Muslim elites of north-eastern Bosnia for public safety and potential consequences of escalating violence against their ethnic fellows, albeit without any mention of the terrorizing and deportation of Serbs to Ustaša camps. The making of the Bijeljina Resolution seems to have been related in some way to conflict between military circles and the influential local elite there, led by Murat-beg Pašić, who was likely the motive force behind the resolution, insofar as he retained the signed original.[54] A sympathizer, the Grand Prefect of the Great County of Posavje Dr Vladimir Sabolić interpreted the Bijeljina Resolution as an expression of local Muslims' discontent with the military authorities' lack of concern over their safety, but its content indicates that the main goal was to rein in the advocates of revenge and prevent a repetition of Koraj. This is why the behavior of "rogue individuals on both sides" was condemned equally and both Catholic and Muslim Ustašas and "Greek-Easterner" rebels were called upon to refrain from bloodletting and acts of vengeance "which will only lead to our general ruin and extermination." The Tuzla Resolution was the furthest from the civic spirit of the Sarajevo and Banja Luka Resolutions: while insurgent actions were referred to as "unrest" most of whose victims had been Muslims, the anti-Serb campaign was described in terms of "attacks" by rogue elements. As a letter to "presiding minister" Kulenović, the resolution's basic goal was to petition for the "unrest," which had been provoked by the "attacks," to be quashed, if not by purely military means, then through political measures, like holding "all those guilty of illegal acts" responsible and publicly punishing them.[55] Both the Bijeljina and the Tuzla Resolutions were made only

---

53 On the background of and circumstances under which the resolutions were made, See Omer Hamzić, "Podsjećanje na dvije muslimanske rezolucije iz 1941. godine – bijeljinsku i tuzlansku," *Gračanički glasnik* br. 34 (2012): 110–117.

54 HDA, VŽP, HR-HDA-254, kut. 3, 194/1942. *Krilno oružničko zapovjedništvo Tuzla Velikoj župi Posavje – Bosanski Brod. Datum: 14. siječnja 1942.*

55 ATKT, *Ustaška nadzorna služba* (UNS), 5671/64.

when it was already quite clear that the insurgent activities were a serious threat to the safety of the Muslims of north-eastern Bosnia.

The available sources give no indication of the Ustaša authorities being particularly put out by the appearance of the Muslim Resolutions or for that matter inclined to take significant repressive measures against the signatories. Muhamed Hadžijahić wrote that the Ustašas were for once ruled by "cold reason and calculation" and limited themselves to petty reprisals against lower status individuals.[56] He offered no support for his claims about the reactions of leading individuals in the NDH, but the claims of threats against the signatories seem credible enough in themselves. Less credible is the alleged threat by Pavelić "that the Sarajevo asphalt will run with the blood of the authors of the resolution before the NDH government gives up its programme," given that, if authentic, it would have entailed Pavelić admitting to the Ustašas' and his own personal responsibility for the outbreak and spread of the insurgency and the chaos prevailing in the state. The sources indicate, as Hadžijahić confirms, that the dominant Ustaša circles considered the appearance of the resolutions a manifestation of Muslim unreliability and of the fact, as they viewed it, that the Muslim elites were still calculating the odds and did not really see the Croatian state as a long-term framework for their survival and future prosperity. The authorities, however, had no intention of allowing this manifestation to develop as a form of broader-based social capital for the discontented urban elites, and they therefore quashed any replication of the resolutions, which they treated as illegal propaganda.[57] Why were no serious measures taken against the signatories? Principally because there were hundreds of prominent and influential people involved. The signatories had acted, like the participants in the Muslim autonomous movement of two years earlier, as a strong and organized phalange which could only have been broken by a severe and uncertain settling of accounts within society. The last thing Pavelić and the Ustašas needed was to open a new front in a situation already marked by spreading insurgency and the loss of towns and districts across eastern Bosnia.

---

56 Hadžijahić, "Muslimanske rezolucije iz 1941. Godine," 281.
57 Jahić, *Vrijeme izazova*, 350.

While the Ustaša regime thus largely ignored the allegations and demands in the resolutions, for reasons of state, certain individuals nonetheless saw in them an appalling farrago of libel and half-truths directed against the NDH and its Catholic Croat majority. The Catholic Bishop of Banja Luka Jozo Garić, a Franciscan, wrote to the President of the Croatian National Assembly, Marko Došen, that all these Muslim Resolutions were "pamphlet[s] full of damned libel against and hatred for the Catholic Church," by which the Muslims were attempting to "pass their own transgressions and crimes off onto Catholics and so justify themselves to the Serbs."[58] Garić was correct in noting that the resolutions' authors had omitted to mention how many wild Ustaša Muslims had taken part in massacres of the Orthodox. On the other hand, he himself entirely ignored the key role played by those who had issued the orders and by Catholic Ustašas from outside Bosnia, claiming that the bloodletting in the Bosnian border districts had been carried out "exclusively by Muslims," while the tiny Catholic minority, and particularly the priests, had "to a man" acted to protect the innocent Orthodox, even "before a movement arose amongst them for conversion to Catholicism."[59] Garić attacked the Muslims for not having come out with the resolutions while the violence and slaughter were still ongoing, instead of waiting until the German attack on Russia had stalled and of doing so out of fear of Serb reprisals. The bishop was not entirely wrong: the resolutions really were "drawn up" only after the most brutal of the crimes had already been committed. He failed to see, however, that the major motive was nonetheless to condemn and end the violence, which was still threatening Muslim lives and property. The second element

---

58   After Jure Krišto, *Sukob simbola. Politika, vjere i ideologije u Nezavisnoj Državi Hrvatskoj* (Zagreb: Nakladni zavod Globus, 2001), 331. Emphasis in the original.

59   The claim that all the crimes against the Orthodox in 1941 were committed by Muslims was not uncommon in Catholic circles. According to the account given by Hava Hadžiosmanović, a Sister Olga, a teacher at the Jajce nunnery, while telling the children about certain unpleasant events, declared "Children, do not suppose that it's Catholics carrying out this massacre, because that's strictly forbidden by our religion. It is all being done by Muslims and not even one in a hundred of those committing these slaughters of Serbs is a Catholic. They are all Muslims and they will be executed as such." GHB, AIZ, A-809/B-1. *Izvještaj Halima Malkoča, imama iz Jajca.*

of Garić's allegation was groundless, insofar as most of the resolutions had already been signed before the German army became bogged down in front of Moscow, on December 5, 1941.

Catholics were particularly put out by the Banja Luka Resolution, as the comments of an anonymous critic, who was obviously well informed of social conditions in Banja Luka and felt a need to draw attention to certain facts left unmentioned in the resolution, make clear.[60] In his reflection on this "notorious pamphlet," he started by ascribing authorship, on reasonable grounds, to Suljaga Salihagić, an engineer and prominent politician, publicist, and activist in the pro-Serb "Gajret" organization, accusing him of having visited a Serb village during the Great War as a member of the Austrian *Schutzkorps* and having presented himself to an elderly woman as a Muslim Serb. He proceeded to present himself to Serbs for years as always having been a Serb himself, only to issue a brochure during the twilight of Yugoslavia calling for autonomy for Bosnia and Herzegovina.[61] He had placed himself at the head of the Banja Luka Muslims when the NDH was formed and was now "a leading voice" amongst them. The author also accused Salihagić's wife, Ifaket-hanuma, of having declared in front of the mayor, Hakija Bešlagić, at a session of the *Committee to Celebrate the Poglavnik's Name Day*, that she was not in any case herself a Croat, "any more than any other Muslims are." He added that she had also stated that the Muslims had previously played nice with the Serbs "for as long as they had needed them" and would now do the same with the Croats, "so long as they follow through with the promises made at the highest level." Otherwise

---

60 See ABiH, ZKURZ, *Referati*, kut. 7, 82. "Kratki osvrt na prednji infamni pamflet." Unfortunately, the document is not dated or signed. It is not impossible it was written by Bishop Garić, his secretary Kruno Brkić, or a Catholic from their circle.

61 This is about a brochure by Suljaga Salihagić, entitled *Mi bos. herc. muslimani u krilu jugoslovenske zajednice. Kratak politički pogled na našu prošlost od najstarijih vremena do danas*, printed and published in Banja Luka, probably in late 1940. On pages 39–40, Salihagić does mention a conversation from 1915 with "a woman" in a village near Kosjerić, but the purpose of the conversation was rather different from that claimed by the critic. The author had not come to Serbia with the Schutzcorps but as a member of a "Baukumpanija," an engineering regiment, as an engineer in the uniform of an Austrian officer, with a fes on his head.

– they would take things into their own hands. These statements provided the critic with enough ammunition to characterize the reasons behind and background of the resolution. If the worthy signatories, he asked, had viewed what was happening with such concern, what had they done to prevent it? How had they responded to the atrocities committed by their "tribal fellows" in the districts of Cazin, Ključ, Bosanska Krupa, Prijedor, Sanski Most, and Bosanski Nova? How many Catholics had there been at Kulen Vakuf? How had Matijević managed to carry out a massacre of such dimensions on his own? Given that they admitted the existence of perpetrators of their faith, why were they so exercized on behalf of their rabble? What had they done to preserve "fraternity between both parts of the people"? He undermined his serious objections to the signatories, however, by casting all the responsibility on just one element: the author of the reflection reduced all the massacres in the Bosnian borderlands to lawless behavior by irregular Muslim Ustašas, while Orthodox conversions were indeed coerced, but the intention was "to protect themselves from Muslim misdeeds." "Why don't they cite the cases of propaganda reminiscent of the Spanish Inquisition? Where has pressure been put on to convert to Catholicism?" The entire resolution was written "for nefarious purposes," including the malicious misuse of "an unfortunate incident," the death of the imam in Banja Luka. Were conditions in the country different, the person who gave the speech at the grave of the "unfortunate deceased" (Salihagić) would have been sitting under lock and key! This critic saw in the claims of the signatories of the Banja Luka Resolution only a pile of inconsistent allegations and views – but he did not deny, any more than he admitted, the responsibility of Catholic Ustašas for the crimes committed and the major human tragedies, the insurgency that had broken out, and the rupture of societal relations in the districts of the Bosnian frontier area.[62]

---

62   The Muslim Resolutions had a very poor reception in both Croat and Serb circles, to judge by the reaction of a Četnik command unit to a letter from the obscure *Narodna muslimanska organizacija/Popular Muslim Organization*, which was itself a response to accusations set out in a Četnik *Message to the Muslims of Bosnia* and which had pointed out that Muslim leaders had clearly expressed their views of the NDH and the Ustaša crimes in the resolutions signed in all of the major towns. Pouring scorn on the resolutions, the Četnik command unit responded that "The Platonic resolu-

In contrast to works of literary or popular history, critical historiography has expressed some reservations regarding the background, purpose, and significance of the Muslim Resolutions of 1941. Branko Petranović has pointed out that the *El-Hidaje* Resolution of August 14, 1941, "is chauvinistic in that it complains only on behalf of Muslim victims, without mentioning the Serb ones."[63] Robert J. Donia recalls that "historians of the socialist era" emphasized how the resolutions' signatories criticized the crimes as deviant excesses, without however attacking the core Ustaša programme of physical violence to eliminate specific groups. He adds that they did, however, call on the NDH authorities to re-establish order and prevent further violence.[64] Tomislav Dulić has written that prominent Muslims were less forceful in opposing discriminatory measures than actual killings. During the summer of 1941, the signatories of the Banja Luka Resolution failed to call for the restoration of property to Serbs or their reinstatement to official positions. None of the signatories said a word against the racial laws or other anti-Jewish measures. As to discrimination against Serbs, Muslim notables took a similar position to that of most Germans regarding the measures to eliminate Jews from public service and

---

tions of the Muslim intelligensia mean nothing in practice. They may serve as a fine historical document but are in themselves barren. They should have done more and written less." The signatories lacked the courage to join the true struggle, preferring to opt for such "barren resolutions." See GHB, ZRDA, A-810/B. ONS, *II knjiga. Jedna od četničkih komanda. Izvršnom odboru Narodne muslimanske organizacije za Bosnu i Hercegovinu*. No date. This commentary does, of course, reflect the Četnik movement's primary stance towards the Bosniaks, which was informed by the justification of mass crimes as "revenge" for Ustaša crimes against the Serb people during the first months of the NDH. By contrast, two years later, when the Četniks were trying to recruit Bosniaks to their struggle to restore a Yugoslavia on monarchical principles, the Muslim Resolutions are mentioned in a spirit of reconciliation, in the *Poruka denerala Draže Mihailovića muslimanima širom Jugoslavije [General Draža Mihailović's Message to the Muslims of Yugoslavia]*, from 1944, as examples of "conscience and civic courage," with the proviso that, thanks to the Ustaša policy of provoking a fight to the death between the Muslims and Orthodox, they had ultimately been a "cry in the wilderness." Jahić, *Vrijeme izazova*, 474–475.

63   Branko Petranović, *Revolucija i kontrarevolucija u Jugoslaviji (1941–1945)*, vol. 1. (Belgrade: Izdavačka radna organizacija „Rad," 1983), 95.

64   Robert J. Donia, *Sarajevo: biografija grada* (Sarajevo: Institut za istoriju, 2006), 214.

other infringements of their rights. They did not, however, acquiesce in killing or forced conversion, partly to protect their own interests, but also in part because the mass killings that were taking place before their very eyes did offend their moral sensibilities. Dulić notes a tendency on the part of the signatories to individualize the responsibility for crimes committed by members of their own ethnic group, while presenting the sins of "others" in terms of collective guilt and responsibility.[65] Emily Greble has expressed similar views. There is no overlooking the fact that most of the signatories of the Sarajevo Resolution had supported the German and Ustaša agendas of the previous few months. If they were now taking a stand against religious intolerance, twelve of the signatories had nonetheless also signed the anti-Semitic petition of March 1941 to "stop the Jews." There had been criticism but no protests regarding discrimination against and deportation of the Jews. One should understand the Sarajevo Resolution as a product of the situation. It was a direct response to a radicalization of Ustaša policies, as experienced by the Muslim community, and to the subordinate position Muslims found themselves in within the NDH. It was an attempt to rein in the Ustaša approach to governance, but not an attempt to halt genocide.[66] Zlatko Hasanbegović has further pointed out the need to take into account the political and social context within which each of the individual resolutions was made. In his view, any proper evaluation of the resolutions must keep in mind that they were made at a time when the NDH was experiencing an appeasement of "revolutionary chaos" and gradual change to the policy of government repression against defenceless communities and national groups.[67]

In assessing the Muslim Resolutions of 1941, it is important to remain within the framework of the history of the Balkan peoples during the first half of the 20th century and not to ignore the models of collective decision-making and action deployed by their elites. The experiences of the first Yugoslavia had shown what confessionally tinged nationalism could do to

---

65   Dulić, *Utopias of Nation*, 232–235.
66   Emily Greble, *Sarajevo 1941–1945. Muslims, Christians, and Jews in Hitler's Europe* (Ithaca – London: Cornell University Press, 2011), 126–127.
67   Hasanbegović, "Muslimanske rezolucije," 171–172.

the idea of Yugoslav community. This reality was informed by inherited social and political barriers. As Ivo Banac has written, the Austro-Hungarian, Ottoman and post-Ottoman patterns of governance all failed to promote the development of a pluralist political culture, never mind a culture of compromise.[68] In fact, a *particularist* culture informed the forms and scope of collective consciousness and social action. The signatories to the 1941 resolutions should perhaps be considered as members of an small, weak, and unsettled people that had suffered multiple shocks due to the abrupt vagaries of history rather than as fighting for universal human rights, something that at the time was at best a somewhat misty ideal even in politically far more developed societies. In this regard, one should not be surprised by the absence of condemnation of the anti-Jewish measures or the "chauvinistic" concern only for Muslim victims. How could it have been different under the closed and undemocratic social conditions of the time? Moreover, how were the signatories to know what consequences they might suffer for having signed the resolutions? In the NDH, entirely innocent people were killed casually – who was to guarantee that the signatories would not fall under articles 1 and 2 of the *Legal provision for defence of the nation and the state*, which mandated the death penalty for anyone who in any way "offends or has offended against the honor or vital interests of the Croat people or in anyway endangers the survival of the Independent State of Croatia or the government authorities, or attempts to do so to any degree"?[69] Unhappy over the status of their national group in the Kingdom of Yugoslavia, many prominent Bosniaks saw in the breakup of Yugoslavia and the emergence of the NDH a long-desired intimation of better times – even if at the expense of other peoples' and communities' interests. This did not entail the absence of any sense of justice or a disregard for the rights of "others." Both before and during the lifetime

---

68   Ivo Banac, *Nacionalno pitanje u Jugoslaviji. Porijeklo, povijest, politika* (Zagreb: Globus, 1988), 385.

69   *Nezavisna Država Hrvatska. Zakoni, zakonske odredbe, naredbe i t. d. proglašene od 11. travnja do 26. svibnja 1941.* Knjiga I. (svezak 1.–10.) ed. A. Mataić (Zagreb: Knjižare St. Kugli, 1941). *Zakonska odredba za obranu naroda i države od 17. travnja 1941.*

of the NDH, Fehim Spaho made multiple representations on behalf of members of other peoples and faiths. There is no reason to suppose that the members of the senior ulema were governed by different moral norms in their relations towards members of other confessions. The signatories of the resolutions included Muslims who had been closer to the previous regime than they were to their own community. During the period we are writing about (and it may not seem so very different today) the elites felt it incumbent on themselves to act and advocate principally on behalf of the interests of their own people and community, their ethnic, political, or religious group, taking the view that there were other people whose job it was to worry about the rights of "others," and strongly influenced by the view that "enough" injustice had already been done against "us and ours" for it to be high time to put their needs and interests first. This could help explain why, during the years of the Great War, even after having criticized anti-Serb demonstrations and called for neighborliness, Catholic and Muslim religious leaders failed to articulate any reaction to the repressive measures taken by the Austro-Hungarian regime against members of the Serb community. Just as it helps in understanding the absolute silence on the part of Serb political, intellectual, and religious elites at the news of the terrorising and killing of Muslims from Podrinje, eastern Herzegovina, and the Sandžak during the first years of the Kingdom of Serbs, Croats, and Slovenes. We have seen how some Catholic circles reacted to the claims in the resolutions. Not merely was there a lack of sensitivity to the suffering of ordinary people, but the suffering of the members of an entire group was simply ignored. Tomislav Dulić has asked why the Catholic Church in the NDH didn't come out with a protest similar in nature to the resolutions by Muslim intellectuals in Bosnia and Herzegovina. Archbishop Alojzije Stepinac did intervene, Dulić points out, on behalf of individuals and smaller groups, but it never took the form of an open and organized countrywide campaign, while Catholic clerics at the same time engaged with gusto in forced conversions. The situation was not any better on the Orthodox side. The Serbian Orthodox Church refrained from any form of protest against Četnik crimes. Dulić takes the view that many Orthodox and Catholic priests had too much invested in building their new states (whether Yugoslavia or the NDH) to criticize or attack them openly. This was not the case for Muslims, because of their societal marginalization in the Ustaša state, whatever the regime's real intentions regarding Islam or Muslims.[70] Consequently, regardless of how compromised one may feel the intention and value of the Muslim Resolutions to have been by the narrow class and ethnic interests of the signatories or their unwillingness to give their major complaints a broader civil import, there can be little doubt that these important social documents remain a shining example of courage and responsibility on the part of concrete individuals, who, under conditions of fascist occupation, staked their names and their integrity on behalf of a new order in which a dangerous and bloody anarchy and religious and nationalist hatred and exclusivity would not prevail.

The assessment of the pre-war politician and publicist Šukrija Kurtović is here entirely apt, namely that the Muslim Resolutions were, as he pointed out after the war, the only voice of protest, the only exclamation against inhumanity and fratricide, even if, as he pointed out, they were formally prompted by the interests and the need to save the Bosnian Muslims – at a time when other "bourgeois circles across Yugoslavia failed to make any type of noise, never mind a similar one."[71] The Muslim Resolutions of 1941 were not aimed directly at the occupier or fascism, but they did have an anti-Ustaša character and intention, which is of some historical importance, given the fact that the Ustaša NDH was a satellite of Hitler's Germany and Mussolini's Italy. The resolutions indirectly, and in some points quite directly, condemned any trampling of basic human rights and any segregation or humiliation of people on the basis of differences. Through the resolutions the Bosnian Muslim elite of the day retained some measure of honor and show that human dignity has no price or at least should not have one.

---

70 Dulić, *Utopias of Nation*, 235–236.

71 "Dokumenti iz perioda narodnooslobodilačke borbe. Stav sarajevskih muslimana 1941 godine," *Glasnik Vrhovnog islamskog starješinstva u Federativnoj Narodnoj Republici Jugoslaviji* br. 1–3 (1951): 24–25.

Safet Bandžović

THE 1941 MUSLIM RESOLUTIONS AND THEIR ECHO*

The swift progress of events in 1941, distrust, and uncertainty over the ultimate intentions of the Ustašas and their goals all made a deep impression on Bosniak consciousness. The propaganda machinery's constant stress on the unity and togetherness of Muslims and Catholics within a single Croat people received little real affirmation in practice. That Muslims and Catholics were treated differently was obvious in how the new authorities behaved, chose personnel, and the unmistakable preferential treatment of Catholics, for all the tirades about equality. There were very few Bosniaks in the senior ranks of the Armed Forces, whether the Croat Home Guard or the Ustaša military.[1] For all his constant appeals to the Bosniak people and their "Croatness," Pavelić was on record as favoring *one country, one*

---

* This is a shortened translation of *"Odjek 'Muslimanskih Rezolucija' iz 1941. godine"*, from *Arhivska praksa*, no. 14, 2011, 433-466.

1 In early August 1941, a group of Banja Luka Bosniaks sent a complaint to Ladislav Aleman, Grand Prefect of Sana Luka County, about Mayor Rudolf Ertl and his treatment of local Bosniaks. The complaint included the claim that "Muslims are being passed over for appointment as heads of various offices to replace Serbs who have been dismissed or moved away," and that "Catholic villages [are being joined] to the municipality of Banja Luka," with a view to "ensuring Muslims are outnumbered by a Catholic majority." Thus, following the dismissal of Hakija Bešlagić, "who provided no pretext of any sort for such action to be taken against him," a Catholic was appointed to lead the town of Banja Luka, a position in which "not even under the worst regime of the former Yugoslavia was a non-Muslim ever found," in a process accompanied by pomp and "the participation of military, musical, and Ustaša units." The complaint further reads that "as a result, Mr Ertl fired 48 Muslims at the beginning of August, depriving 48 Muslim families of their daily crust. He has also pensioned off five Muslims, most of whom were still capable of working and serving the municipality," only for Mr Ertl to then take on nine new officials, eight of them Catholics – cited after *Zločini na jugoslovenskim prostorima*, I, 461-462.

faith. The close relations between the upper echelons of the NDH and a segment of the senior Catholic clergy and Ustaša ideology itself both essentially ruled out recognition or acceptance of the Bosniak segment of the population as an equal community within the NDH. This negative attitude regarding Bosniak rights, even where they were in the majority, was bound to provoke open protest and remonstration. The relevant population was unhappy about Ustaša machinations aimed at deepening the chasm between Bosniaks and Serbs, which naturally fostered Bosniak disgruntlement with the regime. There were growing calls for the situation to be normalized and Ustaša organizations to be disbanded. According to Italian sources, Bosniaks "were equally appalled by Croat chauvinism and Serb nationalism, which has pushed them to seek the protection of a powerful regime." From September 1941, there was a pronounced tendency for Bosniaks to seek German protection and place themselves under German administration, if the Ustašas proved unwilling to change their policy.[2]

The Ustaša policy of persecuting Serbs gathered momentum during the summer of 1941. Groups of volunteers were quickly dispatched to anywhere Serb resistance appeared, tasked with breaking the insurgents' resistance. The Ustašas tried to implicate Bosniaks in their anti-Serb violence, adding to the escalation of interethnic conflict by how they conducted their operations against Serbs, viz. donning the fes and referring to each other by Bosniak names in order to deflect Serb hatred and revenge primarily towards Bosniaks.[3] The Ustašas of Ljubuški and Široki Brijeg used Muslim names when on operations in eastern Herzegovina in order to accentuate tensions between Serbs and Bosniaks.[4] The Bosniak complaints

---

2   Emily Greble, author of *Sarajevo 1941-1945: Muslims, Christians, and Jews in Hitler's Europe*, is of the view that "many Muslim leaders saw alliance with the Germans as the best way to resist secularization and the subordination of Islam to the Ustaša regime as the best way to protect Muslim victims from Četnik terror, and also the best way to protect Islam from the rising threat of Communist forces," cited after *Slobodna Bosna*, Sarajevo, January 13, 2011, 63.

3   M. Hadžijahić, *Posebnost Bosne i Hercegovine i stradanja Muslimana*, Sarajevo 1991, 52-53.

4   N. Bajić, "Komunistička partija Jugoslavije u Hercegovini u ustanku 1941. godine," *Prilozi*, no. 2, Sarajevo 1966, 210. Hafiz Abdulah ef. Budimlija pointed out that the

of 1941 testified to concerted Ustaša attempts to paint Bosniaks as responsible for their crimes and present events as "a mutual settling of accounts between Muslims and Orthodox." These remonstrations include the claim that the Ustašas frequently donned the fes, "to carry out all sorts of abuses, while referring to each other with Muslim names."[5] On the territory of Ljubinje, the Ustašas, feses on their heads, killed Serbs they had rounded up and then threw them into a dyke at Kapavica, commenting to each other that "he" would carry the can for it all – pointing at the fes.[6] According to some sources, the Bjelovar regiment ordered 5000 feses from Sarajevo workshops.[7] A home guard division "composed predominantly of Croats wearing feses on their heads" set off from Sarajevo for Višegrad.[8] Similarly, Ustašas from western Herzegovina, with feses on their heads, arrived in the municipalities of Goražde and Pothranjen, amongst other places in

---

Ustašas also wore the fes in Srijem when attacking the Serbs: "the Ustašas put on the fes and and it was all 'grab hold of him, Mujo, get him, Haso.' And off they all went in columns through Rača and Bijeljina to Serbia, as refugees. And when they got to Rača there were Muslims waiting for them in *šajkače*, which are ordinary Croat caps, and not in feses at all. And they were all bewildered and told us all about it, there in Bijeljina. And we took them to freshen up, to wash themselves, gave them coffee to drink, something to eat if they were hungry. And they said, 'what are you?' Muslims. And they said that it was Muslims who had chased them off there and now Croats were giving them a nice welcome here at Rača. But it was the other way round. And we told them what was going on and how things really were." Cited after *Arhiv Tuzlanskog kantona, Fond memoarske, Kazivanje hafiza Abdulaha ef. Budimlije o "Bijeljinskoj rezoluciji,"* 3.

5   I. Banac, "Hrvati i Bošnjaci," *Behar*, no. 32--33, Zagreb 1997.

6   H. Eminović, "Promoviran predložak za film o Čavkarici," *Preporod*, no. 7/945, Sarajevo, 1 April, 2011, 36.

7   Cf. H. Kamberović, "Muslimani i NDH," *Preporod*, no. 22/509, Sarajevo, 15 November 1991. In a declaration of the regional committee of the Communist Party of Yugoslavia to the peoples of Bosnia and Herzegovina in August 1941, Bosniaks were warned, amongst other things, not to fall for the deceptive policy of the Ustašas: "Are you aware that the Ustašas are putting on feses and going around Serb villages and killing and torturing Serb peasants, women, and children in order to stir up the righteous revenge of Serb villagers against you?" – cited after Z. Antonić, "Napori KPJ na sprovođenju politike bratstva i jedinstva u istočnoj i centralnoj Bosni 1941. godine," *Prilozi*, no. 5, Sarajevo 1969, 71, note 30.

8   I. Kljun, *Višegrad – hronika genocida nad Bošnjacima*, Zenica 1996., 69.

south-eastern Bosnia.⁹ Nazif Alić from Rogatica wrote in the summer of 1941 that he had been working on the railway lines when he saw soldiers disembarking from a railway car "wearing olive-green uniforms and feses on their heads, who had difficulty speaking in [Štokavian, op. trans.] Serbo-Croatian, because they were from Zagorje [in Northwestern Croatia, where they speak Čajkavian, op. trans.]."¹⁰ Dr Asim-beg Ćemerlić, a physician in Srebrenica, saved the lives of around 80 Serbs in June 1941. With other prominent Bosniaks from the town, he prevented even a single Srebrenica Serb falling into the hands of the Ustašas. Murat Dervišević and a group of Bosniak villagers from Kravica, which is on the road from Konjević Polje to Bratunac, stood up to the Ustašas on July 31, 1941, by refusing to take up arms and move against the Serbs.¹¹ During the month in which it controlled the district of Foča, out of a total of 38,000 Bosniaks there "the Ustaša regime managed to mobilize no more than a dozen or so individuals into the Ustašas. Largely because they were using anti-Serb watchwords. Those who did join were mostly outsiders or members of the proletariat, who did not represent the local Muslims in any real way." Not even one reputable citizen of Foča expressed approval for Ustaša behavior in any way.¹² There were thus many examples of Bosniak solidarity with

---

9   K. Čeljo, "Muslimanske milicije u BiH 1941-1945," *Glasnik*, Rijaset IZ u BiH, no. 11-12, Sarajevo, 2007, 1136.

10 N. Alić, "Svjedočenja i sjećanja o pokoljima Muslimana od strane Četnika u okolini Rogatice," manuscript, BZK Preporod, Sarajevo. Cf. S. Bandžović, "Prilog proučavanju četničkog genocida nad Muslimanima u istočnoj Bosni," *Istorijski zbornik,* no. 10, Banja Luka, 1989, 157-175.

11 A. Gruhonjić, "Zlo stiže sa strane," *Oslobođenje*, Sarajevo, 11 September 1991.

12 Cited after S. Jaskić, *Srbokomunistički zločin nad Bosnom,* reprint, Tuzla 2003, 59- 60. Jaskić cites A. Zulfikarpašić's *Put u Foču*. According to Rodoljub Čolaković "for the sake of historical truth, one should point out that the Ustašas in eastern Bosnia had nowhere near the same influence as they did, for example, in western Herzegovina (Široki Brijeg, Čapljina, Ljubuški) or in central Bosnia and the Bosnian borderlands (Travnik, Bugojno, Kupres, Livno). As a result, we did not see a similar number of mass crimes in eastern Bosnia immediately following the occupation as in those areas, and as a rule they were carried out by Ustašas sent from Sarajevo to particular places (Vlasenica, Brčko, and elsewhere). In 1941, the Ustašas intended to create a 'military border' in eastern Bosnia in the areas along the Drina, having first expelled the Serb population. The outbreak of the insurgency hindered them in their plans" – cited

the persecuted and discriminated-against Serbs.[13] The *Doglavnik* [deputy to the *Poglavnik* of the NDH, op. trans.] Adem-aga Mešić opposed Ustaša atrocities, trying without success to influence Ante Pavelić and get him to put an end to the criminal acts.[14] Two months after the establishment of the NDH, Adem Osmanbegović, the acting district chief in Gračanica, was doing whatever he could to save his Serb fellow-citizens from Ustaša persecution. He found a way to inform those for whom warrants were coming from higher authorities for their arrest or expulsion, warning them to get clear, or even withholding the executive order. Midhat Muratbegović, a teacher from Doborovci, and certain other prominent individuals from Gračanica, took similar measures. Although acting entirely off his own bat, Osmanbegović nonetheless kept a number of prominent townsfolk informed of his intentions in order to keep them on board with his activities. Thanks to his engagement, quite a few Serb families were saved from certain death. In practical terms, he snatched Serbs from the clutches of the Ustašas, "protecting them, even if, naturally enough, he did not succeed in protecting everyone." As a result, the Ustašas requested his dismissal on the grounds that he was openly protecting Serbs. In

---

after R. Čolaković, *O društveno-političkim prilikama u istočnoj Bosni uoći izbijanja ustanka 1941.*, 21.

13   O. Marasović, *Narodnooslobodilački pokret u gradu i prvoj godini ustanka*, in *Sarajevo u revoluciji*, vol. 2, Sarajevo 1977, 488.

14   Mešić would later point out that the entire time he was himself resident in Tešanj district, up to October 1943, there was no persecution or killing of Serbs or Jews and that no one from Tešanj was killed or sent to a camp, and that no property was seized from any Serbs or Jews. For more, see S. Kurtić, *Adem-aga Mešić u svom vremenu*, Tešanj 2004, 118-119. Halid Kadrić, a literary author, has spoken of how Mešić saved people without regard to who came from which nation: "It is well known that no one in Tešanj suffered during the war. He saved whole groups of people that were being sent to the camp by train.... Look – he could have refused to collaborate and to become *doglavnik*. He consulted his friends – if he had not accepted, the Ustašas would have come and taken everyone away and burnt it all down. They objected to him – will you be able to sleep soundly, as you look at cemeteries full of people you could have saved? What then? He accepted and succeeded in ensuring that the Ustaša boot and blade did not oppress his national fellows. Even the Serbs asked later for him to be freed because he had protected them." – cited after *Preporod*, no. 24/938, Sarajevo, 15 December 2010, 39.

early August, he was dismissed and transferred to Banja Luka.¹⁵ He was replaced by Franjo Šajkaš and a reign of looting Serb and Jewish families, extortion, and deportation followed in Gračanica.¹⁶ The Jews were nonetheless spared mass persecution up till April 1943.¹⁷ The Ustašas had at best only a few individual sympathizers in Tuzla and there were many examples in the town of vulnerable Serb and Jewish groups being helped.¹⁸ Having learned of a plan to arrest individual Serbs in and around Tuzla, Ragib Čapljić, the Grand Župan or Prefect of the Grand County of Usora and Soli, informed them through intermediaries to hide.¹⁹ His attempts

---

15   E. Tihić – O. Hamzić, *Gračanica i okolina u NOB-u i revoluciji,* Gračanica 1988, 124-125. Bosniak villagers forced the villagers who looted abandoned Serb houses to return the things and livestock they had taken to their real owners in Gornja Lohinja and Lendići. Individuals who were particularly prominent in such moves to return Serb property included Musto Kovač from Sladna, Šahbaz Mujić from Gornja Orahovica, Meho Delić from Sokol, and Jusuf Spahić from Piskavica.

16   O. Hamzić, "Prva organizacija KPJ u Gračanici i njeno antifašističko djelovanje u toku Drugog svjetskog rata – od osnivanja, u proljeće 1941., do raspuštanja, u jesen 1944. godine," *Gračanički glasnik,* no. 24, Gračanica, 2007, 66, 75.

17   Nihad Halilbegović writes that the local authorities in Gračanica were well disposed towards the Jews, "There were no problems until 1943, when orders arrived from the Ustaša headquarters in Tuzla to deal with the Jews. But the Bosniaks opposed it, so on February 28, 1943, they helped a large number of intellectuals, particularly doctors, to get to free territory. At that time, they moved Dr Hinko Marić and his son Petar, Dr Ivo Levi, the pharmacist Vinko Koloman, his wife Helena and their 11 month-old daughter Nada, who Suljo Mujić took in his car, to Ozren" – For more, see A. Malagić, "Kako smo spasili malu Jevrejku u Gračanici," *Dnevni avaz,* Sarajevo, 24 January 2009.

18   According to Edina Kamenica, "A Bosnian story about the holocaust might begin with the Džaferbey Mahala in Tuzla, where a group of Nazi officers burst into a house where had heard there was a two-month-old baby whose father was a Jew. Just a few minutes before, the baby was snatched from its mother's arms by Nermina Hukić, who smuggled her to safety. The baby's savior later brought the baby secretly to her mother on a number of occasions and finally restored it to her in 1945" – See E. Kamenica, "Vizental je BiH otvorio medijska vrata u Americi," *Oslobođenje,* Sarajevo, 28 January 2008, 4.

19   V. Mujbegović, "O prvoj ratnoj godini u okupiranoj Tuzli," in *Tuzla u radničkom pokretu i revoluciji,* vol. II, Tuzla 1984, 242. Serb insurgents around Rogatica had captured Taiba, Čapljić's daughter. She was quickly ransomed for some salt and other goods. See V. Mujbegović, "O prvoj ratnoj godini u okupiranoj Tuzli," 241.

to find out the truth about the disappearance of dozens of arrested Serbs left Čapljić exposed to Ustaša accusations and calls for his dismissal as someone who could not be relied upon to carry out the duties entrusted to him.[20] Sead-beg Kulović, the mayor of Tuzla, was an advocate of autonomy for Bosnia and Herzegovina and considered the Ustaša regime "temporary and artificial." According to statements by a number of Serb families from the town, he helped Serbs and protected them from Ustaša fury "not just in Tuzla but in a number of smaller places around eastern Bosnia."[21] After a group of Ustašas were killed on Mount Ozren at the end of August 1941, the Ustašas summoned Vječeslav Montanije, the district head in Brčko notorious for his brutal persecution of Jews and Serbs, to Tuzla, where he was expected to deploy his Ustašas to help them take their revenge on the Serb population of the town. The plan was for the Serb quarter to be razed to the ground and the population killed or sent to the camps. Prominent Bosniak Tuzlans organized a conference once they had learned of the plan with a view to preventing the planned crime. The conference was held at the premises of the Senate Craft Association. After the conference, three prominent local citizens, led by the mufti, Muhamed efendi Kurt, sought out the German commandant, Hochbauer, and Lt Col Vist to express Bosniak opposition to Ustaša plans. Apprised in this way of the seriousness of the situation, the German commanders issued a written order to the Ustašas forbidding them to take any reprisal measures without prior approval.[22] Because of his attempt to discover the

---

20 A. Jahić, *Muslimanske formacije tuzlanskog kraja u Drugom svjetskom ratu*, Tuzla, 1995, 23; E. Redžić, *Bosna i Herzegovina u Drugom svjetskom ratu*, Sarajevo 1998, 313. Adnan Jahić points out that in addition to Čapljić, the former Tuzla mayors, Lutfi-beg Sijerčić and Hasan-aga Pašić, the Mufti Muhamed Šefket ef. Kurt, Nurija Pašić, and other prominent citizens were involved in the move to protect the rights of Serb inhabitants.

21 He further claimed "that he had even personally intervened to have several dozen imprisoned partisans released from Tuzla gaol" – according to D. Sušić, *Parergon (bilješke uz roman o Talu)*, Sarajevo, 1980, 213.

22 A. Sarajlić, "Otpor u okupiranoj Tuzli 1941. godine," *Vojnoistorijski glasnik*, no. 2, Belgrade, 1971, 307. In Tuzla, resistance to the terrorising of Serbs is particularly associated with the shining example of Muhamed efendi Kurt, the Mufti of Tuzla, who "exerted all his prestige to put an end to the bloody dance, which would have been far

truth about the disappearance of several dozen Serbs arrested in Rogatica, Ragib Čapljić, the Grand Prefect of Usora and Soli Grand County, was the object of Ustaša accusations and there were demands for his dismissal as untrustworthy.[23] Bosniaks and Croats all around the Bosnian frontier areas "protected and hid Serb families from Ustaša persecution, often at the cost of their own lives." There were many examples in Herzegovina of solidarity and help offered "by Croats and Muslims to vulnerable Serbs, their neighbors, whom they informed of Ustaša plans and hid in their houses, even openly standing up to the Ustašas and snatching their intended victims from their clutches as they led them to the killing fields." A group of mobilized Bosniaks from the village of Mulje in the district of Gacko fled their houses to avoid participating in the persecution of Serbs.

---

worse and bloodier in Tuzla had this resistance not been there." The Mufti exerted himself to protect the Serb population and particularly to prevent the blowing up of an Orthodox church full of worshippers on January 6, 1942, and the plans to execute a large number of families in the Serb quarter in Tuzla. According to Seka Brkljača, the behavior of a number of Muslim leaders, both individually and in concert, represented more than just disagreement with Ustaša policy. It was a form of public, albeit passive resistance to what was going on and to ideas and their consequences that went against the human and religious sentiments and beliefs of those who did put up resistance. When some of them joined the organized liberation movement, that resistance took on a qualitatively different form. The solidarity of the people of some of the occupied territories with the persecuted categories of the population was particularly marked not just by individual or even concerted efforts to protect them but to hide vulnerable members of these persecuted categories. It is in this context that Brkljača mentions the Tuzla Mufti: "Mufti Kurt's position grew from his faith, his personal character, and the quality of personal relations in the town of Tuzla and around the country, which he didn't approach from a theoretical perspective, but on the basis of his lived experience, resisting in deeds and not just mute disapproval a policy that denied and desecrated that understanding in blood. The fact of Kurt's understanding of the common character of religious life, alongside the many other examples that "illustrate" this question better and more clearly, is all the more significant, humane, and courageous once we appreciate the degree of general insecurity and the threat to physical survival that prevailed in the region at the time." Cf. V. Mujbegović, "O prvoj ratnoj godini u okupiranoj Tuzli," 259; S. Brkljača, "Neka razmatranja muslimanskog poimanja o dobru i zlu u Bosni i Hercegovini u II svjetskom ratu," *Dijalog*, no. 1, Sarajevo, 1997, 143-144.

23 E. Redžić, *Bosna i Hercegovina u Drugom svjetskom ratu*, 313.

Meho Dželilović, a laborer from Čapljina, was mobilized by the Ustašas and led to a pit at the Monastery in Humac, near Ljubuški, where he too was killed and thrown in for refusing to participate in the execution of the arrested Serbs.[24] When the Ustašas at Bileća rounded up a number of Serbs, prominent local Bosniaks took a stand against it and forced them to release the prisoners. A number of Bosniaks from Jablanica refused to serve as gendarmes and were shot.

The Ustaša crimes against the Serbs provoked responses from Serb insurgents that were influenced by Greater Serb propaganda, the motto of "Serb Bosnia," and "the struggle against the Turks and the Šokci [slang for Catholic Croats, op. trans.]," and which consequently had a chauvinist character.[25] The *revanchism* of the first waves of the Serb insurgency, under a blanket of resurgent nationalist and atavistic language, was a serious obstacle to local Bosniaks participating in any large numbers. Violence became an essential component of day-to-day experience and social and mental reality. Dr Dušan Lukač claims that the Bosniak and Croat masses, "offended by the persecution and ruthless exploitation of the greater Serbian regime before the war and strongly influenced by the propaganda of the Ustaša and the Occupier, were unprepared for the uprising of the Serb masses and, threatened by individual insurgent groups, found themselves entirely outside the insurgency at that stage."[26] The approach taken by the insurgents themselves towards cooperation with Croats or Bosniaks in many areas was hardly such as to encourage either group to join the insurgency. Bosniak Communists associated with insurgent units generally

---

24   Z. Sulejmanpašić, *13. SS divizija "Handžar": istine i laži,* Zagreb, 2000, 36. According to Sulejmanpašić "Individuals do not change the situation: Bosniaks in eastern Herzegovina, and not just there, who took part in the persecutions were not just caught in the Ustaša propaganda trap, but bound over night to the movement in blood, which caused enormous problems for their own people."

25   R. Hurem, "Politička orijentacija ustanika u Bosni i Hercegovini 1941. godine i uloga KPJ," *Godišnjak Društva istoričara Bosne i Hercegovine,* god. XXVIII-XXX, Sarajevo, 1979, 259; see also: S. Čekić, "Četnički zločini u jugoistočnoj Bosni i Sandžaku 1941.-1943.," *Preporod,* Sarajevo, 15 November 1991.

26   D. Lukač, "Prilog izučavanju nacionalnog pitanja u BiH," *Prilozi,* no. 4, Sarajevo 1968., 457.

had to live and act under assumed Serb names.²⁷ Several examples have been recorded of insurgents in the Bosnian borderlands expressing hatred and enmity towards Croats and Bosniaks, looting and burning Bosniak villages, and slaughtering Bosniaks, including both women and children. In many cases, the insurgents refused to cooperate with Bosniaks or Croats in any way. In fact, there were insurgent groups who joined the insurgency explicitly as a struggle against "the Turks," while commanders were replaced at the insistence of the insurgents simply for being Bosniak. In eastern Herzegovina, some representatives of divisions of the People's Army spent most of their energy steering the insurgents towards a settling of accounts with Bosniaks. This approach was particularly popular amongst the wealthier peasantry, who hoped eradication of the Bosniaks would leave them in possession of the latters' houses and property. Insurgents in eastern Bosnia displayed similar intolerance towards Bosniaks. In August of that year, they carried out mass atrocities against the Bosniak population and historiography has still to provide an adequate account of

---

27 Adil Zulfikarpašić pointed out that the first partisans included quite a few Bosniaks, but that the Communist Party of Yugoslavia issued a directive that they, Jews, and often Croats were to use Serb names in the field: "Hasan Brkić was Aco [Aleksandar], Oskar Danon was Jovo, and I was also Aco... It looked as if the entire command crew and first enlisters in Bosnia were entirely made up of Serbs! And I must mention that Serb villagers often asked us: What about the Turks?! Where are they?! Why aren't they in the partisans?! In fact, a Serb boss, the local headsman, asked me precisely that question at a meeting. And we were sitting there, Lakišić, Avdagić, Čengić, Hamović, Kovačević, Zulfikarpašić ... and we said nothing! This is how an anti-Muslim atmosphere developed. Instead of the Communist Party of Yugoslavia openly saying we were there to defend their villages together with our brother Serbs, they renamed all those Communist cadres and fighters! I still don't quite understand why we were forced to hide our real names, because it had a very negative impact on the Serb masses." According to Zulfikarpašić, the order for the Muslims to hide their identity was a fatal mistake and demoralising for those who were partisans. None of the many Muslims who left for Romania to join the Kalinovik division were allowed to bear Muslim names. By his account, the order was issued by the Regional Committee of the Communist Party for Bosnia and Herzegovina, "Rodoljub Čolaković, Iso Jovanović... Djuro Pucar did not apply it, but he was in a somewhat different and better situation. But in Herzegovina and eastern and central Bosnia, Muslims used Serb names" – cited after M. Galić, *Politika u emigraciji*, Zagreb 1990, 83; S. Bandžović, *Ratne tragedije Muslimana,* Novi Pazar, 1993, 20.

the slaughter of innocent Bosniaks who joined the insurgency in 1941 for the most noble of reasons on the grounds that "you can't trust a Turk."[28] The first visible results of Bosniak recruitment to the national liberation movement (beyond a few individual cases) came in August 1941, when a larger group of Bosniaks, mostly from the villages of Šatorovići, Okruglo, and Osovo, joined the partisan division in Romania *en masse*. In mid-October, the first Bosniak partisan unit was formed. Referred to as Mujo's company, it grew to become a battalion by December. A similar unit was formed a little later in the Zenica region.[29]

The Ustašas used their attempts to croatize the Bosniak population and their genocidal operations against the Serb, Jewish, and Roma populations to feed the flame of chauvinistic wildfire and kindle atavistic elements of religious, nationalist, political, and class antagonisms and irrationalism. Matters only became more complicated with the appearance of the Četnik Ravna Gora movement of Draža Mihajlović on the political and military scene, given its goals of creating a greater Serbian state "cleansed" of non-Serb elements and of Muslims especially. Anti-Croatism, anti-Muslimism, and anti-Yugoslavism were the pillars of Četnik ideology. The "Turkish yoke" functioned as a sort of historical indulgence, justifying in advance and providing an *a priori* amnesty for anything done in the name of the "nation."[30] The Četnik oath made clear the two basic

---

28 According to Atif Purivatra in 1991, "the awful impalement on a stake of Avdo Dovadžija by new-minted Četniks speaks to our current reality too in every respect. This dramatic event has not been worked through in any literary work" – See "Muslimani su svoji na svome," *Islamska misao*, no. 146, Sarajevo, February 1991, 7. In addition to this example, another recorded case involved Halid-beg Batotić, who was impaled on a spit and roasted alive. His brother Dadi-beg was first outfitted with horseshoes and then cut down on the bridge in Foča. Hadžija Tahirović (Foča) was skinned by the Četniks from her knees up her back to her neck. They threw her skin over her head and put a sign on her that read "Muslim Woman in a Burka." See further A Gruhonjić, "Ko poubija preko 200 imama," *Preporod*, no. 23/510, Sarajevo, December 1, 1991, 19.

29 Kazazović, "Formiranje muslimanskih partizanskih jedinica u istočnoj Bosni" in *Istočna Bosna u NOB-u*, II, 188-189.

30 D. Stojanović, "U ogledalu 'drugih,'" in *Novosti iz prošlosti: znanje, neznanje, upotreba i zloupotreba istorije*, Belgrade, 2010, 27-28. In a pamphlet from 1941, approved by

components of their ideology: the struggle for Serbia ("the Serb people") and revenge. As a practical expression of greater Serbian ambitions, the Četnik movement put significant emphasis on its "historical mission" of liberation, preserving "the biological essence of the Serbs," and spreading the idea of an ethnically homogenous "Greater Serbia" to be created on the basis of the pre-war platform of the Serb Cultural Club within the framework of war-torn Yugoslavia. These programmatic documents took as their starting point and guiding idea "a homogenous Greater Serbia," established on the assumption that the Serbs were destined to be the key nation of the Balkans.[31] The path to creating this homogenous Serb nation state was envisaged in Četnik plans as to be accomplished during the war by a thoroughgoing cleansing of the Sandžak and Bosnia and Herzegovina of both Bosniaks and Croats. The plan was to throw up ramparts around the Serb lands and so avoid a repetition of 1918.[32] The machete

---

Boško Todorović, the senior Četnik commandant in Bosnia, we find the following explanation of the Četnik war aim: "Once we achieve freedom, golden Serbian freedom, then, freely and without bloodshed and by way of free elections such as we were used to in King Petar's Serbia, the Serb nation will take destiny in our own hands and freely state whether we prefer our own independent Greater Serbia, cleansed of Turks and other non-Serbs, or some other form of state, in which Turks and Jews will again be ministers, commissars, officers, or comrades."

31 In the view of Milorad Ekmečić, the historical project of a Greater Serbia is a legitimate conceptualization of the right of the Serb people to bring together all areas in which Serbs live within common political borders: "As with every other European example, this meant not just bringing together those lands where the Serb people formed the ethnic majority and so would already have had a statistical justification for it, but also non-border zones in which they had a significant ethnic presence but were not in the majority numerically" – cited after V. Šešelj, *Rimokatolički zločinački projekat veštačke hrvatske nacije*, Belgrade, 2007, 894; M. Ekmečić, "Pojam velike Srbije prema evropskim uzorima," in *Velika Srbija – istine, zablude, zloupotrebe*, Belgrade, 2003, 16.

32 The Četniks, who did the most harm to the Bosniaks, were collaborators with the Occupier but declared themselves in the post-Yugoslav period to have been anti-fascists, by resolutions of their assemblies, despite several of them, like Pavle Đurišić, having received Nazi medals. According to Čedomir Antić, "[t]he crimes committed by the Četnik forces against other national groups are not just hardly comparable in scale to the Ustaša genocide of the Serb people, but are also less significant than the crimes committed by Croat and Muslim forces against the Serb people in the recent

was, according to Dobrica Ćosić, "the weapon of choice of that bearded army in *šubaras* [cockarded woollen caps traditionally worn by bandits and insurgents, op. trans.]."³³

As members of a party whose idea of revolutionary action informed their programme and operational approach from the beginning of the struggle in 1941, the Communists dismantled the pre-war system of governance, creating new bodies and promoting a more tolerant policy on nationalities that reflected a rejection of earlier negative experiences with government and in political and social life. Extreme situations, such as outlawry, repression, and war, were precisely what the Communist organization of "professional revolutionaries," with its disciplined and self-sacrificing cadres, had been created for, given their two guiding characteristics: their internationalism and their commitment to their life goals.³⁴ Overall the policy of the Yugoslav Communist movement was not grounded in any recognition of Bosniak national identity, however, given

---

war" – cited after Č. Antić, "Srbija, 'nova istorija' i fašizam," *Politika*, Belgrade, 23 December, 2010. This is part of an environment in which the adoption of institutional mechanisms for collective rehabilitation of the quisling forces is being facilitated by the passing of rehabilitation laws that represent a direct violation of international norms on the punishment of crimes against humanity, which envisage no statute of limitations on the criminal prosecution of such acts.

33   He continues that in Serbia fear of the Četnik machete, "which was carried by Serbs armed with English machine guns, with their beards and hair down to their shoulders, chanting their laments for Serbia, freedom, king, and fatherland," ran "deeper and stronger than their fear of the Germans, the occupier, or the Gestapo, so that Serbia felt equal portions of relief and joy in the autumn of 1944 over its liberation from the Germans and from the Četniks" – cited after D. Ćosić, "Prijatelji mog veka," a special feature, *Politika*, Belgrade, May 5-6, 2011. On the other hand, he would write of the Communists' "inequitable victory" in the Second World War: "It was an inequitable victory for our Croat, Slovene, Muslim, and Macedonian 'brothers', given that the main burden and sacrifice for that victory was again borne by the Serb people. An inequitable victory in the name of naïve idealism, in the name of a Communist illusion of brotherhood and unity. How is a rational person supposed to believe in brotherhood with a people, with people that have carried out genocide?" – cited after D. Ćosić, *U tuđem veku*, Belgrade, 2011, 224.

34   E. Hobsbawm, *Doba extrema: Istorija kratkog dvadesetog veka 1914.-1991.*, Belgrade, 2002, 130.

that the Communists were generally cautious and reserved with regard to "nations," which they regarded as historically contingent creations.[35] The Communist Party of Yugoslavia's position on the Muslims of Bosnia and Herzegovina as a separate ethnic entity has been quite variously interpreted for a fairly long time.[36] In fact, the national liberation movement did not take a consistent or firm position on the Bosniaks. A review of various relevant Communist Party documents makes clear that the creators felt little need to take a hard and realistic look at the position the Bosniaks found themselves in or of real-world problems affecting their survival or, indeed, the functional role of the "Muslim militia" units protecting their communities, preferring to treat them from a sectarian viewpoint as opponents of the national liberation movement.[37] In one of his writings, Kardelj included the "Muslim militias" amongst the Ustaša formations, which entailed condemnation by both the Communist Party of Yugoslavia and the partisans. In reality, however, not all the "Muslim militias" or their members should have been considered opponents, as there was a relatively large number of sympathizers of the national liberation movement

---

35   M. Filipović, *Bošnjačka politika*, 83. In 1938, Edvard Kardelj wrote that the Bosniaks were not a nation, "even if, on an individual basis, they do not consider themselves Serbs or Croats and consequently certainly do comprise a special ethnic group" – cited after E. Kardelj, *Razvoj slovenačkog nacionalnog pitanja*, Belgrade, 1960, 104. Nenad Filipović writes the following about the "wartime" use of the capital and small letter "M": "Making any sort of big deal of the famous use of the capital letter is quite risky, given that the documents of the so-called people's government were generally written at a very low level of literacy. You find capitals and small letters both where they should be and where they have no place" – cited after N. Filipović, "O jednom nasilnom istezanju bošnjačkih nogu," in *Bosna i bošnjaštvo*, Sarajevo, 1990, 176.

36   A. Purivatra, *Nacionalni i politički razvitak Muslimana*, Sarajevo 1969, 57. According to Dr Purivatra, "in the understanding of leading individuals [resistance to creating a Republic of Bosnia and Herzegovina based on equality at Jajce] had no chance of overcoming the fact that in the end a Muslim is just that, a Muslim. That caused resistance." See A. Purivatra, "Muslimani su svoji na svome," *Islamska misao*, no. 146, Sarajevo, February 1990. Cf. F. Saltaga, *Muslimanska nacija u Jugoslaviji*, Sarajevo 1991., 175, and D. Petrović, "Avnojska Jugoslavija-kompozicija i granice," in *Stvaranje i razaranje Jugoslavije*, Belgrade 1996, 125.

37   E. Redžić, *Sto godina muslimanske politike u tezama i kontroverzama istorijske nauke*, 164.

amongst their ranks, including some members of the Communist Party and the Young Communist Movement (SKOJ). Where partisan commanders were not themselves excessively nationalist or dogmatic, they did differentiate and allowed a significant number of these people to join the partisans, as defenders of their villages and homes.[38]

During the conflict of 1941, a significant portion of the Bosniak population was forced to leave their homes to save themselves from the threat of physical annihilation. Their movement *en masse* and abandonment of their homes and the various things that happened to them on their way to find "salvation" in refugee camps and the grim but "safe" outskirts of the major towns, where want, disease, and silent death awaited them, filled the horizons of their lives, their reality, reaffirming the truth that "there is no fate worse than exile." These long columns of refugees were largely oriented towards the interior of the country, and, aside from some temporary detours, moved from village to town or from town to town, across large distances, including journeys from eastern Bosnia all the way to the Bosnian border with Croatia in the West. A few of the refugees withdrew across the border into Srijem, Slavonia, the Sandžak, Zagreb, and Dubrovnik, just as Bosniak refugees were also arriving in Bosnia and Herzegovina from the Sandžak, following the same trajectory that people knew well from as far back as 1914. These mass movements of an unprotected population were accompanied by great want and suffering: violently forced to abandon their homes in terror, their sufferings on the road not infrequently ended in violent persecution, as in Berkovići, Kulen Vakuf, Koraj, and all across eastern Bosnia, during 1941, but particularly in seven districts: Foča, Čajniće, Goražde, Višegrad, Vlasenica, Srebrenica, and Rogatica, where the exiles suffered alongside the locals, wherever they fell into the hands of the insurgents. Those who managed to get away sought safety in Sarajevo and other towns. This powerful migratory wave began in 1941 and gathered steam over the years that followed.

---

38 M. Imamović, *Bošnjaci u emigraciji: Monografija Bosanskih pogleda 1955-1967*, Sarajevo 1996, 83.

It was not the people or ethnic groups of Bosnia and Herzegovina that were in conflict, though such tendencies did exist. It was political and military movements.[39] Once the war had begun in 1941, the Bosniaks found themselves, as the historiographical literature generally makes clear, between the hammer and the anvil – of Greater Serbian and Greater Croatian policies, which only served to further complicate the situation.[40] Ustaša atrocities and their brutal persecution of Serbs and Jews, on the one hand, and insurgent atrocities, on the other, provoked a response and open protest on the part of most of the prominent Bosniaks across the country. It was "a concrete reflection of the profound concern" that gripped all Bosnian civilian politicians. During the second half of 1941, as armed conflict raged across Bosnia and Herzegovina, the conviction grew amongst Bosniaks that the Ustaša regime would not protect them and that the Armed Forces of the NDH could not offer them sufficient security. The very survival of the Bosniak people was increasingly at risk. Such views spread amongst prominent Bosniak individuals and leaders, who searched for solutions to ensure the survival of their people.[41] During the summer of 1941, during a visit to Sarajevo by the Minister of foreign affairs Andrija Artuković, "prominent individuals from the Muslim population" expressed the desire "of Muslims to live peacefully with the members of other confessions, because anger and vengeance would certainly take its greatest toll on the Muslims themselves."[42] The Bosniak citizenry in many places also took a determined stand to protect the Roma from persecution and deportation. A committee formed in Sarajevo for the purpose put together a detailed petition demonstrating that any attack on the so-called "white Gypsies" was in fact an attack on Bosniaks. The petition was delivered to both the Ustaša and the German authorities, and in

---

39 Cf. R. Hurem-S. Brkljača, "Historiografska literatura o Bosni i Hercegovini u Drugom svjetskom ratu objavljena nakon 1980. godine u zemlji i inostranstvu," *Prilozi*, no. 29, Sarajevo 2000., 144; H. Sundhaussen, "Od mita regije do 'države na silu': metamorfoze u Bosni i Hercegovini," *Prilozi*, no. 38, Sarajevo 2009, 23.

40 M. Imamović, *Historija Bošnjaka*, 535.

41 R. Hurem, "Neke karakteristike ustanka u Bosni i Hercegovini 1941. godine," *Godišnjak Društva istoričara Bosne i Hercegovine,* god. XVIII, Sarajevo, 1970, 209.

42 N. Duraković, *Prokletstvo Muslimana*, Sarajevo, 1993, 185, fn. 58.

late August 1941 the Ministry of the Interior of the NDH, anxious over the prospect of further protest by Bosniaks, issued an order canceling the persecution and deportation of "white gypsies" from Bosnia and Herzegovina.[43]

By the end of the summer and in the autumn of 1941, most of the Bosniak bourgeoisie had, via a series of resolutions, distanced itself explicitly from the Ustaša policy of persecution and eradication of Serbs and Jews.[44] These important resolutions, and especially the Sarajevo one, are considered to have their origin in a declaration made by the assembly of the *El-Hidaje Association of Muslim Clerics* on August 14, 1941, expressing public protest against the atrocities and killings.[45] Mehmed efendi Handžić, the head of *El-Hidaje*, was the *spiritus movens* and author of the text. *El-Hidaje* called on Muslims to refrain, in the spirit of Islam, from any wrongdoing and on the government authorities "to restore law and order as soon as possible to all areas and prevent unauthorized action so that innocent people do not suffer." This position is even more important when one takes into account the exceptionally complex circumstances in which the resolution was passed.[46] It came at a time when

---

43 *ABC Muslimana*, 36.

44 Cf. M. Imamović, *Historija Bošnjaka*, 535; B. Petranović, *Revolucija i kontrarevolucija u Jugoslaviji (1941.-1945.)*, vol. I, Belgrade, 1983, 94-96.

45 Art. 4 of the resolution reads as follows: "It is with pain in our hearts and profound condolences that we remember all the innocent Muslim victims struck down through no fault of their own in the unrest that has recently taken place in various places. We condemn any and all individual Muslims who have committed any form of attack or violence independently and at their own initiative. We declare that the only people capable of doing such a thing are rogue elements and uncivilized individuals, whose stain we reject both for ourselves and for all Muslims. We call on all Muslims to refrain from such evil acts, in the spirit of the exalted tenets of their religion, Islam, and in the interests of the state. We call on the government authorities to restore law and order as soon as possible to all areas and prevent unauthorized action so that innocent people do not suffer." Cf M. Imamović, *Bošnjaci u emigraciji*, 149, and N. Duraković, *Prokletstvo Muslimana*, 186. The resolution was sent to the most senior functionaries of the NDH, as well as to Muslims in NDH organs, viz. Osman and Džafer Kulenović, Adem-aga Mešić, Hilmija Bešlagić, and Hakija Hadžić.

46 The American historian Robert J. Donia has, however, pointed out that the resolution

some senior functionaries of the regime, like Džafer Kulenović, were assuring the public that all Muslims belonged in the Ustaša movement and the Ustaša authorities were taking significant steps to shore up support for the regime. According to a report of the Headquarters of the Croat Ministry for Homeland Defence on the general internal situation in the country during the second half of September 1941, "the Muslims have a developed sense of fellow feeling and are entirely unwilling to accept rough and inhumane action against their neighbors, even if they are their religious or political adversaries. They see a desire to set Muslims against Serbs and expect a Serb revolt will jeopardize Muslim lives and property" and are therefore demanding "the urgent establishment of regular government and military authorities and the immediate disbanding of Ustaša organizations."[47] Francine Friedman believes that most Bosniaks found "fascist operations so distasteful that they denounced them."[48] From early autumn to the end of the year, antifascist and anti-Ustaša resolutions appeared from bourgeois Bosniak groups across Bosnia and Herzegovina. The Prijedor Resolution was promulgated on September 23, the Sarajevo one on October 18, the Mostar one on October 21, the Banja Luka one on November 12, the Bijeljina one on December 2, and the Tuzla one on December 11. The last two were made in response to an Ustaša/Četnik massacre on November 28, 1941, of several hundred Bosniaks at the village of Koraj. Some Ustaša elements tried to use the

---

"did not assign guilt to any individual or group. As historians of the Socialist period have stressed, the Muslim signatories to the resolutions criticized the crimes as deviant excesses but did not attack the core Ustaša program of physically eliminating particular groups by force. However, they did call on the NDH authorities to establish order and prevent further violence. They clearly pointed out that that the regime's actions in the first months of the occupation had led to them distancing themselves from the Ustaša movement" – after R. Donia, *Sarajevo: biografija grada*, Sarajevo, 2006, 214.

47 R. Hurem, "Pokušaj nekih građanskih muslimanskih političara da Bosnu i Hercegovinu izdvoje iz okvira Nezavisne Države Hrvatske," 198, fnn. 29 and 30.

48 F. Friedman, "Islam kao nacionalni identitet: bosanskohercegovački Muslimani slavenskog porijekla (s osvrtom na Muslimane Novopazarskog sandžaka)," *Forum Bosnae*, no. 18, Sarajevo, 2002, 97. She refers for more detail on Bosniak protests against anti-Serb violence to "Ustašas," in the *South Slav Journal*, Summer 1982 (pp. 31-33) and Autumn 1983, (pp. 37-39).

massacre as incitement to vengeance, as had been done with mobilization into Francetić's Black Legion, but instead the patriotic citizens of Bijeljina and Tuzla grouped together and condemned the crimes in targeted resolutions. The Bijeljina Resolution was passed after a long process of consultation and two meetings of delegates from the town of Bijeljina and all of the town lands of Bijeljina district, held in the Muslim reading room (kiraethana). At the meetings, they discussed the status, future, and survival of Bosniaks in Bosnia and Herzegovina and more particularly in that region. The many speakers included Prof Enver Pozderović, who called on those present to have the courage to sign the resolution before them.[49] The resolution bears the signatures of 73 local citizens, mostly of whom were village headsmen (*muhtari* or *knezovi*) and municipal mayors.[50] The initial text of the Tuzla Resolution was composed using very strong language, but the organizers decided that it would be less dangerous for a delegation of 11 Bosniaks from the town and three Croat peasants to present their protest orally in Zagreb, rather than as a written text. In the meantime, they nonetheless published the resolution in a more moderate form, with the signatures of 22 townsfolk. There are some grounds for believing that similar resolutions were also passed in Bosanska Dubica, Visoko, and elsewhere.

At the time when they were produced, according to Dr Šaćir Filandra, the resolutions expressed through their pens and their signatures "the peace-loving disposition of this people, their principled rejection of dictatorship, discrimination, genocide, proselytism, and terror, and a commitment to the establishment of the principle of co-existence. As a protest against disorder, lawlessness, and legalized annihilation, particularly of the

---

49 A few months before the resolution was published, a home guard killed Mustafa-Mujo Hajrić, a laborer, in Jabanuša, not far from Bijeljina. The killing called forth considerable hard feeling amongst the Bosniaks of Bijeljina. Hajrić's funeral was attended by a large number of Bosniaks and processed along most of the town's streets, as a way of making clear the hard feeling and of protesting against the killers. Murat-beg Pašić and Prof Enver Pozderović spoke. Pašić emphasized the demand for the autonomy of Bosnia and Herzegovina in his speech – after A. Budimlija, "Nešto o Bijeljinskoj rezoluciji 1941.," *Hikmet*, no. 9-10, Tuzla 1993, 336.

50 AVII, NDH, no. reg. 42/4-4, k. 114.

Serb and Muslim peoples in Bosnia and Herzegovina, they were also an indicator of the political condition of the Muslim people at that moment in time, caught up in the course of events, vulnerable, insecure, disoriented, off-guard, as would later become clear in how they lost their way, both intellectually and in practice, their excesses, their lows, and their highs."[51] The text of the Sarajevo Resolution stresses that Bosniaks "have neither committed nor intended any harm to anyone, as is clearly shown by the fact that all and any Muslims who served in the Yugoslav army handed over their arms as soon as the conflict ended. Even in the past, during Turkish times, when the Muslims were the only masters, they tolerated all religions without distinction and terrorized none." The signatories to the resolution called for the introduction of "real security of life, honor, property, and measures that apply to all citizens of the state without distinction of any kind," which is to say for both Serbs and Jews as well. They also called for the authorities "to disallow any future form of action likely by its nature to provoke popular insurrection and bloodletting," as well as to bring "all the real culprits, including all those who have committed any form of violence or atrocity, to justice before the courts, regardless of religious affiliation, and to punish them severely under the law, along with all those who ordered or enabled their criminal acts." In the Mostar Resolution, the signatories stressed that "The countless crimes, injustices, lawless acts, and violent acts of conversion done and still being done to Orthodox Serbs and other fellow citizens are entirely repugnant to the soul of any Muslim. Every real Muslim, ennobled by the exalted tenets of Islam, condemns these crimes, from whatever quarter, fully cognizant that for the Islamic faith the murder and torture of the innocent are the gravest of sins, as are the looting of other people's possessions and conversion under conditions that exclude free will. The handful of so-called Muslims who have committed such transgressions have by that very fact transgressed against the exalted tenets of Islam and will inevitably face God's punishment and human justice." In the Banja Luka Resolution, we find: "The most basic of individual rights are trampled upon without scruple. Personal safety and

---

51 Š. Filandra, "Prilog rastakanju ontologije zla," *Književna revija*, no. 31, Sarajevo, April 1990.

security of property, freedom of religion and conscience have all ceased to exist for a large part of the people of these regions." It also contains a condemnation of the looting of Serb and Jewish property, citing Banja Luka as an example "where the property of expelled or fled Serbs and Jews has been made a source of booty and enrichment for certain individuals, their families, and friends." With regard to the scramble for Serb and Jewish workshops and shops, we read "We reject with contempt the allegation that we have designs ourselves on the workshops in question."[52] The Tuzla Resolution includes the statement: "Our Muslim community, inspired by the spirit of Islamic culture and ethics, condemns any form of disorder. This noble characteristic of Muslims is well known, but misinformation has been being maliciously spread that Muslims are actually responsible for these actions against the Serbs, and all the blame for them is now directed against Muslims and everything is presented as though it were all just a settling of scores between Serbs and Muslims." The signatories to the resolutions were public representatives of the Bosniaks, officials of the

---

52   *Zločini na jugoslovenskim prostorima*, I, 835; "Dvije muslimanske rezolucije iz 1941. i 1992.," *Preporod*, no. 8/946, Sarajevo, 15 April 2011, 30-31. Fadil Ademović cites a report from the Banja Luka Ustaša headquarters (no. 11/42, dated January 16 1942) about the Banja Luka and Mostar Resolutions, which includes the following: "This office has tried to attract the Muslim element, which bowed it head before the war to each and every regime, and offer it the possibility of the closest possible cooperation in the Ustaša movement, but I have to report that all the efforts I have made in this regard have been pointless. The Muslim element has not at all shown the response expected. Withdrawn into his own narrow circle, the Muslim experiences life in much the same way as during the age of religious hatred towards Catholicism, and looks with equally great lack of trust on all events taking place not just here but throughout Europe, in the assumption that the situation will not be maintained and that the old order will be restored, and so is inclined to test the terrain so as to 'ensure' his future, and so engage in various forms of promotion and, in this concrete case, representations and remonstrations about the Ustašas and casting of blame on the Ustaša movement for everything that is happening on the territory of the county, and indeed throughout the entire country of Bosnia and Herzegovina" – cited after F. Ademović, *Novinstvo i ustaška propaganda u Nezavisnoj Državi Hrvatskoj*, Sarajevo 2000., 325. See also M. Hadžijahić, *"Muslimanske rezolucije iz 1941. godine,"* in *1941. u istoriji naroda Bosne i Hercegovine*, 280-281.

Islamic community and of various societies and associations, businessmen, landlords, intellectuals, and other prominent citizens.

The appearance of these anti-Ustaša resolutions was an expression of moral and critical resistance on the part of the Bosniak public towards a lawless regime and it unmasked and refuted the Ustaša propaganda claim that "Croats of Islamic religious affiliation" represented a pillar of the Ustaša order in Bosnia and Herzegovina.[53] The resolutions express a clear lack of confidence in the Ustaša regime and its plans, a condemnation of the Ustaša terror, and a call for the immediate ensuring of personal and religious safety and security of property "for all citizens of the state without distinction of any sort." The signatories called for "all forms of religious intolerance to be prevented," for the "innocent" to be protected, and for all those responsible for crimes to be held to account, regardless of religious affiliation, including those who had ordered or facilitated the crimes. They also sharply condemned any Bosniaks who had taken part in crimes and distanced themselves from the crimes. They rejected any attempts to make Bosniaks collectively responsible for Ustaša crimes. The signatories set out the facts regarding Ustaša persecution of Bosniaks, while also raising their voices against "unfounded acts of vengeance" against innocent Bosniaks.[54] Morality and justice do not require consensus. The resolutions showed that most of the Bosnian bourgeoisie was against religious or racial discrimination and distanced itself from the Ustaša crimes, condemning them in no uncertain terms, "which was without doubt an act of great civil bravery, but did not in itself call into question the NDH regime or occupation of the country, which was not really possible under the circumstances."[55]

---

53 Cf. E. Redžić, *Sto godina muslimanske politike u tezama i kontroverzama istorijske nauke*, 150; Idem, *Nacionalni odnosi u Bosni i Hercegovini 1941.-1945. u analizama jugoslavenske istoriografije,* Sarajevo, 1988, 49.

54 R. Hurem, "Narodi Bosne i Hercegovine prema ustanku 1941.-1942.," *Prilozi*, no. 23, Sarajevo, 1987, 160.

55 Serb patriarch Gavrilo Dožić claimed in his memoirs: "We appealed to the followers of Dr Mehmed Spaho, and even before our appeal they had been trying to do what they could to halt the massacre and slaughter of Serb civilians. They received our appeal favorably and tried to do something about it. Taken overall, the Muslims' representatives behaved correctly and well towards the Serbs and condemned the Ustaša

They were read out in mosques and at home and presented to the public in a variety of ways. Members of the "Young Muslims" reproduced the

crimes publicly and courageously" - cited after M. Huković, "Bošnjaci su naj, naj, naj...," *Oslobođenje*, Sarajevo, October 3, 2009, 10. In March 1961, *Bosanski pogledi* published a letter from Miloš Pudarić that included commentary on the contents of the Mostar Resolution, which it suggested spoke to the honor of the Muslims of Bosnia and Herzegovina: "It is a document of historical importance and an achievement worthy of a noble and courageous race who were fully aware that every day could see 'darkness fall without a dawn.'" In April 1962, the same paper carried an article by "Naša reč", an organ of the Serb democratic "Oslobođenje" [Liberation] collective, whose members had for the most part belonged to the Četnik movement of Draža Mihaljović during the war. In 1961, "Naša reč" published a text entitled "Borba protiv ustaških pokolja- reakcije Muslimana i Slovenaca" [The struggle against Ustaša slaughter - the Muslim and Slovene responses], which includes the following: "While there is very rarely any mention in Serb and even less in Croat public life, whether at home or amongst the diaspora, of the struggle that was taken up immediately in 1941 against the Ustaša slaughter – "Naša Reč" wants to use this opportunity to make clear that the first political resistance to the Ustaša massacres came from the Muslims of Bosnia and Herzegovina. Dozens of intellectuals and citizens of Sarajevo, led by Mehmed-Ali ef. Ćerimović, the president of the Ulema-medžlis, and Dr Šaćir Sikirić, director of the Higher Islamic Sharia Theological School, published their resolution, *with their signatures in full*, on October 12, 1941," and goes on to point out that the resolution "could hardly have been more belligerent during that time of Ustaša terror." The same paper also characterizes the "Mostar Resolution" as "even more belligerent" than the Sarajevo one. In the autumn of 1962, *Bosanski pogledi* carried a text by Ratko Parežanin, the editor of the émigré publication *Iskra*, in which he said that the Muslim masses had never wanted to go to extremes, sensing that such a path would lead to disaster, given the conditions prevailing on the ground. During the Second World War, only a few individual Muslims had joined the Ustašas, while the vast majority of the Muslim population of Herceg-Bosna had supported the famous resolutions in which prominent Muslims from a number of the larger towns around Bosnia and Herzegovina had condemned the Ustaša crimes and distanced themselves from Pavelić's 'independence'." Petar II Karađorđević, the deposed Yugoslav king, also mentioned the resolutions at the fifth pan- Serb Congress, held at the end of June, 1963, in Chicago, saying "We Serbs should not forget that the first people to stand up to defend the Serb population of the Independent State of Croatia from the Ustaša crimes were leading Muslims. True, there were Muslim renegades amongst the Ustašas too, but such rabble have always existed everywhere and amongst all peoples. A people is not, however, judged by its rabble but by its elites", after *Bosanski pogledi*, 126, 163, 193, 238, 317.

resolutions and distributed them.⁵⁶ Some of them were translated into foreign languages and sent secretly abroad. The Communists also drew attention to them. Partisan headquarters and institutions mentioned them in their newspapers, as did the Communist Party of Bosnia and Herzegovina regional committee.⁵⁷

The appearance of the resolutions was evidence of the existence of a strong oppositional current amongst Bosniaks to the NDH. Their contents reveal that the political mood of very many Bosniaks was quite different than Ustaša propaganda suggested. In contrast to the much insisted upon support for the NDH, they offered a very different picture of

---

56 On this, A. Izetbegović, a former member of the Young Muslims, had the following to say: "None of us, literally no one, joined the Ustaša movement or became an Ustaša functionary, just as no one joined the SS division or any German unit, and in fact the vast majority of us were military deserters. Some of those drafted went into the home guard, because you had to, but nobody joined the Ustašas. This was not a matter of chance. For some people to resile from the Ustašas in 1943 and 1944 was understandable, as by then it was already clear who was going to lose, but none of us had joined them even in 1941-2, when the Germans were at the height of their power. In fact, some of our people were close to the circles that issued the resolutions against the Ustaša and German regimes. We were all too young to be signatories of the resolutions, but we made copies of them and passed them around. In the signatories we saw reflected our own ideals, we saw in them our spiritual fathers, or simply mentors. Accordingly, we were close to a certain humanist opposition to the regime of the day. We considered the Ustaša and the German system simply unacceptable." See further S. Trhulj, *Mladi Muslimani,* Sarajevo, 1995, 60-61.

57 In November 1941, in a report to the regional committee of the Communist Party of Yugoslavia for Bosnia and Herzegovina, Avdo Humo stated "I am also sending you two resolutions, from Mostar and Sarajevo. There is considerable ferment here amongst the Muslims. One hears quite often: 'there is a great rift between us and them' [the Ustašas, op. S. B.]. The Sarajevo Resolution is perhaps not quite as direct, but it has been really very well received by the Serbs. The signatories are very prominent Muslims. Given all this ferment amongst the Muslims and the unanimous condemnation of the Ustaša authorities everywhere, which can be most clearly seen reflected in the resolution, there is an obvious need for a flyer to be put out signed by Headquarters that will clearly set out the occupiers' policy, which the Muslim masses are not really aware of yet. It needs to make really clear and demolish any illusion that the Muslims have anything to hope for from the occupier, any form of salvation" – after *Zbornik NOR-a,* Vol. IV, Bk. 2, Doc. no. 65.

overall conditions in Bosnia and Herzegovina and of the mood amongst Bosniaks. Hafiz Abdulah efendi Budimlija, a signatory of the Bijeljina Resolution, spoke in 2007 of the difficult circumstances in the Bijeljina region, particularly after the massacre of Bosniaks at Koraj, and about the atmosphere within which the resolution was signed, with Bosniaks just a "drop in the sea. The entire area around Bijeljina is Serb, from the Drina to the Sava. So, what were we to think, if they rose up, would happen to us?" In his view, the signatories to the resolution were "staking their own heads, because it was going to be either/or," once "the Germans went to march through Russia. And here we were, asking... for Serbs and Jews to be treated equally, and the Roma too. So, everything that was done was done with a dose of fear," he explained, continuing, "and after signing the resolution, many were too afraid to sleep in their own homes. They went to other people's houses to sleep, while waiting for it to calm down, for it to settle a bit."[58] The appearance of the resolutions angered the Ustašas. Ante Pavelić threatened "the streets of Sarajevo will flow with the blood of the authors of the resolutions before the NDH government gives up its programme." The Ustaša councillor, Jure Francetić, announced that "all of the signatories [in Sarajevo] will be sent to concentration camps." According to some sources, however, the Ustašas backed down from the plan to send the signatories to the concentration camp at Jasenovac out of concern the British would use such a move for propaganda purposes in the Islamic world. Pro-Ustaša elements in Prijedor organized the signing by Bosniaks of counter-resolutions and declarations of a desire to cooperate "within the framework of Ustaša institutions." The "Prijedor resolutionaries" were attacked as intending "to incite hatred against the Ustašas, the Ustaša movement, and thereby the Poglavnik and the State of Croatia." Jozo Garić, the Bishop of Banja Luka, characterized the resolutions as nothing more than "a pamphlet full of damned libel and hatred for the

---

58 He goes on to point out, "Generally, when someone asks me: well, okay, hafiz, you signed that resolution in 1941 to save the Serbs, who were killing your own people, burning them alive in Foča, that same year. Would you do the same thing again now – they ask. Yes, I would, as a human being. How could I not? If it is a matter of saving people, honest people, how could I not? ... as Muslims, we have a responsibility to do so" - after *Kazivanje hafiza Abdulaha ef. Budimlije o "Bijeljinskoj rezoluciji,"* 5.

Catholic Church," accusing the Bosniaks of persecuting, plundering, and killing the Serb population of Bihać, Sanski Most, Cazin, and Bosanska Krupa.[59] The Germans explained the Muslim Resolutions as the product of happenings that had alarmed, frightened, and threatened the Bosniaks, not least the burning of Serb villages and the widespread plundering. According to these German analyses, the Bosniaks were pointing out that representatives of the regime were enriching themselves by seizure and looting. What stood behind their appeals were a desire for security, religious tolerance, legal protection, and for criminals to be punished.[60] A report by the commander of the Third Home Guard Corps of late December, 1941, throws considerable light on conditions in Bosnia and Herzegovina from this perspective. Regarding the mood of "the Muslim part of the population on the Corps' territory, one may say that it is unsatisfactory. The population has lost 'confidence in the authorities,'" and "we may one day be surprised by the severity of internal events, that is by a public revolt on the part of the common people, without distinction of religion."

The Ustašas were not ready to settle accounts radically with the signatories of the resolutions, and they satisfied themselves with petty reprisals, generally against individuals (firings, blocking promotions, et cetera). They were aware that open persecution would, at this dramatic juncture, have added fuel to and reinforced Bosniak revolt, as well as to the Bosniak bourgeoisie's aspiration for Bosnia and Herzegovina to separate off from the framework of an unstable NDH, giving rise to a new inter-ethnic conflict, which they had no desire for in an already complex situation.[61] The

---

59 M. Konjević, "Neke informacije Hrvatskom državnom saboru o prilikama u Bosni 1942. i 1943.godine," in *AVNOJ i Narodnooslobodilačka borba u Bosni i Hercegovini*, 170-171; D. Lukač, *Banja Luka i okolica u ratu i revoluciji*, Banja Luka, 1968, 149. At the end of May 1942, reports were being received from the Bosnian borderlands that the Ustašas would move on to "a final settling of accounts with the Muslims, once they finish with the Jews and the Serbs." These reports "gave rise to considerable concern amongst the broader Muslim masses," which were only accentuated by intemperate statements by various official representatives of the authorities. A song of the time went "hey now, Ante, loose our hands and let us kill Turks in Bosnia."

60 B. Petranović, *Revolucija i kontrarevolucija u Jugoslaviji (1941.-1945.)*, I, 94.

61 H. Matković, *Bosansko-hercegovački muslimani u programu ustaške emigracije i politi-*

situation remained tense. In Sarajevo, more than a thousand people were quickly rounded up and arrested, including more than 300 Bosniaks.[62] These arrests called forth more public unrest. For the Ustaša regime, the policy towards Bosniaks would increasingly obviously take on the character of a special question, whose "resolve" would depend primarily upon the application of direct political pressure. The Germans increasingly began to issue warnings to this effect within the context of their occupation policy, the main goal of which was to maintain a stable and peaceful situation on the territory of the NDH, and particularly in Bosnia and Herzegovina, where their economic interests were more strongly expressed.[63]

According to Mile Konjević, it had become evident that the Bosniak people was unwilling to follow an exclusive circle of pro-Ustaša political cronies and Ustaša appointees, and that they could not be won over by the distribution of ministerial appointments, promises of religious autonomy, and paeans about their political maturity or similar demagogic promises. The resolutions were hardly capable of putting an end to conflict or the uncontrolled and chauvinist rampages, but they were an attempt to open everyone's eyes and call for the restoration of peace at a time of general insecurity.[64] The Ustašas were quite simply not up to dealing with the complex political situation in Bosnia and Herzegovina and in no position to impose their will on the Bosniaks, who were in the process of becoming the masters of their own national, social, and political development. Consequently, the Ustaša policy in Bosnia and Herzegovina, particularly towards the Bosniaks, was clearly failing by the end of 1941.[65] On 1 October

---

ci Nezavisne Države Hrvatske, 1034-1035. A circular from Eugen Dido Kvaternik, the director of the Ustaša intelligence services, from March 1942, announced special measures in Bosnia and Herzegovina to ensure that any future disagreement with NDH policy "be most energetically suppressed, by applying the most drastic methods."

62 R. Hurem, *Narodi BiH prema ustanku 1941.-1942.,* 161. For Bosniak suffering in the camps, see N. Halilbegović, *Bošnjaci u jasenovačkom logoru,* Vijeće Kongresa bošnjačkih intelektualaca, Sarajevo 2006.

63 F. Jelić-Butić, *Ustaša i Nezavisna Država Hrvatska 1941.-1945.,* Zagreb 1977, 202.

64 F. Jelić-Butić, *Ustaša i Nezavisna Država Hrvatska 1941.-1945.,* 202.

65 M. Konjević, *O nekim pitanjima politike ustaša prema bosanskohercegovačkim musli-*

1941, in Banja Luka, Josip Babić Barun, an Ustaša from Pavelić's own personal guard, killed Edhem Hodžić, a mentally ill imam from the village of Hrujića, near Kozarac, in the courtyard of the National Hospital. Trampling on the corpse of the murdered imam worsened relations "between the clerical-Ustašas and the Muslim currents, the latter of which is supported by significant part of the Muslim population." A group of Bosniaks protested the murder with the Grand Prefect. At the murdered imam's funeral, in the presence of around 500 people, repugnance was expressed in protest against arbitrary Ustaša action in the town and the state as a whole. One of the speakers at the funeral, according to the report of an Ustaša agent present, said "You have all come here to protest what has been done. Let us pray to God that He deliver us from such things." To which those present responded by shouting "We will free ourselves. Down with them."[66] Relations worsened through October across the Bosnian borderlands. A German intelligence officer then making his way around Bosnia informed the relevant authorities at the end of the month, that "recently Muslim distancing from Zagreb has gone so far that there is now quite open talk in some Muslim ranks of Bosnian autonomy to be guaranteed by Germany, while other circles are giving consideration to stronger links with Serbia, particularly if Serbia becomes a German protectorate."[67] A report on conditions in Sarajevo and "the rest of Bosnia" sent by the NDH Ministry of the Interior to the Ministry for Homeland Defence in early November 1941 included the claim that there was a growing rift between Croat Catholics and Muslims, as Muslims are "not nationally conscious Croats as yet," as they were very conscious of their *din* [religious faith and obligations, op. trans.], and that one had with Muslims "to have a firm hand at times, and a soft one at other times. To be unyielding in important matters, generous in minor ones."[68]

"The declarations against the State of Croatia and against the Ustaša order," as the resolutions were referred to in some Ustaša pamphlets, could

---

manima 1941. godine, 273.
66 D. Lukač, *Banja Luka i okolica u ratu i revoluciji*, 146.
67 D. Lukač, *Banja Luka i okolica u ratu i revoluciji*, 147, note 49.
68 *Zločini na jugoslovenskim prostorima*, I, 814.

do little to change the situation in Bosnia and Herzegovina drastically, but they did represent an open and courageous manifestation of Bosniak disagreement with the Ustaša policy of discrimination and a conscious act on the part of the signatories who were well aware that they too could end up at the receiving end of repressive policies.[69] It is somewhat difficult today to understand fully what it must have meant some seven decades ago, in an atmosphere of such great uncertainty, fear, and undeniable suffering, to sign and distribute the Muslim Resolutions in 1941. This was a society in which, as hafiz Abdulah Budimlija later wrote, the most responsible and mindful citizens did nothing, by word or deed, to have a positive impact on society, preferring to live passively, in isolation, withdrawn into themselves, and waiting for evermore awful events, in which each individual would feel lost and disoriented.[70] The resolutions deserve a place of honor amongst the dramatic events of 1941, when the Axis forces were in a major push of conquest, and the victory of Nazi fascism seemed on the horizon. These were the circumstances under which the "clear voice" of antifascist Bosniak protest was heard.

According to Tacitus, "the main task of the historian is to ensure no great deed falls into oblivion, and that evil words and deeds receive eternal condemnation." The resolutions were an act of civic bravery and responsibility, a humane act under circumstances that made any attempt to stand upright and against fear difficult, in a tense environment, in which the unprotected individual was above all exposed. They were an expression of unrest and of resistance to a grim reality and "a time of the unbearable lightness of dying," a stand against war, destruction, and the propagation of hatred. This was not a simple question of spiritual redemption or

---

69 M. Hadžijahić, *Posebnost Bosne i Hercegovine i stradanja Muslimana*, 47-53. Draža Mihailović also referred to these resolutions in 1944: "the memorandum of the Banja Luka Muslims sent to the Muslim ministers in the Pavelić government in August 1941, followed by the resolutions from the Sarajevo, Mostar, Prijedor, and Tuzla Muslim leaders, is an example of conscience and civic courage" – cited after M. Hadžijahić, *Muslimanske rezolucije iz 1941. godine*, 275; Idem, *Posebnost Bosne i Hercegovine i stradanja Muslimana*, 56.

70 A. Budimlija, ""Adžaibi" (čuda)," *Preporod*, no. 4/870, Sarajevo, 15 February 2008, 15.

the temporary easing of conscience. According to Gandhi, nonviolence represents the highest degree of human dignity. By uncovering and documenting the various practices and discourses through which opposition to war is made manifest, despite all the limitations to such action, we may reaffirm that history is above all a matter of choice, if not always in the same way and to the same degree for all elements in society. Responsibility largely depends upon social status.[71] Antifascism is something the Bosniaks as a people can be proud of and that gives them a right to walk tall through the history of civilization. Attempts to deny Bosniak antifascism generally serve as cover for anti-Bosniak policies with imperialist and expansionist goals, which involve, amongst other things, an attempt to cover over and obscure responsibility. Any stand against any form of hatred, xenophobia, and racism is of great importance. One must always stand against abuses in the interpretation of historical events, impassioned prejudices, and quasi-historical analyses intended to support ongoing political goals, no matter the cost to inter-ethnic relations and intensified tensions and distance between peoples.

---

71 D. MacDonald, "Living Together or Hating Each Other?" *Confronting the Yugoslav Controversies: A Scholars' Initiative*, eds. Charles Ingrao and Thomas Emmert, Purdue University Press, 2nd Edition, 2012, 380.

Xavier Bougarel

THE MUSLIM RESOLUTIONS OF 1941: BETWEEN MORAL COURAGE AND POLITICAL IMPOTENCE

Between August and December 1941, representatives of the Bosnian Muslim community in several cities adopted resolutions addressed to the Ustaša authorities of the Independent State of Croatia (NDH). These resolutions were published in a particularly difficult context for the Muslim community: after its proclamation on 10 April 1941, the Independent State of Croatia had introduced a series of discriminatory laws against Serbs, Jews, and Roma living on its territory and, from June onwards, the Ustaša militias committed numerous massacres of Serbs in the regions where they were in the majority. In response, Serbs in the NDH rebelled and, in some places, took revenge by attacking neighboring Muslim villages. The Muslim community thus found itself caught in a cycle of violence that it had not provoked, and it is primarily to this dramatic situation that the Muslim Resolutions of 1941 wanted to draw attention. The resolution adopted in Sarajevo on 12 October 1941 wrote, for example, that "The Muslims of Bosnia and Herzegovina today find themselves in great difficulty. It is no exaggeration to say that the Muslims of these parts have never experienced such difficult times in all their history." The signatories denounced the violence committed against the Serb community and, in a less explicit way, against the Jewish community, and blamed the local representatives of the Ustaša movement and other uncontrolled elements. They admitted that some Muslim individuals may have participated in the massacres of Serbs but also accused the Ustašas of deliberately wearing the fes or using Muslim names among themselves in order to start a cycle of violence and counter-violence between Serbs and Muslims. In addition, some resolutions denounced the forced conversions to Catholicism supported by part of the Catholic Church and compared these practices to the medieval Inquisition. Against this background, the Muslim Resolutions demanded that the NDH authorities put an end to the violence and restore order and the rule of law. The first resolution adopted on 14 August 1941 by *El-Hidaje*, the association of *ilmije*, for example, called on the Ustaša authorities "to restore law and order as soon as possible to all areas and prevent unauthorized action so that innocent people do not suffer."

The Muslim Resolutions of 1941 first expressed a demand for security and protection addressed to the central authorities of the NDH. However, they were also a moral condemnation, in the name of Islam, of the violence provoked by this same central power. Perhaps the most explicit resolution on this point was that of Mostar, which declared that "Every true Muslim, ennobled by the exalted tenets of Islam, condemns these crimes, from whatever quarter, fully cognizant that the Islamic faith considers the murder and torture of the innocent, looting of other people's possessions, and conversion under conditions that exclude free will, amongst the worst of sins." Other resolutions contrasted the intolerance of the NDH with the tolerance that Muslims had showed during the Ottoman era. The Bijeljina Resolution stated for example that "For hundreds of years, Bosnian Muslims have lived in harmony and brotherly love with all other Bosnians, regardless of faith, just as their exalted Islam commands them to. Even when all the power was in their hands, they did not commit evil deeds against their fellow citizens of other faiths or sow religious or tribal hatred." From this point of view, the 1941 resolutions prove that the Muslim elites of Bosnia and Herzegovina did not share the racist and criminal ideology of the Ustašas and remained attached to the inter-religious coexistence that had traditionally characterized Bosnia and Herzegovina. The Bijeljina Resolution proclaimed therefore that "Bosnia's salvation lies in the unity and fraternity of Bosnians, not in blood feud and hatred." Yet, on the political level, none of these resolutions broke completely with the NDH. Their authors continued to assure the leaders of the NDH of their loyalty and to consider them the only ones capable of restoring order and security, and the *El-Hidaje* association even advocated the inclusion of the Sandžak region into the NDH.[1] This must be seen as an extension of an attitude of the Muslim elites that dates back at least to the Austro-Hungarian period, consisting in pledging allegiance to the central power in order to obtain its protection. What the signatories of the 1941 resolutions did not seem to understand is that the context of the 1940s was not that of the end of the 19th century.

A strong and courageous moral protest in the context of the Second World War, the Muslim Resolutions of 1941 were at the same time a testimony to the political hesitations of Muslim elites in the face of extreme violence. The mere fact that the first resolution of 14 August 1941 was published by a religious association underlines the silence of the political elites of the inter-war period. Elsewhere, the initiators of the resolutions were sometimes relatively marginal individuals or notables with a complex political career. Thus, in Prijedor, it was a Muslim married to a Serb who had spent part of his life in Belgrade, Muharem Sadiković, who encouraged the local religious institutions to adopt the resolution of 23 September 1941.[2] In Bijeljina, on the other hand, one of the authors of the resolution of 2 December 1941 was the landowner Murat-beg Pašić, a deputy of the Yugoslav Radical Community (JRZ) in the inter-war period, who in April 1941 became commander of the local Ustaša militia and as such was involved in the violence against the Serbs and Jews of the town. It was not until the massacre of a hundred Muslim villagers in Koraj on 25 November 1941 that Murat-beg Pašić distanced himself from the Ustaša regime and remembered the tradition of tolerance of Bosnian society.[3] If the condemnation of the Ustaša violence by the resolutions of 1941 thus reflected a sentiment widely shared by the Muslims of Bosnia and Herzegovina, it should

---

1   The Sandžak region is located on the border between Serbia and Montenegro and is populated by Muslims and Orthodox. Between 1941 and 1945, it was attached to Montenegro under Italian occupation.
2   See Tomislav Dulić, *Utopias of Nation. Local Mass Killing in Bosnia and Herzegovina 1941-1942*, Uppsala: Acta Universitatis Upsaliensis, 2005, pp. 226-228 and 236-241.
3   See Xavier Bougarel, *La division Handschar. Waffen-SS de Bosnie 1943-1945*, Paris: Humensis, 2020, pp. 42 and 46-47.

not create the illusion of a population united and mobilized around its traditional elites: on the contrary, what characterized the Bosnian Muslim community during the Second World War was dispersion, disorientation and, as a consequence, political impotence.

To illustrate this reality, one needs only to look at other resolutions adopted later by representatives of the Muslim community, and less known than those of 1941. On 10 November 1942, for example, Muslim notables from eastern and central Bosnia assembled in Tuzla addressed a petition to General Rudolf Lüters, commander-in-chief of the German troops in Croatia. In their communication, they asserted that the physical existence of Bosnian Muslims was threatened by the massacres committed by the Četniks, and that the NDH was incapable of ensuring their protection. They also explained that a delegation had met with the *Poglavnik* Ante Pavelić on 30 October to ask him to support the creation of Muslim self-defense militias, but that he had replied that such a decision depended on the German military authorities. The signatories of the resolution therefore asked the commander of the German troops in Croatia to authorize the creation of Muslim militias on the model of the one led in Tuzla by Muhamed Hadžiefendić, and to provide them with weapons.[4] This resolution of 10 November 1942 is different from those of 1941: it was not addressed to the Ustaša leaders, but to the German authorities, and it did not seek the protection of the central power, but rather to provide the Muslim community with the means to defend itself. It corresponds to the state of mind of those traditional Muslim elites who were distancing themselves more and more from the NDH: two months earlier, on 26 August 1942, nearly 300 Muslim notables had formed in Sarajevo a People's Salvation Committee (*Odbor narodnog spasa*) chaired by Mehmed Handžić of the *El-Hidaje* association and including several signatories of the 1941 resolutions. This committee instructed Muhamed Pandža, one of the leaders of the Islamic Religious Community, to seek weapons to organize the defense of the Muslims of Bosnia and Herzegovina. But this search for arms led some representatives

---

4   "An dem komandierenden General der deutschen Wehrmacht im Unabhängigen Staaate Kroatien in Agram," Archives of the armed forces of Serbia, collection NDH, box 40G, fascicule 3, document 25.

of the Muslim community – beginning with Muhamed Pandža – to support in 1943 the project of an SS division composed of Bosnian Muslims, and some of those who had opposed the violence of the Ustaša state in 1941 thus fell into collaboration with Nazi Germany. In this context, it is not surprising to find among the imams of the SS division three young Islamic clerics who had signed the Sarajevo Resolution of 12 October 1941, namely Husein Đozo, Hasan Bajraktarević, and Ahmed Skaka.

Far from giving rise to an organized resistance movement, the signatories of the 1941 resolutions later became passive or, for some, succumbed to the temptation of collaboration. In the final years of the war, their disorientation and lack of perspective became even more apparent. On 20 October 1943, the *El-Hidaje* association published a communiqué in which it recalled that the religious duty of Muslims was to "heroically defend themselves against anyone who threatens their lives," while refraining from looting, killing innocent people or committing any other act contrary to the Islamic religion. *El-Hidaje* also emphasized that "we must behave with our [Christian] neighbors who do us no harm as required by good neighborliness [*komšiluk*] and our most sacred traditions."[5] Eleven months later, on 15 September 1944, *El-Hidaje* and several other Muslim associations called on the citizens of Sarajevo to organize in self-defense "on a broad and multi-religious basis where the neighbor of one faith will if necessary defend the member of a second or third community and thus avoid unnecessary victims," and invited representatives of the Orthodox and Catholic communities to discuss measures to be taken in the event of an attack against the city by an undefined enemy.[6] But as German troops began to leave Bosnia and Herzegovina, and the victory of Tito's partisans was no longer in doubt, these general considerations did little to mask the difficulty for the representatives of the Muslim community to develop new strategies and alliances. More generally, the case of the resolutions adopted by certain representatives

---

5   "Svim jedinicama i prijateljima El-Hidaje," Historical Museum of Bosnia and Herzegovina, collection UNS, box 10, document 2460A.

6   "Rezolucija muslimanskih društava u Sarajevu," Historical Museum of Bosnia and Herzegovina, collection UNS, box 16, document 3779.

of the Bosnian Muslim community between 1941 and 1944 reveals the limits of a peaceful mode of action, limited to the notables alone and inherited from the Ottoman and Austro-Hungarian periods, at a time when the world was witnessing the violent confrontation of the nationalist projects and totalitarian ideologies of the 20th century.

Marko Attila Hoare

MUSLIM BOSNIAK RESISTANCE TO THE USTAŠAS AND THE MUSLIM RESOLUTIONS OF 1941

The Muslim Resolutions issues by notables from the ranks of the Muslim Bosniak elites in 1941 expressed the opposition of members of the Muslim Bosniak elite to the genocidal crimes of the Ustašas. They reflected the revulsion of Muslim notables and Muslims and Bosnians more generally in the face of the horrific crimes. They reflected also the opposition of Muslim notables to the forcible inclusion of their nation and country within the Ustaša puppet-state, the so-called "Independent State of Croatia" (NDH), involving the erasing of Bosnia and Herzegovina and the forced inclusion of Muslims within the Croat nation as supposed "Muslim Croats." They also reflected awareness that the Ustaša genocide of Serbs was provoking a Serb-rebel backlash involving massacres of Muslim civilians, and that this had been deliberately intended by at least some elements within the Ustaša regime to sow conflict between Serbs and Muslims. The Muslim Resolutions were linked with other Muslim expressions of resistance to the Ustaša regime; these expressions were the work of Muslim notables who were not necessarily anti-fascist or anti-occupier - many were in fact collaborationist vis-à-vis the German and Italian occupiers of Yugoslavia, and some were explicitly pro-Nazi. But they all manifested, at some level, a desire to preserve the Muslims as a community in the face of the threat represented by the Ustašas and the pogromist Serb rebels who were coalescing as the Četnik movement. Thus, the Resolutions were not simply humanitarian in motivation.

The Ustaša project of a Great Croatia incorporating all of Bosnia and Herzegovina, required the latter be forcibly assimilated, contrary to the wishes of most of its inhabitants. The NDH was divided into twenty-two administrative units or "Great župas/counties." This was intended to erase the border between Croatia and Bosnia and Herzegovina.[1] Meanwhile, the Ustaša regime relied particularly on former members of the minority pro-Croat faction among the Muslim Bosniaks, the so-called "Muslim Branch of the Croat Peasant Party," to implement its policy in Bosnia and Herzegovina, particularly Hakija Hadžić. Hadžić's purge from the state apparatus of the older and politically mainstream Muslim notables began the process by which the Muslim elite would be wholly alienated from the NDH.[2] Furthermore, all levels of the NDH apparatus, its armed forces, and the Ustaša movement would be dominated by Catholic Croats, while Muslims were underrepresented in all of them.[3]

The NDH was treated like a colony by the Germans and Italians. Its raw materials, industrial installations and military assets were systematically and continuously seized and plundered by the Axis powers. The NDH was forced to pay Germany its share of the Yugoslav debt, while foreign trade between the NDH and the Axis powers was manipulated at the NDH's expense. The NDH had to pay the costs of the German-Italian occupation of its territory. It had also to feed and house the German and Italian troops on its territory and provide civilian labor for German military needs. The cost of financing this occupation massively strained the NDH's economy, generating huge inflation. Even before the outbreak of the civil war in the summer of 1941, the NDH barely possessed the agricultural resources to feed its inhabitants. Civil war inevitably made an adequate supply of food to the population impossible. The flight of refugees from the countryside to the towns; rebel control over large food-producing areas, the rebel cutting of transport lines and rebel sieges combined with massive inflation to produce serious food-shortages in the towns of the NDH. The efforts of the regime to force the peasants to cultivate specific crops and to

---

1 Fikreta Jelic-Butić, *Ustaša i Nezavisna Država Hrvatska 1941-1945*, Sveučilišna Naklada Liber, Zagreb, 1978, 105; Hrvoje Matković, *Povijest Nezavisne Države Hrvatske*, Naklada Pavičić, Zagreb, 1994, 70.

2 *Istorija građanskih stranaka u Jugoslaviji*, vol. 2, SUP, Belgrade, 1952, pp. 111-112.

3 Jelić-Butić, *Ustaša i NDH*, pp. 99-100.; Mehmedalija Bojić, *Historija Bosne i Bošnjaka (VII-XX vijek)*, TKD Šahinpašić, Sarajevo, 2001, 200-202.

impose compulsory delivery quotas on food products could not resolve the problem, while imports from Romania and elsewhere were sufficient only to avoid the complete collapse of the NDH government and armed forces. Shortages of food and other goods created a lively smuggling trade. While the state supply of food dwindled, black-market food prices rose exponentially.[4] The Axis exploitation and oppression of the NDH including Bosnia and Herzegovina, through the medium of the Ustaša puppet-state, catalysed the growing Muslim resentment of the NDH.

Most Muslims reacted with reserve to the establishment of the NDH. Politically conscious Muslims bided their time while waiting for the outcome of the war to become clearer. Their sympathies generally neither with the Axis nor the Allies, those Muslims who sought guidance from abroad tended to look to Turkey, the former imperial matrix and now studiously neutral.[5] The Muslims also resented the breakdown of law and order, the behavior of Italian troops who collaborated systematically with the Četniks, the loss of East Bosnian territory to the rebels, and the inability or unwillingness of the NDH to protect the Muslims there. They feared the possibility of mobilization for service on the Russian front, of an Axis attack on Turkey, and above all that the regime would attempt their mass conversion to Catholicism.

Consequently, Muslim opinion steadily turned against the Ustaša regime. The growing Muslim resistance took a number of different forms, ranging from Muslim entry into the Četniks, through Muslim autonomist agitation on an anti-Ustaša but pro-German basis, to Muslim entry into the Communist-led Partisans. But all currents of the anti-Ustaša Muslim opposition were united behind a shared goal: a Bosnia and Herzegovina enjoying some element of autonomy, in which Muslim individuality would be protected. The different Muslim currents tended not to view each other as real enemies, but rather as fellow travellers who had simply chosen

---

4   This summary of Axis exploitation of the NDH is based on information provided by Jozo Tomasevich, *War and Revolution in Yugoslavia, 1941-1945: Occupation and Collaboration*, Stanford California Press, Stanford, 2001, chs 6-10.

5   Historical Museum of Bosnia and Herzegovina (HMBiH) Collection UNS, box 4, docs. 1101 + 1110; box 6, doc. 2094; box 7, doc. 2463.

different strategies to achieve national liberation. Muslim opposition to the Ustašas was spurred above all by their anti-Serb campaign, something that provoked a massive anti-Muslim backlash among the Bosnian Serbs and that threatened to decimate Bosnia and Herzegovina.

In the first weeks of the NDH's existence, a group of Bosnian Muslim, Serb and Croat politicians, who were anti-Ustaša but nevertheless ready to collaborate with the occupiers, delivered a memorandum to the German military government contesting the validity of the inclusion of Bosnia and Herzegovina in the NDH and demanding a direct German military administration over the whole of Bosnia and Herzegovina. The initiative for this came from Uzeiraga Hadžihasanović. The other signatories were the Muslims Husein Kadić and Asim Šeremet, the Serbs Milan Božić, Vojislav Besarović, Dušan Jeftanović and Milan Jojkić, and the Croats Luka Čabrajić and possibly Vjekoslav Jelavić. Members of this group then visited Hakija Hadžić to demand that Bosnia and Herzegovina be granted autonomy. This effort at cross-confessional collaboration by members of the Bosnian elites against the Ustaša genocide came to an abrupt end when the Ustašas responded by arresting Božic, Besarović and Jeftanović, all of whom were later executed, while the Muslims were warned to desist from such activities.[6]

Hadžihasanović, as the *de facto* leader of the pro-German but anti-Ustaša wing of the Muslim elite, thereupon ceased lobbying the Ustašas directly and adopted a back-seat role in channeling Muslim autonomist opposition. He and Kulenović summoned leading members of the former JMO to a meeting at a private residence in the north-Bosnian town of Doboj, some time in the summer of 1941, to adopt a new strategy. With Hadžihasanović's support, and despite the opposition of a majority of those present, Kulenović resolved to enter the NDH government in order to act as a counterweight to Hadžić and the Muslim Branch. His entry

---

6   Rasim Hurem, "Pokušaj nekih građanskih muslimanskih političara da Bosnu i Hercegovinu izdvoje iz okvira Nezavisne Države Hrvatske," *Godišnjak Društva istoričara Bosne i Hercegovine*, no. 16, 1965, 197-198; Filandra, *Bošnjačka politika u XX. stoljeću*, 172-173; Enver Redžić, *Bosna i Hercegovina u Drugom svjetskom ratu*, Sarajevo, OKO, 1998, 303.

was furthermore urged by two Bosnian Serb politicians, Savo Besarović and Dušan Kecmanović, who hoped thereby to improve the position of the Serbs in the NDH. On 14 August, a delegation of Muslim notables led by Kulenović and Hadžihasanović was received by the Ustaša leader Ante Pavelić and delivered to him a declaration of Muslim loyalty, after which Kulenović replaced his brother Osman as vice-president of the government in November. The pro-NDH wing of the Muslim elite would be henceforth divided into two hostile camps: the collaborationist wing of the former Yugoslav Muslim Organization and the genuine ideological Ustašas who had emerged from the Muslim Branch.[7]

This Muslim autonomist opposition to the Ustašas then manifested itself in the series of resolutions issued in September-December 1941 by representatives of the Muslim elite in the principal Bosnian towns, addressed to the German and NDH authorities and condemning the persecution of the Serbs. These resolutions were couched in Bosnian-patriotic terms. The event heralding these resolutions occurred on 14 August, while Pavelić was receiving Kulenović's delegation. On that date the assembly in Sarajevo of El-Hidaje, representing the Muslim clergy of the NDH, "expressed its concern for the disturbances that had come about and the deaths caused by these disturbances, and in the name of all Muslims condemned and disassociated itself from those Muslims who had participated in acts of violence."[8] This was followed by resolutions issued by assemblies of Muslim notables in Prijedor (23 September) Sarajevo (12 October), Mostar (21 October), Banja Luka (12 November), Bijeljina (2 December) and Tuzla (11 December). The resolutions, with varying degrees of forthrightness,

---

7   *Istorija građanskih stranaka u Jugoslaviji*, vol. 2, 112-114; Redžić, *BiH u Drugom svjetskom ratu*, 302; Milica Bodrožić, 'uloga i držanje građanskih stranaka i grupa tokom 1942. godine i prvo zasjedanje AVNOJ-a', in Slavko Odić (ed.), *Prvo zasjedanje Antifašističkog vijeca narodnog oslobođenja Jugoslavije*, Muzej AVNOJ-a i Pounja, Bihać, 1967, 338.

8   Mile Konjević, 'O nekim pitanjima politike Ustaša prema bosanskohercegovačkim Muslimanima 1941. godine', in *1941. u istoriji naroda BiH*, Veselin Masleša, Sarajevo, 1973, 272.

rebuked the Ustašas, for their mistreatment of Muslims and their attempts at turning Muslims and Serbs against one another.

The Prijedor Resolution accused rogue Ustaša elements of killing "perfectly peaceable civilians of the Greek-Eastern rite," while wearing "the fes, creating the misapprehension that all this havoc was being carried out by Muslims," as well as forcing "some Muslims at gunpoint to hack some Greek-Eastern rite villagers to death," in order to turn the Serbs against the Muslims. It complained also that all organs of authority in the district "are exclusively in the hands of Catholics." That "not a single Muslim has been appointed to a senior position in the local authorities… means those self-same authorities can pursue their purely Catholic policy."[9]

The Sarajevo Resolution noted: "Even in the past, during Turkish times, when the Muslims were the only masters, they tolerated all religions without distinction and terrorized none. Consequently, Muslims cannot be painted today as the instigators of these crimes or intolerant of the Greek-Easterners or as causing these disturbances, as some certainly seek to do." It further demanded that the authorities "introduce real security of life, honor, property, and measures that apply to all citizens of the state without distinction of any kind", "bring all the real culprits, including all those who have committed any form of violence or atrocity, to justice before the courts, regardless of religious affiliation, and to punish them severely under the law, along with all those who ordered or enabled their criminal acts", and "counter all forms of religious intolerance and punish severely any guilty of proven transgression in this regard."[10]

The Mostar Resolution lamented: "None can remember days as difficult and eventful or times as fateful as those we are now living through, in the entire history of our beloved homeland, Bosnia and Herzegovina." It claimed to represent "the feelings and intentions of the broadest strata of Muslims throughout this proud country of ours, Bosnia and Herzegovina," in stating that "the countless crimes, injustices, lawless acts, and forced

---

9 HMBiH Collection UNS, box 1, doc. 130/3.
10 Cf. Šemso Tucaković (ed.), *Srpski zločini nad Bošnjacima-Muslimanima 1941-1945*, El-Kalem, Sarajevo, 1995, 220-223.

conversions committed and still being committed against Orthodox Serbs and other fellow citizens are entirely repugnant to the soul of any Muslim." It stated that "[c]ondemning all this, we call for the introduction of absolute equality of status and rights, order, and the rule of law for all, regardless of religious or national identity."[11]

The Banja Luka Resolution condemned: "The slaughter of priests and other leading individuals, without trial or verdict, and the mass shooting and abuse of all too often entirely innocent people, women, even children, and the driving of entire families *en masse* from their homes and their beds with but an hour or two to prepare for deportation to an unknown destination; the alienation and looting of property, forced conversions to Catholicism, all these are facts that cannot but leave any sincere human being aghast and have had a most unsettling effect on us, the local Muslims."[12] Although this Resolution condemned the activities of the Communists, many of its signatories were active in the Communist-led resistance or would become so in the coming months.[13]

The Tuzla Resolution claimed that "[s]o far most, if not all, of the victims of this unrest have been Muslims," as a result of "attacks on Serbs by rogue elements, attacks that are unfortunately continuing and provoking retaliation" against the Muslims. Yet although "our Muslim community, inspired by the spirit of Islamic culture and ethics, condemns any form of disorder," nonetheless, "misinformation has been being maliciously spread that Muslims are actually responsible for these actions against the Serbs, and all the odium for them is now directed against Muslims and everything is presented as though it were all just a settling of scores between Serbs and Muslims."[14]

---

11   Ibid, pp. 219-220.
12   Cf. *Zbornik dokumenata i podataka o narodnooslobodilačkom ratu Jugoslovenskih naroda,* pt 4, vol. 2, Vojnoistorijski institut, Belgrade, 1951, doc. 164, 430-431.
13   Dušanka Kovačević and Zaga Umičević, "Neki podaci o delovanju NOP-a u okupiranoj Banjoj Luci," in *Banja Luka u novijoj istoriji (1878-1945),* Institut za istoriju u Banjoj Luci, Sarajevo, 1978, 595.
14   HMBiH Collection UNS, box 1, doc. 177.

The Bijeljina Resolution denounced in Bosnian-patriotic terms the atrocities being committed by both the Ustašas and the rebels: "Bosnia's salvation lies in the unity and fraternity of Bosnians, not in blood feud and hatred. Religion should not separate us. It should unite us, to positive action on all our parts, and encourage us to be first and foremost people who refuse to be governed by alienated animal impulses to murder and looting, arson and abuse, urges any man of culture must rein in."[15]

Another Muslim initiative against the Ustaša genocide concerned the so-called "white gypsies," a community of largely settled, slavophone and Islamic Roma who were among those destined by the Ustašas for extermination. On 26 May 1941, notables from the ranks of the Muslims of the town of Zenica in Central Bosnia rallied in their defence. According to the meeting's resolution, "The Muslims of Zenica, having convened a meeting over the dispatch of the so-called 'Gypsy' Muslims from Travnik to the concentration camps and rumors that the same is to be done with the other so-called 'Gypsy' Muslims of Herzeg-Bosna…" It demanded the return of the arrested gypsies and an end to their persecution and deportation. Meetings of this kind took place in several places in Bosnia and Herzegovina, and in Sarajevo, a committee was formed to protest the issue. In the face of fierce Muslim opposition, the NDH authorities on 30 August halted all further deportation of the "white gypsies" to concentration camps.[16]

In the months and years that followed, Muslim resistance to the Ustaša regime would develop as part of two currents: the Muslim autonomist resistance on the one hand, which was neither anti-fascist, nor anti-Nazi, nor anti-occupier, but merely anti-Ustaša, and the People's Liberation Movement (NOP) led by the Communist Party of Yugoslavia, which was anti-fascist and anti-occupier, on the other. Some Muslim autonomists such as Hadžihasanović followed an explicitly pro-Nazi line; others were pro-Italian and pro-Četnik. But some Muslim notables, soldiers and their followers gravitated toward the NOP, which explicitly championed Bosnian and Herzegovinian national-liberation, self-rule, and, eventually,

---

15   HMBiH Collection UNS, box 1, doc. 134.
16   Bojić, *Historija Bosne i Bošnjaka*, 190.

statehood. The Muslim Resolutions were thus an early manifestation of Muslim opposition to the Ustaša regime that would eventually find expression in mass Muslim entry into the NOP and participation in a revolution that would destroy it, replacing it with a People's Republic of Bosnia and Herzegovina, as a constituent member of a new federal Yugoslavia.

THE MUSLIM RESOLUTIONS

EL-HIDAJE RESOLUTION	151
PRIJEDOR RESOLUTION	155
SARAJEVO RESOLUTION	165
MOSTAR RESOLUTION	179
BANJALUKA RESOLUTION	183
BIJELJINA RESOLUTION	195
TUZLA RESOLUTION	201
ZENICA RESOLUTION	205
BOSANSKA DUBICA RESOLUTION	211
BUGOJNO RESOLUTION	215

EL-HIDAJE RESOLUTION

The El-Hidaje Resolution, dated August 14, 1941, in Sarajevo, was passed by the General Assembly of the El-Hidaje Association of Muslim Clerics [ilmijje] at its Annual General Meeting. The Resolution was initially published in the El-Hidaje journal, Year 5, No. 1 (22 September 1941), pp. 27-29. Individual copies of the Resolution may be consulted at the Archives of the Islamic Community of Bosnia and Herzegovina in the Gazi Husrev-Bey Library. This translation is based upon the published text.

* * *

The members of *El-Hidaje*, the Organization of ilmijje (the Muslim clergy) of the Independent State of Croatia, gathered in annual assembly, after discussion of issues of importance for the Islamic religious community, have unanimously passed the following resolution:

1. The Assembly notes with satisfaction that the authorities at the highest levels in our country have demonstrated, in many statements, a strong desire to provide Muslims full freedom in their religious affairs, religious education, and matters of *waqf* property. Based on which, the members of the Assembly look forward with raised hopes to the realization of our aspirations in this regard.

2. The assembly members unanimously endorse the work of El-Hidaje to date and [the organization's] participation in [promoting] passage of the new law and statutes of the Islamic religious community and express their agreement with all the principles on which that draft law and statutes are based, which principles were set out in last year's resolution and discussed at this assembly. It has been affirmed as an urgent requirement of the Islamic religious community, and our association has previously expressed its position on the law and statutes and the principles on which they have been drafted. The assembly members do not believe there are any good reasons

for putting off this issue to some undetermined date. Our participation in this work does not entail any marks of party-political affiliation and aims only at the common good of the Islamic religious community.

3. The assembly members note that the absolute equality of the Islamic and Catholic religions in the Independent State of Croatia has been repeatedly publicly and clearly stated and emphasized at the highest levels in the state. It is vital that the entire Croat people act and think in line with the spirit of this exalted idea. Our most fundamental duty is therefore absolute tolerance and fraternal cooperation between all the members of the Croat people in building our young state. Any intolerance or unequal treatment in religion is detrimental to our common national and state cause.

4. It is with pain in our hearts and profound condolences that we remember all the innocent Muslim victims struck down through no fault of their own in the unrest that has recently taken place in various places. We condemn any and all individual Muslims who have committed any form of attack or violence independently and on their own initiative. We declare that the only people capable of doing such a thing are rogue elements and uncivilized individuals, whose stain we reject both for ourselves and for all Muslims. We call on all Muslims to refrain from such evil acts, in the spirit of the exalted tenets of their religion and in the interests of the state. We call on the government authorities to restore law and order as soon as possible to all areas and prevent unauthorized action so that innocent people do not suffer.

5. The assembly members note that the higher religious authorities have recently been neglecting both religious preaching and religious propaganda among Muslims, even though a special institution already exists for this in the Ulema-medžlis. The consequences of this neglect are evident among Muslims. Appropriate attention to the issue is needed.

6. All Islamic religious ministers, and especially the muallims, are carrying out their pious religious and cultural duties and contributing to the spiritual betterment of our people. Most are also in highly straitened financial and material circumstances, especially today, hindering and in some cases preventing their valuable work. Given that state officials are currently

receiving special consideration and financial assistance, the assembly members declare that both the religious and government authorities should accomodate Islamic religious officials in this regard.

7. El-Hidaje has always advocated the absolute unity of Muslims in terms of religious rules and regulations. The assembly members note the imperative that all Muslims adhere to this principle, especially under current circumstances.

8. The Novi Pazar Sandžak is historically an integral part of Bosnia and Herzegovina and the Sandžak Muslims an inalienable part of the Muslim component of the Croat people. The General Assembly therefore petitions all the relevant authorities to promote the inclusion of the Sandžak within the framework of the Independent State of Croatia. By force of circumstance, that part of the Islamic religious community left in Sandžak have no recourse to the legal regulations on the Islamic religious community, and we ask the authorities to give this issue due consideration and take remedial action regarding the financial and material situation of Islamic religious officials in the Sandžak area.

PRIJEDOR RESOLUTION

The Prijedor Resolution was promulgated on September 22, 1941, in Prijedor, by the Prijedor District Waqf and Educational Committee and signed by leading Bosniak citizens of Prijedor. The specific individual(s) to whom it is addressed is not recorded. There are transcribed copies, entitled "The Declaration of Prijedor Muslims" at the Historical Museum of Bosnia and Herzegovina, *the* Bosniak Institute, *and the* Archives of the Islamic Community of Bosnia and Herzegovina *in the* Gazi Husrev-Bey Library.[1]

***

On August 23 (the second night of Ramadan), this year, the Prijedor district *Waqf and Educational Committee,* as religious representative of all 24,000 Croat Muslims in the district, convened a public meeting of Muslims of all social classes at their express universal request and decided to address you in this way and present the situation of the Muslims of this district, which is generally similar to that of the entire C[roatian] Bosnian Krajina, and petition you to do your fraternal and Muslim best to find a remedy for it.

There have been almost daily public statements at the highest levels, since the Independent State of Croatia was founded, referring to us, the Muslim Croats, as "the flower of the Croat people" and "the beating heart of the state" and to our [country of] Bosnia, which we have brought with us into the Independent State of Croatia, as "the heart of the state, without which there is no life within our state," et cetera. There have also been any number of articles published stressing how Croat Muslim representatives and leaders in the government of the Independent State of Croatia are

---

1   Historical Museum of Bosnia and Herzegovina (HMBiH Collection UNS, box 1, doc. 130/3.); Gazi Husrev-Bey Library, Archives of the Islamic Community of Bosnia and Herzegovina (GHB, ZRDA, A-810/B. ONS); Archive of the Bosniak Institute, (Drugi svjetski rat, DSR 3/VIII-2).

acting on our behalf, that is on the behalf of the Muslim Croats of Bosnia and Herzegovina.

Despite all such or similar statements, the Croat Muslim people of the Bosnian borderlands have been forsaken and our parlous condition has still not materially improved. The reason is the local authorities, whose activities here and in all the surrounding areas are quite contrary to the stated intentions of senior government officials. The local authorities act as they do only because there is no one to oversee how they treat Muslims. No senior religious or political representative from our side has made any effort to visit or check on the situation and our needs in the field. Or rather, when such officials have come to Prijedor, as for example both Mr Ademaga Mešić, the Deputy *Poglavnik*, and Mr Hakija Hadžić, the government commissioner, have done, Muslims here were unaware of their coming, because the local authorities forbore to inform them. Consequently, their reception and brief stay proceeded rather differently than we Muslims would have wished. We are as a result abandoned to our own resources and private initiative, and our affairs have been poorly managed by various Muslim delegations, as it is largely a matter of chance whether they will be received by the authorities, make progress, or see their legitimate petitions, which are always as small as possible, given due consideration.

There are the following government institutions locally: the Ustaša *Logor*, the district presidency, and a district court, a tax office, the land registry, a railway station and railway maintenance office, a construction office, the forestry service, the gendarmerie, a junior grammar school, a post office, etc. All these institutions are exclusively in the hands of Catholics, as though it were a rule that senior positions can only be filled by Catholics.

Our attempts to have at least one Muslim department head appointed have all been unsuccessful, brushed aside on the pretext that no attention is paid to who is Catholic and who Muslim. But precisely this fact that not a single Muslim has been appointed to a senior position in the local authorities is what means those self-same authorities can pursue their purely Catholic policy. The following examples may serve as proof:

Only Catholics have come to the Ustaša *Logor* in Prijedor, including some with a rather unpleasant history, even if our district contains 24,000 Muslims and only 8,000 Catholics, a little more than half of whom are locals and Croats by nationality.

Muslim young men have been and continue to be arrested on the *Logor's* orders as alleged Communists, though there is hardly ever any real evidence of it. The *Logor* head has ordered that Muslim students, even in the lower grades at the grammar school, be refused their political conduct and work detail certificates, which they need for school enrolment. When they are issued certificates, it is only after soliciting information about them from Catholic classmates, who often denounce them without grounds.

The *Logor* head has refused for several months to issue certificates to Muslims seeking government jobs, and their papers are not being forwarded to the main Ustaša Headquarters in Zagreb, so that their applications cannot be dealt with in good time by the relevant authorities.

With the support of the *Logor*, all positions in government and private business are being filled by Catholics. This includes some who neither deserve nor have any particular need of [such employment]. Meanwhile, not a single Muslim local has been employed in any official capacity since the formation of the Independent State of Croatia, even though plenty of situations have become available since the Serbs were expelled.

The *Tabornik*[2] at the *Logor* has stated publicly that Muslims are not to be entrusted with positions of responsibility because of the lack of confidence in them, though everyone knows that more than 75% of all National Guard and Croatian Army officers are Muslim and that they shoulder most of the burden of ensuring the continued existence of the state. Equally notorious is the fact that some Muslims in this district were persecuted before the foundation of the Independent State of Croatia for identifying as Croat. The *Logor* and the district leadership (district authorities), whose head has been changed five times in just five months, have been manipulating the *Order on conversion* any way they can, protecting those who convert

---

2   Translator's note: Station Chief.

to Catholicism, while forcing those who convert to Islam to re-convert to Catholicism, and, during the Prijedor insurrection, even stripping some Muslims of their freedom-of-movement badges, on the grounds they had no right to such permits.

During the insurrection, without consulting any of the Muslims, the *Logor* included amongst those it armed the worst rabble, and even gypsies, and deployed these types alongside the Ustaša irregulars to kill perfectly peaceable civilians of the Greek-Eastern rite. This was later worked up to suggest that only Muslims had committed atrocities and that the Catholic Church consequently offered the only safe haven from Muslim terror.

Showing Muslims in an ugly light like this has gone so far that some mobile Catholic Ustašas have hauled the women of captured rebels before the courts to get them to testify that their husbands did not flee into the forests to escape "the perfectly correct behavior of the Ustaša irregulars but because of terror imposed by local Muslims, who joined the Ustašas in order to loot and kill without mercy."

In a nearby branch office in Kozarac, some Ustaša irregulars who have since gone to ground forced some Muslims at gunpoint to hack some Greek-Eastern rite villagers to death and later presented it as a settling of long-standing accounts between the Muslims and the villagers. With the *Logor's* complicity, Ustaša irregulars put on the fes, creating the misapprehension that all this havoc was being carried out by Muslims. Even the name of the Ustaša officer who gave the first order for killing in the locality, one Tomislav Dizdar, has been used to prove that the commander was a Muslim.[3]

Indigent local Muslims have been court-martialed, condemned to death, and executed for allegedly extracting a few gold crowns from the jaws of the already dead, but no attention has been paid to the disappearance of property worth millions, carried off in broad daylight during the insurrection, though a complaint has been forwarded to the relevant authorities.

---

3   Translator's note: Dizdar is a Muslim surname, but Tomislav is a Croat or Catholic first name.

The recent joint attempt by honest Muslims and Catholics to have the *Logor* staff replaced with good Catholics and Muslims has so far been unsuccessful, not least because the petition to that effect sent by all the local Muslim cultural societies to Mr. Blaž Lorković via the local office does not seem to have reached its destination.

The grammar school in Prijedor, which has been here for many years, has now been cut back to just the four junior grades, with a negative impact on the poor Muslim locals as well as Muslims from the nearby districts of Bosanski Novi, Sanski Most, and Ključ, who send their children to school here. In nearby Banja Luka, where there is a public grammar school, they have opened a further two new private grammar schools, open to the general public and run by the Sisters of the Precious Blood of Jesus, but here we have no Muslim [representative prepared] to act on our behalf and preserve this local institution.

Just listing all the cases of this sort would take a long time, as would listing all the various subterranean activities to compromise us, which, if continued, risk undermining loyal cooperation.

It is now the month of Ramadan, when all Muslims dedicate themselves to thoughts of God and the welfare of their religious community. We are sending you this letter with just a couple of examples for you to think on in the coming days.

As good Muslim Croats, we are pained by these negative local happenings and profoundly convinced senior government levels cannot be aware of them and, more particularly, that the *Poglavnik* knows nothing of them. We therefore ask you to use your access to those levels and put your full weight behind efforts to ensure that the most senior levels put a stop to these painful happenings. We, the undersigned Muslims, who guarantee the truth of these allegations with our signatures, will repay you with our unwavering support.

In that spirit, we offer you all our best wishes for a happy Ramadan and our fraternal greetings of peace.

Prijedor, September 23, 1941.

Smajlbeg Beširović, Hasan Džananović, Jusuf Habibović, Ramadan Ramadanović, Ibrahim Alagić, Mustafa Jahić, Edhem Kahrić, Alija Ćehić, Bešir Bašić, Reuf Sarić, Fadil Salihbegović, Mehmed Babić, Edhem Alagić, Mumin Habibović, Salko Cepić, Ahmed Cipranić, Teufik Brekić, SmailAlišić, UzeirAlišić, Alija Bašić, Omer Bikić, Hilmija Hadžalić, Nurija Mešić, Mehmed Hergić, Kasim Goretić, Smajo Habibović, Ishak Habibović, Sadik Blekić, Mehmed Beganović, Salih h. Selimbegović, Halid Kapetanović, Rahim Bajramović, Esad Selimbegović, Hakija Hadžalić, Kasim Šehović, Pašo Pehlić, Adem Kurović, Salih Ćepić, Susnija Burazerović, Smail Jakubović, Muharem Midžić, Fehim Čaušević, Ahmed Babić, Suljo Arnautović, Muhamed Trepić, Smail Šehić, Uzeir Trepić, Omer Suljanović, Kasim Hrustanović, Abdulah Hadžalić, Muharem Softić, Chair of the Waqf and Educational Committee, hafiz Husein Cikota, Idriz Selimbegović, Fuad Širkinagić, Muhamed Sadiković, Suljo Arnautović, Ibrahim Hergić, Dževad Midžić, SulejmanAlišić, Nijaz Softić, Mustafa Habibović, Jakub Alihodžić, Fehim Kahrić, hafiz Smail Kodžić, Omer Jogić, Osman Jakubović, Safer Kurtović, Enver Petrović, Mustafa Selimbegović, Muhamed Ćumurija, Ahmet Serhatlić, Muhamed Kahrić, Esad Petrović, Šerif Đulkić, Ibrahim Mešić, Alija Jahić, AvdoAlišić, Sulejman Đulkić.

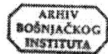

PRIJEDORSKA REZOLUCIJA

Kotarsko vakufsko-mearifsko povjerenstvo u Prijedoru, kao vjersko prestavništvo svih 24.000 Hrvata muslimana ovoga kotara, na širem sastanku muslimana svih slojeva, održanom po izričitom traženju svih muslimana, dana 23 rujna t.g./drugu noć remazana/, odlučilo je da vam se obrati ovim putem, te da Vam izloži stanje muslimana ovoga kotara, koje uglavnom odgovara stanju cijele H.Bosanske krajine i da Vas zamoli, da se bratski i muslimanski zauzmete da se ovom stanju nađe lijeka.

Od osnivanja NDH skoro svakodnevno u javnosti i to s najviših mjesta daju se izjave o nama muslimanima Hrvatima, koje nazivaju "ovijetom hrvatskog naroda", "srčikom ove države", a naša Bosna koju mi unosimo u sklop NDH "srcem države, bez kojeg nema života samoj državi" i t.d. Isto tako vrlo se često u javnosti opažaju članci o prestavnicima i vođama Hrvata muslimana, koji učestvuju u vladi NDH, na dobrobit nas bosansko-hercegovačkih muslimana hrvata.

Pa ipak i pored svih tih i takovih izjava naš hrvatski muslimanski svijet u Bosanskoj Krajini je zapostavljen, te se njegovo loše stanje do danas nije stvarno poboljšalo. Uzrok tome je rad mjesnih vlasti koje i u našem mjestu kao i u ostalim okolnim mjestima rade sasvim suprotno onome što govore visoki državni funkcioneri. Mjesne vlasti mogu tako da rade zbog toga što ih niko ne kontrolira u pogledu postupka prema muslimanima. Niko od naših visokih ni vjerskih ni političkih prestavnika ne zadaje sebi truda, da nas obiđe te da se na terenu se uvjeri o našim prilikama i potrebama. Ako se i desilo, da je neko od tih funkcionera došao, kao što je slučaj s dolaskom g. Ademage Mešića, doglavnika i g. Hakije Hadžića, vladinog povjerenika, u Prijedor, niko od muslimana o njihovu dolasku nije ništa znao, jer o tome mjesne vlasti nisu htjele, da ih obavjeste, te je i njihov doček i kratki boravak izgledao drugačije nego što žele muslimani. Stoga su prepušteni samom sebi i privatnoj inicijativi, te se sve naše stvari slabo svršavaju preko raznih delegacija muslimana, koju su prepušteni slučaju da li će biti na nadležnom mjestu primljeni i sreći, da li će se njihovi zahtjevi, koji su uvijek minimalni i opravdani uvažiti.

U našem mjestu postoje slijedeće državne ustanove: ustaški logor, kotarsko prestojništvo, kotarski sud, poreski ured, katasterska uprava, željeznička stanica, sekcija za održavanje pruge, građevinska sekcija, šumska uprava, državna žandarmerija, niža gimnazija, pošta itd. Sve te ustanove nalaze se isključivo u rukama katolika, t.j. kao po nekom pravilu na sva mjesta za šefove dolaze samo katolici. Pod izgovo-

The Prijedor Resolution of 1941

2

rom da se ne gleda ko je katolik a ko musliman,svi naši napori da
barem na jedno mjesto dovedemo za šefa muslimana ostali su bez us=
pjeha.A baš zbog toga što kod tih mjesnih vlasti nema ni na jednom
uglednom mjestu nitko od muslimana mogu te vlasti da vode čisto kat
ličku politiku,za dokaz čega neka Vam služe ovi primjeri:

U ustaški logor u prijedoru došli su isključivo katolici,a
među njima i neki vrlo nezgodne prošlosti,mada u našem kotaru ima
24000 muslimana a katolika 8000,od kojih pravih starosjedioca i po
narodnosti "rvata ima nešto više od polovine.

Po nalogu toga logora hapšeni su a i danas se hapse musliman
ski mladići,zato što su navodno komunisti,mada za to skoro u svim s
slučajevima se pokazalo da nema nikakovih stvarnih dokaza.Po nalogu
logornika odbija se đacima muslimanima,pa čak i iz nižih razreda
gimnazije izdavanje potvrda o političkom vladanju i radnoj slu
bi,koje su im potrebne radi upisa u školu.Ukoliko im se ovakova pot
vrde i izdaju,za to se traže o njima informacije od njihovih drugov
katoličke vjere,koji ih bezrazložno često puta denuncirajų.

Ovaj logornik zadržava po nekoliko mjeseci ,davanje potvrd
muslimanima, koji traže državnu službu,i njihove stvari ne dostavljaj
Glavnom ustaškom stanu u Zagrebu,te time ometa pravovremeno rješava
nje njihovih molbi kod nadležnih vlasti.Podrškom toga logora,na sva
mjesta u državnoj i privatnoj službi namještaju se samo katolici,pa
čak i oni koji to i nezaslužuju i nije im služba čak ni potrebna,do
se od osnivanja NDH nije nijedan musliman mještanin zaposlio u ma k
kovoj službi iako je poslije istjerivanja Srba ostalo dovoljno mjes

Tabornik u ovome logoru javno izjavljuje,da se muslimanima
ne mogu povjeriti odgovorne službe,jer ne uživaju povjerenje,ma da
je svakom poznato,da preko 75 % svih domobrana i časnika hrvatske
vojske daju muslimani i da oni snose najviše terete oko očuvanja op
stanka ove države i premda je istome poznato,da u samom našem kotar
ima muslimana koji su prije osnivanja NDH,bili zbog Hrvatstva progo
njeni.Ovaj logor u suradnji sa kotarskim prestojništvom/kotarskom o
lasti/u kome se za 5 mjeseci izmijenilo 5 pretstojnika na sve moguć
načine izigrava uredbu o prelasku na vjeru,te dok je lica koja prel
ze na katoličanstvo štitio,dotle je sva lica koja sū prešla na isla
silio da ponovo pređu na katoličku vjeru,pa čak i pojedinim muslima
ma,za vrijeme pobune u Prijedoru,skidao trake za slobodno kretanje,
nazivajući ih nedostojnim tih dozvola.

Za vrijeme pobune u okolini mjesta,bez pitanja ma koga od m
slimana naoružavao je ovaj logor među ostalim i najgori ološ,pa čak
i cigane,te ovakove tipove upotrebljavao uz suradnju divljih ustaša

The Prijedor Resolution of 1941

3

za ubijanje mirnog građanskog stanovništva grko-istočne vjere, a to se poslije rabilo u cilju da se prikaže kako su samo jedino muslimani zulum činili i da je jedino katolička crkva sigurno mjesto za zaštitu ovih ljudi od muslimanskog zuluma.

Prikazivanje muslimana u ružnom svijetlu ide tako daleko da pojedine pokretne ustaše katoličke vjere čak i sudovima privode žene pohapšenih pobunjenika i pokušavaju da svjedoče kako njihovi muževi nisu pobjegli u šumu od"korektnog ponašanja tih divljih ustaša već od zuluma mještana muslimana koji pristaju uz te ustaše te pljačkaju i ubijaju bez milosti."

U obližnjoj ispostavi Kozarcu divlje ustaše, kojima se sada ne može uhvatiti traga, s naperenim puškama sile muslimane da sjekirama ubijaju seljake grko-istočne vjere, a poslije se to prikazuj kao neko likvidiranje starih računa između muslimana i tih seljaka Znanjem toga logora divlje ustaše nose fesove te se stvara zabuna da sve zlo vrše muslimani. Čak i ime Tomislava Dizdara nekakvog ustaškog zapovjednika koji je prvi izdao naredbu za masovno ubijanje iskorišćava se da se prikaže kao da je i taj zapovjednik musliman

Siromašni mještani muslimani stavljaju se pred prijeki sud, osuđuju na smrt i strijeljaju zbog toga što su navodno iščupali nekoliko zlatnih zuba iz vilice poubijanih ljudi, dok se niko ne osvrće na nestanak milijonskih imetaka, koji su usred bijeloga dana i to za vrijeme pobune od drugih razneseni, o čemu je otišla pritužba na nadležno mjesto.

Skorašnji zajednički pokušaj poštenih muslimana i katolika, da se ovaj logor zamjeni i u njega dovedu dobri i katolici i muslimani, zasada je ostao bez uspjeha, jer takav zahtjev svih ovdašnjih muslimanskih kulturnih društava upućen g. Blažu Lorkoviću, putem ovdašnjeg predstoništva izgleda nije do dospio nanadležno mjesto.

U Prijedoru se ukida puna gimnazija koja je tu postojala više godina i svodi na 4 razreda ma da se time pogađaju siromašni muslimanski mještani kao i muslimani iz obližnjih kotareva Bos. Novog, Sanskog Mosta, Ključa, koji su ovdje slali svoju djecu u školu, dok se u susjednoj Banjoj Luci pored pune državne gimnazije otvaraju istovremeno dvije nove privatne gimnazije sa pravom javnosti, ali pod patronatom časnih sestara dragocjene krvi Isusove, a niko od muslima nema da se zauzme da nam se ova mjesna ustanova sačuva.

Dugo bi nas odvelo nabrajanje sličnih pojava. Dugo bi nas odvelo nabrajanje raznih podzemnih akcija, upravljenih na to da nas kompromituju, koji ako se produže prijete da onemoguć svaku lojalnu saradnju.

Sada je mjesec ramazan, kada se svi muslimani posvećuju

The Prijedor Resolution of 1941

4

mislima na Boga i dobro svoje vjerske zajednice.Dostavljamo Vam pute ovoga pisma ovo nekoliko primjera,da o njima u ova dana razmislite.

Mi kao dobri Hrvati muslimani gledamo s bolom na ove mjesne negativne pojave i duboko smo uvjereni,da se za ove pojave ne zna na visokim državnim mjestima,a specijalno da o ovim pojavama nije ništa poznato Poglavniku.Zato molimo Vas,koji imate mogućnosti,da lakše dođete do tih mjesta,da uložite sav svoj ugled,da se ovim bolnim pojavama stane na put s najvišega mjesta,a mi muslimani koji za istinitost navedenoga jamčimo svojim potpisima odužićemo vam se našim jednodušnim povjerenjem.

U to ime čestitamo Vam svima ramazani-šerif,uz bratski mahsu selam. U Prijedoru ,dana 23.rujna 1941.godine

Beširović Smajlbeg v.r.
Hasan Džananović v.r.
Jusuf Habibović v.r.
Ramadan Ramadanović v.r.
Ibrahim Alagić v.r.
Mustafa Šahić v.r.
Edhem Šahrić v.r.
Ćehić Alija v.r.
Bašić Bešir v.r.
Sarić Reuf v.r.
Salihbegović Fadil v.r.
Babić Mehmed v.r.
Alagić Edhem v.r.
Mumin Habibović v.r.
Selko Ćepić v.r.
Ahmed Cipramić v.r.
Teufik Brekić v.r.
Smail Ališić v.r.
Uzeir Ališić v.r.
Alija Bašić v.r.
Omer Bikić v.r.
Hilmija Hadžalić v.r.
Nurija Mešić v.r.
Mehmed Mergić v.r.
Kadim Goretić v.r.
Smajo Habibović v.r.
Ishak Habibović v.r.
Sadik Blekić v.r.
Mehmed Beganović v.r.
Salih H.Selimbegović v.r.
Halid Kapetanović v.r.
Rahim Bajramović v.r.
Esad Selimbegović v.r.
Hakija Hadžalić v.r.
Kasim Šehović v.r.
Pašo Pehlić v.r.
Adem Kurović v.r.
Salih Ćepić v.r.
Husnija Burazerović v.r.
Smail Jakubović v.r.
Muharem Midžić v.r.
Fehim Čauševič v.r.
Ahmed Babić v.r.

Midžić Muharem v.r.
Čaušević Fehim v.r.
Babić Ahmet v.r.
Suljo Arnautović v.r.
Muhamed Trepić v.r.
Smail Šehić v.r.
Trepić Uzeir v.r.
Suljanović Omer v.r.
Ing Kasim Hrustanvić v.r.
Abdulah Hadžalić v.r.
Muharem Softić pret.vak.povj.v.
Hafiz Husein Cikota v.r.
Idriz Selimbegović v.r.
Fuad Čirkinagić v.r.
Muhamed Sadiković v.r.
Suljo Arganutović v.r.
Ibrahim Hergić v.r.
Dževad Midžić v.r.
Sulejman Ališić v.r.
Nijaz Softić v.r.
Mustafa Habibović v.r.
Jakub Alihodžić v.r.
Fehim Kahrić v.r.
Hafiz Smail Kodžać v.r.
Omer Jogić v.r.
Osman Jakupović v.r.
Safet Kurtović v.r.
Enver Petrović v.r.
Mustafa Selimbegović v.r.
Muhamed Ćumurija v.r.
Ahmed Seyhatlić v.r.
Muhamed Šahrić v.r.
Esad Petrović v.r.
Šerif Djulkić v.r.
Ibrahim Mešić v.r.
Alija Jahić v.r.
Avdo Ališić v.r.
Sulejman Djulkić v.r.

Da je ovaj prepis vjeran svome orginalu koji se nalazi u arhivi ovog Povjereništva tvrdi: Pretsjednik vakufskog povjerenstva
M.Softić v.r.

PEČAT

The Prijedor Resolution of 1941

SARAJEVO RESOLUTION

The Sarajevo Resolution, published on October 12, 1941, in Sarajevo, was signed by an informal group of Bosniak citizens of Sarajevo, but initiated and supported by leading members of El-Hidaje. *The final sentence suggests it was intended for circulation as a general appeal to government officials and more specifically Muslim office holders and religious officials. The original is kept in the Archives of the Islamic Community of Bosnia and Herzegovina in the Gazi Husrev-Bey Library.[1] Some segments of this Resolution overlap with the text of the August El-Hidaje Resolution.*

* * *

Given the difficult and daily worsening conditions in which the Croat Muslims of Bosnia and Herzegovina currently find themselves, both as followers of the sublime religion of Islam and as individuals, we, the undersigned Muslims, feel an obligation to respond to the call of the executive board of *El-Hidaje*, the official organization of the ilmija (Muslim clergy), and present the following clear statement and petition for a remedy to their present misfortunes.

1. The Muslims of Bosnia and Herzegovina today find themselves in great difficulty. It is no exaggeration to say that the Muslims of these parts have never experienced such difficult times in all their history. Muslims form the great majority of casualties in raids by Communists and insurgent Orthodox Serbs. This is because they generally live mixed up with the Orthodox Christian population in these areas. In this unrest, it has been the peaceful citizenry and innocent who are suffering. Tens of thousands have lost their lives and all their property has been destroyed; villages have been burned, their inhabitants forced to move or flee, escaping to relocate on a

---

[1] Gazi Husrev-Bey Library, Archives of the Islamic Community of Bosnia and Herzegovina (GHB, ARIZBIH, A-318/B (A-3200/TO)).

daily basis in larger towns, without possessions. Hundreds and even thousands of parentless orphans cry out for help and vie for protection. We state this to make clear these are not sacrifices the patriotic must bear for their native land. This is a general and widening disturbance that threatens the Muslims of Bosnia and Herzegovina with ruin. Despite the daily cries rising from every side to bring an end to all this and the soothing statements made by responsible officialdom, the situation is not improving. In fact, it is getting worse by the day and beginning to threaten areas previously unaffected directly by significant disturbances. Even worse, there have been and continue to be moves by individual authorities that will only provoke harsh retaliation from the insurgents and expose the wretched and unprotected population to even more unwarranted suffering. All this is undermining confidence in public safety and adding fuel to attempts, grounded in the course of events themselves and, to some degree, in Communist propaganda, to convince the uninformed masses that there is a systematic plan behind it all that is being consciously prosecuted.

2. Many Catholics have intentionally been assigning the blame for all recent misdeeds to Muslims and representing these events exclusively as the settling of personal scores between Muslims and Orthodox. Some of the Orthodox themselves share this opinion of Muslim responsibility. On closer and fairer inspection, however, it is clear that Muslims are not to blame and they most strenuously reject all such allegations. The fact that some individuals with Muslim names may have been amongst the culprits of these various atrocities hardly means all the blame and responsibility for them can be put off on Muslims. Muslims as a group had already distanced themselves from such evil acts, as for example with the inclusion of the following article in the *Resolution* passed at the main assembly of *El-Hidaje*, the Organization of Muslim Clerics, on August 14 of this year:

4. "It is with pain in our hearts and profound condolences that we remember all the innocent Muslim victims struck down through no fault of their own in the unrest that has recently taken place in various places. <u>We condemn any and all individual Muslims who have committed any form of attack or violence independently and on their own initiative. We declare</u>

that the only people capable of doing such a thing are rogue elements and uncivilized individuals, whose stain we reject both for ourselves and for all Muslims. We call on all Muslims to refrain from such evil acts, in the spirit of the exalted tenets of their religion, Islam, and in the interests of the state. We call on the government authorities to restore law and order as soon as possible to all areas and prevent unauthorized action so that innocent people do not suffer."

We once again declare that only rabble and habitual criminals, such as exist in every community, could possibly commit such evil acts. We also declare that they did not take such action independently, but only once they had been given weapons, uniforms, authorization, and, in many cases, orders. There is no way that Muslims as a group should bear the responsibility for the criminal actions of these men, nor are they the initiators of those actions. We also declare that the *fes* and Muslim names have been used to transfer responsibility for these evil deeds to Muslims. That is, the *fes*, which has been introduced as part of the uniform for the Bosnian military, was distributed to non-Muslims carrying out these crimes, who also used Muslim names to refer to each other throughout. Muslims as a group have neither committed nor intended any harm to anyone, as is clearly shown by the fact that all and any Muslims who served in the Yugoslav army handed over their arms as soon as the conflict ended.[2] Even in the past, during Turkish times, when the Muslims were the only masters, they tolerated all religions without distinction and terrorized none. Consequently, Muslims cannot be painted today as the instigators of these crimes or intolerant of the Greek-Easterners or as causing these disturbances, as some certainly seek to do.

3. Under these difficult circumstances, intolerance of Islam has also surfaced amongst some Catholics. This is reflected in writings, private and public discourse, and unequal treatment of the Catholic and Islamic religions. It is there to be seen, regardless of statements at the highest levels

---

2   Translator's note: i.e. the April War/Axis Invasion and establishment of the Independent State of Croatia.

that speak of the equal status and rights of both religions. We are prepared to back-up our allegations with concrete examples.

Following these declarations, we call on all the relevant authorities and all Muslim religious and political representatives in all positions of authority to take action:

1. to introduce real security of life, honor, property, and measures that apply to all citizens of the state without distinction of any kind;

2. to provide the innocent population with real protection through a strong military and defensive capacity;

3. to disallow any future form of action likely by its nature to provoke popular insurrection and bloodletting;

4. to bring all the real culprits, including all those who have committed any form of violence or atrocity, to justice before the courts, regardless of religious affiliation, and to punish them severely under the law, along with all those who ordered or enabled their criminal acts;

5. to allow only the regular authorities and regular army to enforce the law;

6. to counter all forms of religious intolerance and punish severely any guilty of proven transgression in this regard; and

7. to provide urgent adequate assistance to those who have suffered unjustly in the recent unrest.

In Sarajevo, on Laylat al-Qadr, 27 Ramadan 1360 (18 October 1941)

H. Mehmed Hadžić, President of *El-Hidaje,* Muhamed Pašić, Director of the Sharia High School, Mustafa Varešanović, Deputy President of the Association of Jaamat imams, hafiz Hasib Fazlić, President of the Muallim Society, Dr Vejsil Bičakčić, Chief Physician of the Worker's Insurance Department Sarajevo, Ešref Berberović, President of the Muslim Society *Trezvenost,* Abdulah Dervišević, President of the *El-Hidaje* Sarajevo District Board, Kasim Dobrača, member of the *El-Hidaje* Main Board, hafiz Ramiz Jusufović, Secretary of the Association of Imams and Muallims and President of *El-Hidaje* Sarajevo District Board, Mahmud Traljić, student, Fejzulah Hadžibajrić, member of the *El-Hidaje* Main Board, Husein Đozo, member of the *El-Hidaje* Main Board, Mehmed Mujezinović, Secretary of the *El-Hidaje* Main Board, Muhamed Fočak, member of the *El-Hidaje* Main Board, Hamdija Zulfikarpašić, businessman from Sarajevo, Jusuf Čengić, businessman, Salih Fočo, businessman, Mustafa Bičakčić, businessman, Derviš Atić, industrialist, Šerif Vranić, businessman, Tajib Saračević, Director of the Lower District Madrasah, Šaćir Mesihović, member of the Ulema Council, retired, Abdulah Mulić, teacher, hajji hfz. Ibrahim Redžić, Sharia Justice, retired, Husein Kadić, Asim Hadžišabanović, industrialist, hfz. Akif Handžić, Imam at the State Hospital, hfz. Ibrahim Prohić, teacher, Hasan Zulfikarpašić, businessman, hfz. Muhamed Pandža, member of the Ulema Council, Mehmed-Ali Ćerimović, Mehmed Šahinagić, landlord, Asim Šeremet, engineer and Senior Agricultural Advisor retired, Ahmed Mešinović, businessman, Edhem Fočo, businessman, Asim Arslanagić, businessman, Sulejman Gorušanović, businessman, Sulejman Muhasilović, businessman, Halid Čaušević, Kemal Čaušević, hafiz Ibrahim Riđanović, Mehmed Kučukalić, businessman, Uzeir H. Hasanović, businessman, Mustafa Softić, Hamdija Mujičić, Hašim Skopljak, Edhem Ćejvanija, hfz. Omer Mušić, teacher, Salem Muharemagić, Salim Džino, H. Hasan Nezirhodžić, businessman, Hamdija Đukić, businessman, H[azim] Šabanović, author, Ahmed Burek, Director of the Gazi Husrev-Bey Madrasah, Muhamed Kemura, Dr Šaćir Sikirić, Rector of the Higher Islamic Sharia and Theological School, Ismet Njemčević, businessman, Dr Kasim Turković, former member of the Waqf and Educational Committee, Hamdija Kapidžić, teacher, Mustafa Drljević, teacher, Nedim Filipović, teacher trainee, Ćazim Nožić, teacher, Salim Ćatić, teacher, Mahmud Bajraktarević, teacher, Derviš M. Korkut, Custodian at the National Museum, Ibrahim Čadordžić, President of the District Waqf and Educational Committee in Sarajevo and Sharia Justice, Dr Hazim Muftić, Vakuf Director, Mahmud Bahtijarević, member of the Ulema Council, retired, Osman Sokolović, Secretary of the Chamber of Commerce, retired, Bekir Omersoftić, Assistant Attorney General,

Dr Behaudin Salihagić, Judge, Besim Korkut, teacher, Ahmed Kasumović, teacher, Prašo Sejid, Ahmed Tabaković, businessman, H. Šabanović Fejzulah, Edhem Bičakčić, former Managing Director of the City Savings and Loan, hafiz Džemaludin Hadžijahić, Muhamed Nanić, Edhem Đulizarević, Ismet Sulejmanović, Faik Musakadić, President of the Muslim Society *Bratstvo,* Hamdija Đukić, Ahmed Tuzlić, teacher trainee, Ibrahim Trebinjac, teacher trainee, Muhamed Hazim Tulić, teacher, Ahmed Tufo, businessman, Hasan Bajraktarević, student, Ahmed Skaka, R. E. teacher, Abdulah Skaka, craftsman, Kasim Bukvić, student, H. M[ustafa] Merhemić, Abdulah Fočak, hfz. Mustafa Mujezinović, Edhem Mulabdić, Hasan O. Užičanin, craftsman, Dr Asim Musakadić, physician, H. Alija Aganović, Nasib Repovac, Judge, Dr Husein Mašić, Judge, Dr Muhamed Kulenović, President of the Sarajevo Court, Osman Sikirić, Council Member of the Ban's Court in Sarajevo, Mehmedbeg Fidahić, Council Member of the Supreme Court in Sarajevo, Osman Forta, Sharia Justice, Munir Tarabar, trainee at the Sharia Court, hafiz Sulejman Kulenović, Sharia Justice, Ahmed Selimović, Sharia Justice, Osman Omerhodžić, Sharia Justice.

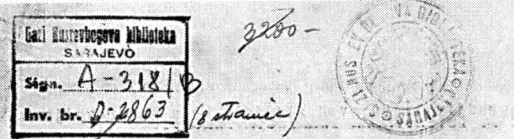

Potpisani muslimani razmotrivši po prijedlogu Glavnog odbora El-Hidaje, organizacije ilmijje /muslimanskog svećenstva/ teško stanje u kome se danas nalaze muslimani Bosne i Hercegovine i uočivši da se to stanje iz d na u dan pogoršava osjetili su se i kao pripadnici svoje uzvišene vjere i lama i kao ljudi dužnim da konstatiraju slijedeće činjenice i da zatraže lijeka nevoljama u kojima se nalaze.

1./ Stanje muslimana u Bosni i Hercegovini je danas vrlo teško. Neće biti pretjerano ako reknemo, da u svojoj povijesti muslimani ovih krajeva nijesu doživjeli težih časova. U akcijama koje poduzimaju komunisti i pobunjeni pravoslavni Srbi stradaju u najvećoj većini samo muslimani. To stoga što su najviše izmiješani muslimani sa pravoslavcima u ovim krajevi U ovim neredima strada mirno građanstvo i nedužni ljudi; stradaju goli ži voti i propada sav imetak; sela se pale, stanovnici prisiljeni da bježe i s le, svakim danom se zbjegavaju u veće gradove bez igdje išta. Na stotine pa čak i na hiljade siročadi ostalih bez svojih roditelja vape za pomoći i po tucaju se tražeći zaštite. Konstatirajući ovo ističemo da ovo nijesu žrtve koje su rodoljubi dužni podnijeti za svoju grudu, nego je ovo opći nered, k ji se sve više širi i vodi propasti muslimane Bosne i Hercegovine. Pored svakodnevnih vapaja sa raznih strana da se ovome stane na kraj i pored ra nih utješljivih izjava od strane odgovornih činbenika, stanje se ne poprav lja nego se svakim danom pogoršava i ugrožava i one krajeve, koji nijesu d sle direktno pogođeni istaknutim nevoljama. Što je još najgore poduzimani su i poduzimaju se taki potezi, koji samo više izazivaju oštre reakcije po bunjenika, pa je na taj način još više bijedno i nezaštićeno stanovništvo nedužno izloženo stradanjima. Sve ovo podrmava svako uvjerenje u sigurnost i daje povoda da se na temelju samog toka činjenica, a nešto možda i komunističkom propagandom stvara u širokim neupućenim slojevima uvjerenje da ovo sve sistem, koji se smišljeno provodi.

2./ Mnogi katolici, svjesno, za sva nedjela, koja su provedjena u po ljednje vrijeme bacaju odgovornost na muslimane i pretstavljaju sve dogadjaje medjusobnim razračunavanjima između muslimana i pravoslavnih. Tako iste mišljenje imaju i neki pravoslavci u pogledu odgovornosti muslimana. Kad se stvari medjutim pravilnije i izbližeg upoznaju, vidi se, da muslimani nijesu krivi i zato oni to nabacivanje najenergičnije od sebe odbijaju. Mu slimani su se i ranije ogradjivali od sveh zlodjela,koja su provodjena te je u rezoluciji,donesenoj na glavnoj godišnjoj skupštini El-Hidaje organizacije ilmijje,održanoj 14 VIII.ove godine unešena i ova tačka:

4./ "Sa bolom u duši i dubokom sućuti sjećamo se svih onih nevinih muslimanskih žrtava,koje nedužno padoše u nemirima,koji se ovih dana mjestimično dogadjaju.Osudjujemo sve one pojedince muslimane,koji su na sve ju ruku sa svoje strane napravili kakav bilo ispad i učinili kakvo nasi lje.Konstatiramo da su tako što mogli učiniti samo neodgovorni elementi i neodgojeni pojedinci,čiju ljagu odbijamo od sebe i od svih muslimana. Pozivamo sve muslimane da se u duhu visokih uputa svoje vjere islama i u interesu države strogo klone svih zlodjela.Molimo državne vlasti, da što prije zakonski zavedu sigurnost u svim krajevima ne dozvaljavajući da se što bilo čini na svoju ruku kako ne bi nevini ljudi stradali." I mi sada konstatiramo da je zlodjela mogao činiti samo sloš i kriminalni tipovi,kojih ima u svakoj zajednici.Konstatiramo i to,da ni oni to nijesu od sebe činili dok im nije dato oružje,uniforma,ovlaštenje,a često puta i naredbe.Stoga ni u kom slučaju za ta zlodjela ne snose muslimani odgovornost niti su im oni inicijatori.Konstatiramo i t da su u svrhu da se odgovornost za nedjela obori na muslimane izrabljivani fes i muslimanska imena.Naime oblačili su fes,koji je zaveden kao uniforma sve bosanske vojske,nemuslimani vršeći razna zlodjela,kojom s se prilikom i nazivali medjusobno muslimanskim imenima.Muslimani nijesu nikom spremali ni mislili nikakva zla,što najbolje potvrdjuju činjenice da su svi muslimani bivši jugoslavenski vojnici,odmah nakon rata predali vojno oružje.Na zahtjev vlasti odmah su muslimani predali i privatno oružje.Muslimani su i u svojoj prošlosti za vrijeme Turske,kada s bili jedini gospodari,tolerirali bez razlike sve vjere i nikom nijesu zla činili.Stoga se ni danas ne mogu muslimani pretstavljati inicijatorima zločina i onima koji ne trpe pravoslavnih i izazivaju sve nered kao što neki to namjerno čine.

3./ U ovakim teškim prilikama pojavljuje se i netrpeljivost prema islamu od nekih katolika.Ta se odražava u pisanju,u privatnim i javnim govorima i nejednakom postupku prema katoličkoj i islamskoj vjeri.To se sve pojavljuje pored raznih izjava sa najviših mjesta u kojima se govori o jednakosti i ravnopravnosti obiju vjera.Ovu našu

The Sarajevo Resolution of 1941

konstataciju spremni smo uvijek potvrditi konkretnim primjerima.

Nakon ovih konstatacija tražimo od svih odgovornih čimbenika, i svih muslimanskih vjerskih i političkih predtavnika da se zauzmu na svim nadležnim mjestima:

1/ da se zavede stvarna sigurnost života, časti, imovine i vjere za sve građjane u državi bez ma kakvih razlika.

2/ da se nevini svijet stvarno zaštiti jačom vojnom obranom.

3/ da se u buduće ne dozvoli da se poduzimaju ma kakve akcije koje će po svojoj naravi izazivati pobune i krvoprolića u narodu.

4/ da se pozovu na sudsku odgovornost svi stvarni krivci, koji s počinili ma kakvo nasilje ili zlodjelo bez razlike kojoj vjeri pripadal te da se najstrožije kazne prema zakonu, kao i oni koji su ovaka zlodjela naredjivali ili za njih dali mogućnost.

5/ da zakone primjenjuje samo redovne vlasti i redovita vojska.

6/ da se onemogući svaka vjerska netrpeljivost i da se najoštrije kazne oni koji u ovem pogledu naprave kakav bilo dokazan izgred.

7/ da se što prije pruži dovoljna materijalna pomoć onima, koji nedužno postradali u ovim neredima.

U Sarajevu, na Lejlei-kadr, 27 ramazana 1360 /18.X.1941./

The Sarajevo Resolution of 1941

The Sarajevo Resolution of 1941

The Sarajevo Resolution of 1941

The Sarajevo Resolution of 1941

The Sarajevo Resolution of 1941

MOSTAR RESOLUTION

The Mostar Resolution is dated October 21, 1941, and was signed in Mostar by an informal group of Bosniak citizens of Mostar. It was initiated and supported by members of the Islamic Community and El-Hidaje. It appears to have been a declaration of concern for general circulation, rather than addressed to a specific individual or even to Muslim office-holders. There are several war-time transcripts of the resolution in the Archive of Bosnia and Herzegovina *while the* Bosniak Institute *and the* Archives of the Islamic Community of Bosnia and Herzegovina *at the* Gazi Husrev-Bey Library *have early copies.*[1]

* * *

None can remember days as difficult and eventful or times as fateful as those we are now living through, in the entire history of our beloved homeland, Bosnia and Herzegovina. For months, we have listened and watched as villages and towns burn, as the innocent children of the country perish, and as people's possessions are looted. All of which forces us to reflect, out of deep concern for the present and future of these sorely afflicted parts, so dear to us. Buoyed up by a sincere belief that we are bearing witness to the feelings and intentions of the broadest strata of Muslims throughout this proud country of ours, Bosnia and Herzegovina, we feel impelled to declare and state the following:

1. The countless crimes, injustices, lawless acts, and forced conversions committed and still being committed against Orthodox Serbs and other fellow citizens are entirely repugnant to the soul of any Muslim. Every true Muslim, ennobled by the exalted tenets of Islam,

---

[1] Archive of Bosnia and Herzegovina (ABiH, *Zemaljska komisija za utvrđivanje zločina okupatora i njihovih pomagača Sarajevo* (henceforth: ZKURZ), *Referati*, kut. 7, 82. *Rezolucija muslimana grada Mostara.);* Gazi Husrev-Bey Library, Archives of the Islamic Community of Bosnia and Herzegovina (GHB, ZRDA, A-810/B. ONS); Archive of the Bosniak Institute, (Drugi svjetski rat, DSR 3/VIII-2).

condemns these crimes, from whatever quarter, fully cognizant that the Islamic faith considers the murder and torture of the innocent, looting of other people's possessions, and conversion under conditions that exclude free will, amongst the worst of sins. The handful of so-called Muslims who have committed such transgressions have by that very fact transgressed against the exalted tenets of Islam and will inevitably face God's punishment and human justice. Condemning all this, we call for the introduction of absolute equality of status and rights, order, and the rule of law for all, regardless of religious or national identity, and for all citizens to be allowed to return to their hearths and for all injustices against them to be rectified.

2. The hard times we are currently struggling to survive, which we neither wanted nor prepared, have caught Muslims up in their vortex. Some ten innocent Muslims from our town alone have paid with their lives, but none of their killers, some of whom are known, have been held responsible or punished. This was to have been just the beginning, a breaking down of our Muslim ranks, with a view to weakening the entire Muslim community. We condemn most strenuously any and all killings and expulsions of Muslims under the banner of purported Serbdom, Communism, Gajret-ism[2], Sokol-ism[3], JNS-ism[4], JRZ-ism[5], and so forth.

3. With utmost indignation, we refuse to allow the honor of the Muslim name be besmirched by responsibility for these things individuals have maliciously accused us of, hoping to transfer their own responsibility onto us. We demand that non-Muslims be banned

---

2 Gajret was a cultural association established in 1903 that promoted Serb identity among the Slavic Muslims of Austria-Hungary and then up to World War Two.

3 Sokol was a highly influential movement in the interwar Yugoslav Kingdom. It was a Serbo-centric organization that promoted brotherhood among South Slavs.

4 Acroynm for the Yugoslav National Party (*Jugoslavenska nacionalna stranka, JeNeSa*), which was the ruling party of Yugoslavia under the authoritarian dictatorship of King Aleksandar from 1929 to 1934.

5 Acroynm for the Yugoslav Radical Union (*Jugoslavenska radikalna zajednica, JeReZa*), the ruling right-wing party of Yugoslavia from 1934 until the 1941 *coup d'état*.

from wearing the *fes*, a symbol of Islamic identity, or calling each other by Muslim names, et cetera, during the conduct of certain forms of armed action, as they have repeatedly and systematically done in order to give the impression it is actually Muslims doing these things.

4. We admonish our brother Muslims to reflect seriously on the real and innermost wishes, and intentions of the many individuals who have either provided intellectual inspiration for or themselves carried out such crimes against our fellow citizens and have then indicated unequivocally, not just in their own private circles, but more or less in public too, that they have something similar in mind for Muslims too.

5. We also stand, in the strongest possible terms, against all who, out of bitterness or lust for plunder, have carried out senseless acts of revenge against innocent Muslims, their wives and children, and their homes and villages. If this continues, we inform them that we will resist it with the greatest determination.

6. We call on all our honest Muslim brothers to live in harmony and love with all their fellow citizens and neighbors, and to keep in mind that only absolute unity, harmony, and closed ranks can save us in these extraordinarily difficult times. Honest Muslims must put aside all earlier grudges, and, with faith in the omnipotence and justice of Almighty Allah, look heads held high towards their future and that of their people.

Our most fraternal wishes of peace:

Hafiz Omer Džabić, Mufti of Herzegovina, retired, Ibrahim Ribica, President of the Waqf and Educational Board, Husein Ćišić, President of the Waqf and Educational Committee, Ibrahim Fejić, President of *El-Hidaje*, hafiz Husein Pužić, Smajo Ćemalović, landlord, Mustafa Pašić, hajji Ibrahim Slipičević, Omer Kalajdžić, Dr Salih Komadina, Sulejman Krpo, Smail Grebo, Smail Džudža, Salih Popovac, Ahmed Avdić, Šaćir Muratović, Ahmed Behlilović.

Mostar, October 21, 1941.

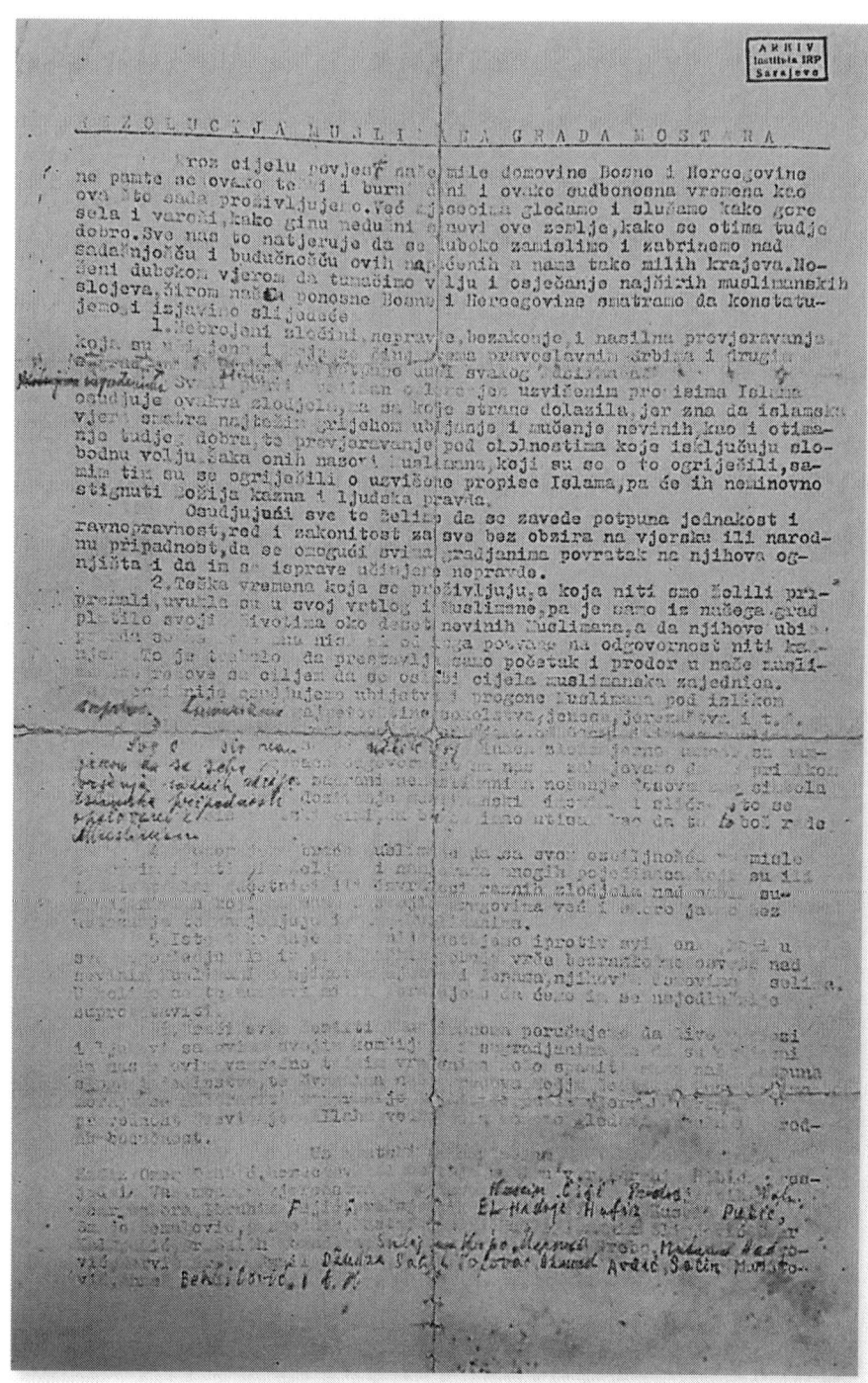

The Mostar Resolution of 1941

BANJA LUKA RESOLUTION

The Banja Luka Resolution is dated November 22, 1941, and it was signed in Banja Luka by an informal group of Bosniak citizens of Banja Luka and initiated and supported by members of the Islamic Community and El-Hidaje. *The resolution took the form of a letter to two senior members of the Independent State of Croatia government. Early copies are located at the* Archive of Bosnia and Herzegovina, *the* Bosniak Institute *and the* Archives of the Islamic Community of Bosnia and Herzegovina *at the* Gazi Husrev-Bey Library.[1]

* * *

To Dr Džafer-beg Kulenović, Vice President of the Government [of the Independent State of Croatia], and Hilmija Bešlagić, B.Sc.Eng., Minister of Communications and Public Works,

Zagreb.

Honorable Ministers,

Ever since this Independent State of Croatia of ours was first established, we Muslims have looked on with great concern as some Ustaša and other regular and rogue elements have committed grievous mistakes and even crimes. The most basic of individual rights are trampled upon without scruple. Personal safety and security of property, freedom of religion and conscience have all ceased to exist for a large part of the people of these regions.

---

1   There is apparently another original copy at the Military Archive in Serbia, which the editors have not seen. Scanned versions of the original are found online but without reference to the source. The text of these scanned originals is identical to the early copies. Archive of Bosnia and Herzegovina (ABIH, fond Zemaljska komisija za utvrdivanje ratnih zločina okupatora i njihovih pomagača, Referati, kutija 7.); Gazi Husrev-Bey Library, Archives of the Islamic Community of Bosnia and Herzegovina (GHB, ZRDA, A-810/B. ONS, *II knjiga. Banjalučka rezolucija od 12. studenog 1941.*); Archive of the Bosniak Institute, Drugi svjetski rat (DSR 3/VIII-2).

The slaughter of priests and other leading individuals, without trial or verdict, and the mass shooting and abuse of all too often entirely innocent people, women, even children, and the driving of entire families *en masse* from their homes and their beds with but an hour or two to prepare for deportation to an unknown destination; the alienation and looting of property, forced conversions to Catholicism, all these are facts that cannot but leave any sincere human being aghast and have had a most unsettling effect on us, the local Muslims.

We never expected and certainly never wanted such operational and administrative methods to be applied here, in our region. Not even under the worst of circumstances in our eventful history have we resorted to such means, not just because Islam forbids it, but because we have always believed, and still believe, that such methods must lead inevitably to the collapse of public peace and order in any state and put its very survival at risk. We do not consider such violence permissible even against the worst of enemies, and doubt examples will be found in the history of any people to equal what has been done here.

The results of this policy, if behavior of this sort can be dignified with such a name, will certainly be terrible, as any man of intelligence must surely have expected. The religious tolerance that, despite our religious differences, has been such a prominent feature of BiH has now been terribly undermined. A certain element amongst the Catholics here has begun to indulge in such frequent and express insulting and provoking of the local Muslims as to force serious reflection. Relations between these two parts of our people, previously so good, are now well on the way to being totally ruined.[2] All the efforts of the Croat nationalists on both sides to promote fraternity between these (two) parts of our people, efforts that have born such good fruit, are now well on the way to absolute collapse.

One group amongst the Catholic clergy judge their time has come and are making unscrupulous use of it. Propaganda for conversion has reached heights that recall the Spanish Inquisition. Under this pressure, and with

---

2   Editor's note: This sentence is not found in all copies or transcriptions of this resolution.

the tacit approval of the public authorities, there have been mass Catholic conversions of the Orthodox. Those who up till recently were denied even a scrap of citizenship or national kinship are thus at a stroke made full and equal citizens and national Croats, purely on the basis of having formally received the Catholic faith. The equal standing of Islam, emphasized so often in writing and by frequent statements from the highest levels, is now all too often put in question, in daily life and practical terms. Conversion to Islam, which we have never pushed, has also never afforded the protection that conversion to the Catholic faith does. Many intellectuals have paid for the attempt with their lives – as was the case in Travnik. Insulting songs are often to be heard from some Catholics – insulting the religious feelings of Muslims and predicting the same destiny for them as for the Orthodox.

An element in the Ustaša army, and not just "irregulars" but regular troops as well, has carried out serious attacks and assaults on not just the Orthodox but on Muslims too, giving rise to apprehension in our ranks. The case of the awful murder of the insane village cleric Edhem-efendi Hodžić here at the hospital, in the hospital yard, in broad daylight, is a terrifying example of the unhinged behavior of the Ustaša Josip Babić. Most regrettably of all, we still do not know today whether the perpetrator has even been arrested, something all of Banja Luka's Muslims, in fact the entire Muslim population, have demanded and still demand.

The spreading uprising in these parts is itself a consequence of this behavior and these mistakes. The uprising bears within itself all the terrible characteristics of rebellion and civil war. The insurgents kill people, women, children in bestial fashion, setting them alight, all too often avenging themselves on those guiltless of their sufferings. The insurgency has even reached the gates of our city and its consequences are increasingly evident. The town has been without water for three days now and shortages of fuel and provisions press us increasingly, forcing us to consider other worse eventualities.

The Communists have taken advantage of the dissatisfaction of a large section of the people and position themselves at the head of the uprising. In the hunt for Communists, we Muslims are suffering unjustly. We have no intention of claiming there are no Communists at all amongst the Muslims in the town, but they are being used as a pretext to justify arresting and persecuting other Muslims who have never been Communists, if they so much as express disapproval of the irregularities taking place. By contrast, many Catholics who were known Communists are not just overlooked but even rewarded with positions and sinecures.

We are particularly disturbed that some of the elements behind the uprising have managed to draw some Muslim rabble in, which we regret and condemn. We are aware of many examples of Ustašas donning the *fes* when going out to kill and slaughter. That was the case in Bos[anski Novi], where four lorries arrived from Prijeko full of Ustašas with *feses* on their heads and joined up with the Muslim rabble to carry out a mass killing of the Orthodox. The same happened at Bos[anska] Kostajnica, where 862 of the Orthodox were killed the same way in a single day. And they did the same in Kulen Vakuf, where the Ustaša Miroslav Matijević, from Vrtoč, played a particularly prominent role. Around 950 Orthodox Christians were slaughtered on that occasion, prompting revenge on the part of the Četniks on August 6, when Kulen Vakuf was set alight and 1365 Muslim men, women, and children paid with their lives. We also know of cases when Catholic Ustašas have attacked Orthodox Christians with cries of "Hit him Mujo, hold him Huso, don't let him get away Meho!" and so forth. We are also aware of cases of whispering in the ears of the Orthodox that we Balije[3] have been killing and slaughtering them in the hope of exterminating them entirely. Had we wanted to exterminate, kill, or convert the Serbs or anyone else, surely we could have done so rather more easily a couple of centuries ago, when our power in the land was greater than today and such behavior easier to justify.

Now that serious conflict has been provoked between us Muslims and the Orthodox, we find ourselves called upon as soldiers to put it down and kill Serbs, and they us, so that we end up slaughtering and exterminating each other, with no idea when it'll stop or what the consequences will be. This fight, which we didn't start, has taken on such dimensions that many

---

3   Translator's note: Ethnic slur for Muslims.

of our villages have been burned and looted and their people, men, women and children, are wandering, naked and barefoot, hungry and thirsty, praying for help and protection looked and unlooked for, and fleeing to our towns, which are already overflowing with them and where there is little help for them. Our people, particularly in the villages, are very inadequately protected, especially in the regions that lie under Italian occupation. There, the Italian army often looks on peacefully as Muslim villages burn. This happened recently in the villages of the Ključ, Petrovac, and Sanski districts, where our own troops failed to offer them assistance either.

Worst of all, the instigators of these disturbances pull back into the background, or parade in their uniforms, and generally amuse themselves with the looting of Serb and Jewish property. We have seen all this clearly here in Banja Luka, where the property of expelled or fled Serbs and Jews has been made a source of booty and enrichment for certain individuals, their families, and friends. No account is taken in all this of their reputation or past or, indeed, the interests of the state. Professional facilities are given over to the untrained, just as property of enormous value is often handed over without valuation or without collateral to individuals who have performed no particular service to the Croatian state. Such things are ordered by individuals who do not have the authority to make such decisions but have usurped it. And where there have been investigations into such irregularities, in the interest of the state or of public morals and decency, there is a rush to undermine it precisely on the part of that person who, unfortunately, occupies the most senior position in Ponova [the Office for Managing Confiscated Property], generally at the behest of those responsible for the actions in question. We reject with contempt the allegation that we have designs ourselves on the workshops in question.

We address your excellencies as ministers and our representatives in the government of the Independent State of Croatia and close counsellors of the *Poglavnik* with our request to inform him of these facts and exercise all your influence as we live through this critical time to bring an end to this awful situation as soon as possible.

We hereby add ours to all the Muslim initiatives of similar intent and particularly the initiative of the Sarajevo Muslims of October 12 of this year, and to that end we join them in petitioning for and proposing the following:

1. That real personal safety, security of property, and freedom of religion be introduced as soon as possible for all inhabitants of the state;

2. That innocent people be provided the protection of a strong military defensive capacity;

3. That no future operations be allowed that might provoke popular resistance;

4. That the perpetrators of any form of violence or criminal act all be brought to trial, regardless of position or religion, along with all those who ordered or assisted such actions, and that they be punished under the law;

5. That the laws be enforced solely by the regular authorities and the regular army;

6. That all religious intolerance be suppressed;

7. That adequate material assistance be provided as soon as possible to the innocent victims of the recent unrest.

Banja Luka, November 12, 1941.

Hajji hafiz Mustafa Nurkić, Mufti, retired, hafiz Idriz Skopljak, *muderis*, Hasan-beg Džinić, former Mayor, Husein Hadžić, private official, Ago Abazagić, retired, Halid-beg Džinić, Vice President of the Waqf and Educational Committee, Derviš Džanić, craftsman, Hamdija Afgan, former Mayor, Avdija Hasić, government official, retired, Ćazim Muftić, President of *Sloga*, Ćerim Ćejvan, President of *Fadileta*, Dr Asim Kulenović, Senior Physician at the National Hospital, Nezir Biberić, member of the Waqf and Educational Committee, Ramiz-beg Begović, former landowner, Muharem Ibrahimbegović, businessman, Kemal Hadžiomerspahić, professor and member of the Waqf and Educational Committee, Dr Ibrahim Ibrahimpašić, prosecutor, Hamzaga Husedžinović, former Mayor, Mustafa

Zuhrić, Sharia Justice, Husein Kapetanović, engineer and retired teacher, Dževad Gluhbegović, bank official, Ibrahim Karaselimović, businessman, Mehmed Jahić, businessman, Asim Krajišnik, member of the Waqf and Educational Committee, Rizah Hadžiomerspahić, engineer and official, Muharem Katana, engineer and forestry official, Halid Buljina, teacher, hajji hafiz Hamid Muftić, Imam, hajji Ćamil Gušić, owner of the baths, hafiz Bakir Demirović, Imam, Bedrudin Gušić, engineer and President of *Bratstvo*, Mustafa Gušić, President of *Islahijet*, hafiz Dr Asim Džinić, lawyer, Latif Demirović, craftsman, Prof. Naim Ćejvan, Ilijas Omerbegović, Seid Ćejvan, Omer Kajtaz, engineer, Forestry Commissioner, Dr Seid Buljina, Šaćir Dedić, teacher, Dr Ali Ćamil-beg Džinić, former Mayor, Bećir Galijašević, bookbinder, Ibrahim Maglajlić, businessman, Ali-beg Gradaščević, landowner, Salih Džođić, private official, Ibrahim Suljić, technical officer, Dr Ihsan Zukanović, physician, Safet Dorocić, teacher, Sulejman Hadžidedić, bank official, Alija Kapidžić, Military Chaplain/Imam, Hamdija Softić, jamaat Imam, Mehmed Ibrahimbegović, landowner, Derviš-beg Kapetanović, han manager, Osman-beg Kulenović, Mujo Gunić, businessman, Abdulah Smajić, official, hafiz Mehmed Zahirović, R. E. teacher, Fehim-aga Bitrić, landowner, Muhamed Tabaković, former Mayor, Muharem Namula, member of the Waqf and Educational Committee, hajji Derviš Numanović, butcher, hafiz Šaćir Kovačević, landowner, Mujo Medić, Secretary of *Bratstvo*, Edhem Baručija, Secretary of *Islahijeta*, Salih Vehabović, businessman.

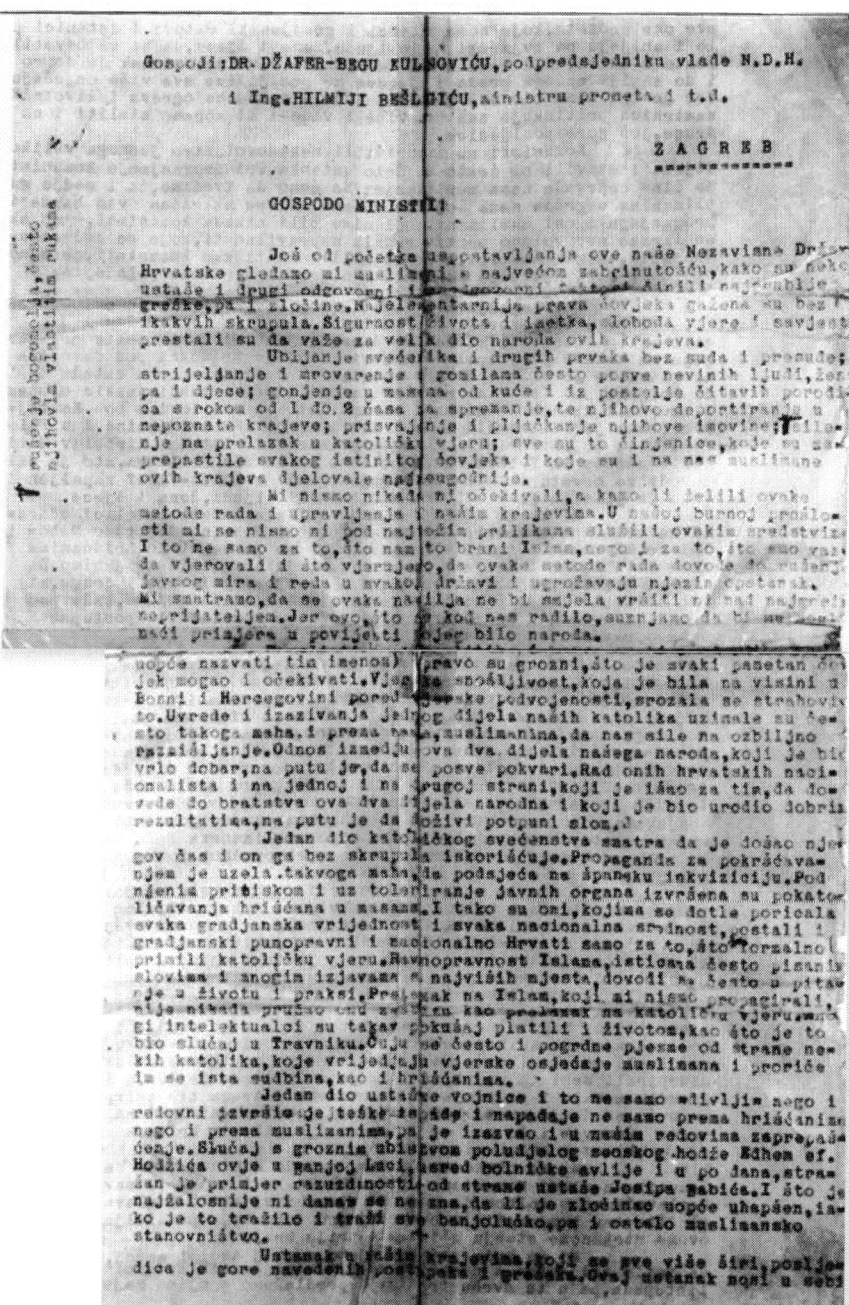

The Banja Luka Resolution of 1941

The Banja Luka Resolution of 1941

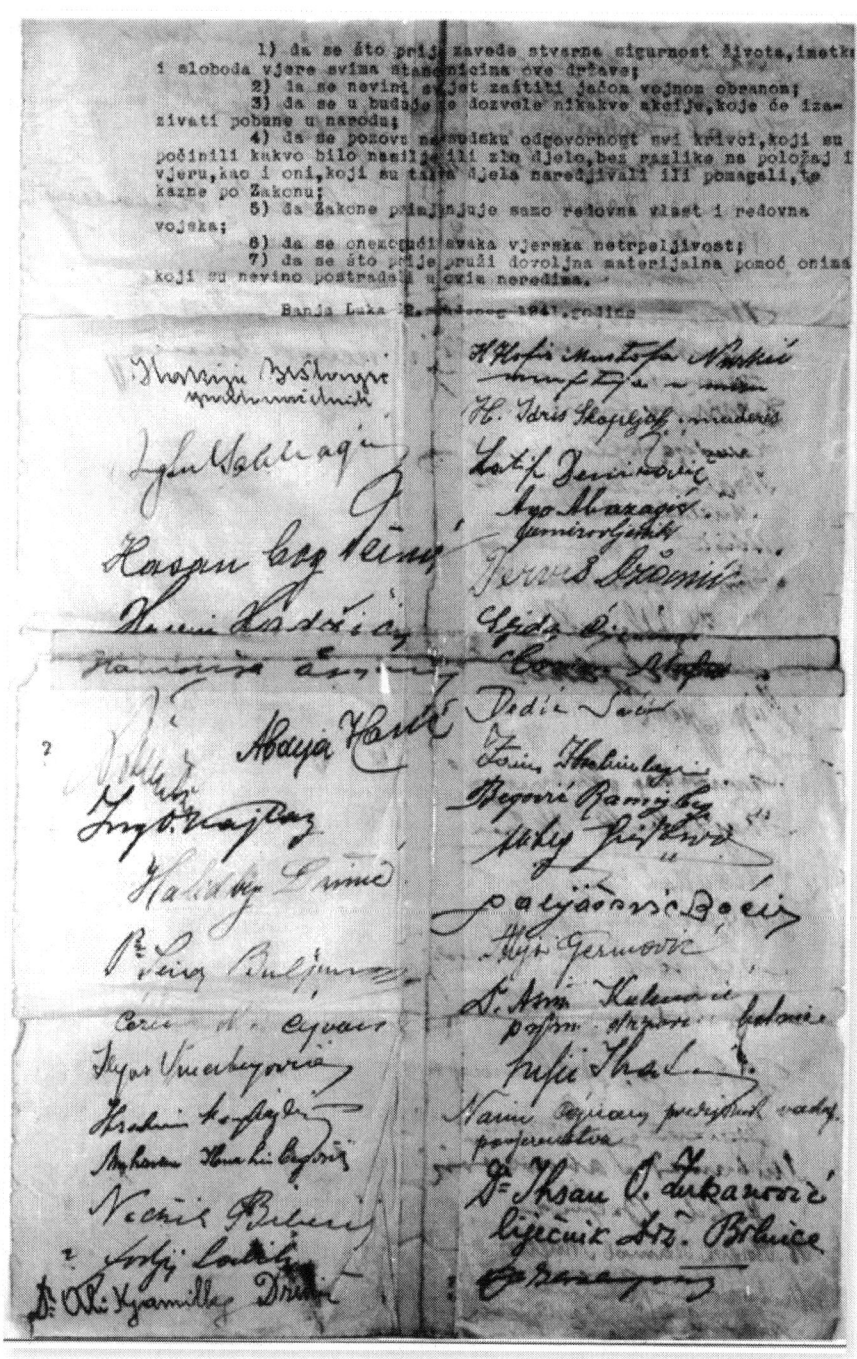

The Banja Luka Resolution of 1941

The Banja Luka Resolution of 1941

BIJELJINA RESOLUTION

The Bijeljina Resolution, dated December 2, 1941, was signed in Bijeljina by an informal group of Bosniak citizens of the town and initiated and supported by members of the Islamic Community. This resolution was sent to the Ustaša authorities in Sarajevo as a "Statement." There is an early transcript in the Historical Museum *in Sarajevo, while the Bosniak Institute has a photocopy of an Ustaša transcript, according to which the original was signed on January 8, 1942, at 18:00, in the reading room of the* Narodna Uzdanica *cultural society in Bijeljina.*[1]

* * *

Statement of the Muslims of the city and district of Bijeljina on 2 December 1941, made on the occasion of the slaughter of hundreds of innocent inhabitants of the Islamic faith of Koraj, in Bijeljina district.

1. The land we live in is Bosnia, where Bosnians have lived and live without distinction of creed or tribe. These parts have been subject to equal levels of Serbian and Croatian influence. We speak the same language, share the same customs, and have equal portions of love for the motherland. We speak primarily as Bosnians, because much of the current trouble has come crashing down precisely on our Bosnia and on us as Bosnians.

2. The sons of these parts carried their mother tongue to the Ottoman court where it became the second official language and the language of diplomacy.

3. Bosnians have their own history and had their own powerful state in the past, just like the Croats and Serbs, and they have played an

---

1   Archive of the Bosniak Institute, Drugi svjetski rat (DSR 3/VIII-2); Historical Museum in Sarajevo (HMBiH, UNS, Box 1, Document 134).

honorable role over the centuries as a bridge between brothers of different [faiths].

4. For hundreds of years, Bosnian Muslims have lived in harmony and brotherly love with all other Bosnians, regardless of faith, just as their exalted Islam commands them to. Even when all the power was in their hands, they did not commit evil deeds against their fellow citizens of other faiths or sow religious or tribal hatred.

5. Muslims in these parts have up until now enjoyed all the same rights as Serbs and Croats, so they seek that we now all be equal under the law and that a secure and peaceful family and religious life and private property be guaranteed to all.

6. Muslims as a whole condemn the behavior of rogue individuals on all sides and reject unconditionally all the evil actions they are falsely alleged to have committed against their fellow citizens of other faiths during these difficult times. They call on the civil and military authorities to behave with equal severity towards all who violate the laws of man and state, regardless of religious affiliation, so that there is no privileged and oppressed, free and vulnerable.

7. Muslims call for all civilians to be disarmed and for military authority to be exercised exclusively by the army, insofar as some citizens are known to have been abusing authorities, they do not have but have assumed of their own accord.

8. Muslims call for adequate protection of life and property to be provided throughout the Independent State of Croatia but particularly in its heartland of Bosnia to all citizens in these areas, as well as to provide the afflicted with urgent and generous assistance, insofar as it is clear that under the current difficult circumstances both Catholic and Muslim, and indeed the righteous Greek-Easterner, but particularly the Muslim Croat are inadequately protected or looked after and that their lives are in danger.

9. Muslims call for love, fraternity, unity, and safety to flourish in these lands, as they did in the past, in the place of the hatred, blood feud,

and senseless slaughter that are currently being sown, and for each citizen of the Independent State of Croatia to be respected not on the basis of their religion but of the industry, integrity, and humanity they show to those closest to them in the course of their lives.

10. Muslims admonish all Bosnians, regardless of religion, but particularly the (Catholic and Muslim) Ustašas and the Greek Eastern rebels, to refrain from revenge, retribution, and bloodletting, as it will lead only to our common ruin and extirpation and is generally carried out against the innocent populace, who, if there were any sin on their conscience, would hardly have waited at home to die instead of evading danger by removing themselves, as those who have actually committed crimes normally do.

This is our last chance to take stock and make it our life's work to calm and settle the situation in the region, where we can and must live beside each other and with each other as brethren brought into blood feud by an evil destiny and the urgings of the enemy.

Bosnia's salvation lies in the unity and fraternity of Bosnians, not in blood feud and hatred. Religion should not separate us. It should unite us, encouraging us, through its blessed action on us all, to be first and foremost people who refuse to be governed by alienated animal impulses to murder and looting, arson and abuse, urges any man of culture must rein in.

Alija Aliefendić, imam and registrar, Hajdar Tešnjaković, imam of the Main Mosque, hafiz Šerif Mujaković, imam and registrar from Teočak, Mustafa Redžić, imam from Atmačići, Alija Sadiković, imam and registrar from Janja, Rifatbeg Rifetbegović, businessman, Jusuf H. Salihović, businessman, Enver Pozderović, teacher, Alija Salihagić, businessman, Husejn (Zijabegov) Pašić, Omer Šehović, businessman, Sinan Halilović from Teočak, Jusuf-beg Pašić, Hasan H. Salihović, Izet Uzejrović, hafiz Ibrahim Islamović, imam of the M. V. Pasha Mosque, Murat-beg Pašić, Mayor, Murat-beg Osmanbegović, Salih Joldić, Hifzi-beg Zulfikarpašić, Ibrahim-beg Muratbegović, Avdo Ljubović, Muharem Pašić, Hasan-beg Ljubović, Husejn Pazarac, Abaz-beg Hadžić, landlord, Emin Hajdarbegović, Bajro Ferhatović, Mustafa Zvizdić, Hašim Merić, Alija Berbatović, Ibro Buljubašić,

Sulejman Mehmedović, Pašan Izić, Hasan Selimović, Huso Ismić, Ibrahim Mulalić, Hasan Sindrić, Emin Račević, Muharem Sejdić, Mustafa Hujdurović, Osman H. Salihović, Salih Hodžić, Safvet-beg Ljubović, Rašid Ašćerić, Adem Šehović, Rašid Pomrčić, Mehmed Efendić, Mustafa Hajrić, Idriz Hodžić, hafiz Abdulah Budimlija, assistant registrar, Dedo Korajkić, Suljo Dizdarević, Adem H. Mujagić, Bajro H. Muhić, Sulejman Žilić, Jusuf Osmanbegović, Salih Salihbegović, Abdulah Pjanić, Rizvan Šečić, Hakija Vidinlić, Emin Bjeljenčević, Meho Jukić, Ahmed Dukić, Suljo Pašalić, Huso Mulalić, Abid Jahić, Mustafa H. Salihović, Hilmo Zečević, Mustajbeg Ljubović, Alija Imamović, Alija Hamzić, hafiz Ilijas Hazurović.

Predmet: Rezolucija muslimana grada
i kotara Bijeljine.

U.N.S. U r e d u II.

O v d j e

        Povjereničtvo U.N.S.-e u Sarajevu dostavilo je rezoluciju muslimana grada i kotara Bijeljine koja je izdana 2.prosinca 1941 a koja glasi:

"R I J E Č muslimana grada i kotara Bijeljine na dan 2. prosinca 1941. izrečeno povodom pokolja izvršenog nad stotinama nedužnih stanovnika islamske vjere u Koraju kotar Bijeljina.

1./ Zemlja u kojoj živimo je Bosna, u kojoj su živili i žive Bosanci bez razlike na vjeru i pleme. U ovim krajevima je bilo isto toliko srpskoga koliko i hrvatskoga uticaja. Govori se istim jezikom isti su običaji i jednaka je ljubav prema rodjenoj grudi. Govorimo na prvom mjestu kao bosanci, jer se je velik dio nesreće sadašnjice srušio baš na našu Bosnu i Bosance.

2./ Na osmanlijskom dvoru sinovi naših krajeva zaveli su naš maternji jezik kao drugo službeni jezik i diplomatski jezik.

3./ Bosanci imaju svoju kolijevku i imali su svoju moćnu državu, a kao što su je imali Hrvati i Srbi a vršili su kroz stoljeća časnu ulogu spone izmedju braće raznih veza.

4./ Stotinama godinama bosanski muslimani su živili u slozi i bratskoj ljubavi sa svim bosancima bez razlike na vjeru, kao što im to uzvišeni Islam naredjuje, a kada su imali svu vlast u svojim rukama, ni tada prema sugradjanima drugih vjera nisu nedjela činili niti vjersku i plemensku vršnju sijali.

5./ Kao što su muslimani do sada u ovim krajevima uživali sva prava koja i srbi i hrvati, tako i sada traže da svi budemo jednakopravni pred zakonom, da nam svima bude obezbjedjen i siguran miran porodični i vjerski život kao i privatna imovina,

6./ Muslimani kao cjelina osudju postupak jednih i drugih neodgovornih lica i odlučno se ogradjuju protiv svih nedjela koja im se zlonamjerno pripisuju, da su ih počinili na sugradjanima druge vjere u ovakvim teškim vremenima, pa traže da vojne i civilne vlasti jednako i najstrožije postupaju prema svim prekršiteljima zemljskih i ljudskih zakona ma koje vjere bili ti prekršitelji, s tim da nema povlaštenih i podvlaštenih slobodnih i ugroženih.

7./ Muslimani traže da se razoružaju sva civilna lica i da vojnu vlast vrši isključivo vojska, jer se ustanovilo da pojedini gradjani zloupotrebljavaju vlast koja im ne pripada, već su je samovoljno prigrabili.

8./ Muslimani traže da se u Nezavisnoj Državi Hrvatskoj, naročito u njenom srcu Bosni pruži dovoljne zaštite života i imetka svim njenim državljanima a u svim krajevima, kao i da se postradalima pruži što hitnija i obilnija pomoć, jer se je pokazala u sadašnjim teškim dogadjajima da nedovoljno zaštićeni nezbrinuti, izloženi životnoj opasnosti i katolik i musliman, kao i ispravan grko-istočnjak, a naročito muslimani hrvati.

9./ Muslimani traže da se u ovim krajevima umjesto posijane mržnje krvne zavade i bezdušnog klanja zavlada ljubav sloga i sigurnost kao što je bilo u prošlosti, i da se svaki državljanin Nezavisne Države Hrvatske cijeni ne prema mjeri vjere prema radu, čestitosti i čovječnosti koje pokazuje u svome životu prema bližnjima.

10./ Muslimani upozoravaju sve bosance bez razlike na vjeru, a naročito ustaše /katolike i muslimane/ kao i pobunjene grko-istočnjake da prestanu sa osvetama, odmazdama i krvoprolićima, koje vode samo našoj općoj propasti, i istrebljenju a vrše se redovno samo nad našim nedužnim stanovnicima, koji kad bi imali
... ... ostali da ginu

The Bijeljina Resolution of 1941

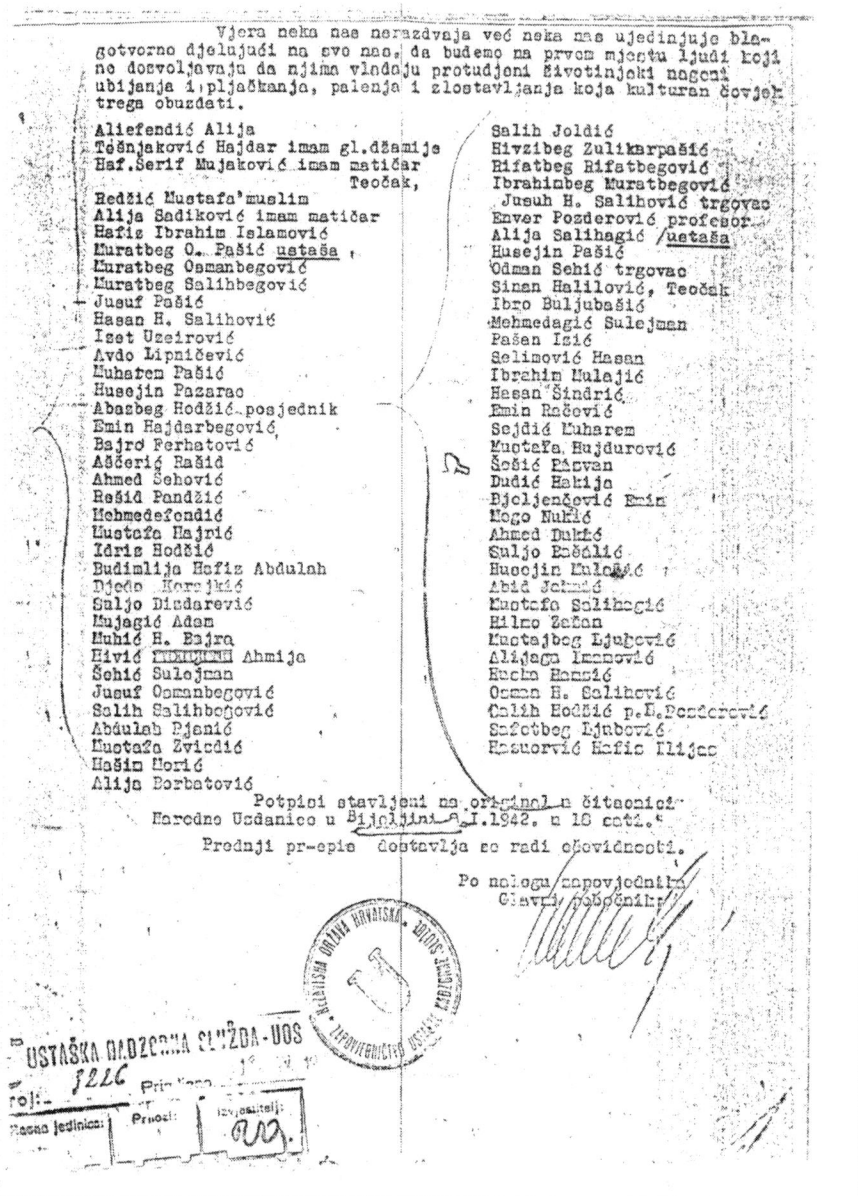

The Bijeljina Resolution of 1941

TUZLA RESOLUTION

The Tuzla Resolution, dated December 11, 1941, was signed in Tuzla by an informal group of Bosniak citizens of the town and initiated and supported by members of the Islamic Community. The resolution was addressed to Džaferbey Kulenović, vice-president of the Independent State of Croatia, as "presiding minister." A transcript is kept at the Historical Museum, *while there is a German translation of the document in the* Military Archives in Serbia.[1]

* * *

To the presiding minister!

Appalled by the difficult circumstances and distressing events currently unfolding all around us, we find it incumbent upon us to address you, as, in our view, the proper representative of Muslims in the government of the Independent State of Croatia, and acquaint you with the situation we find ourselves in here in Tuzla and the Tuzla district.

The well-known actions of the Četnik-Communists are getting closer and closer to Tuzla, and many surrounding Muslim villages have already suffered, including Deveta, Banovići, Cerik near Puračića, Gračanica village, and others. There is fighting near Tuzla, on Ozren, around Karanovac, leaving Tuzla itself, where there are few soldiers left, in serious peril. Knowing what occurred in Koraj, we fear for our people even in our strongest Muslim district.

So far most, if not all, of the victims of this unrest have been Muslims. As you will know, our people are least responsible for these things, insofar as the disorder appears to have been caused by attacks on Serbs by rogue elements, attacks that are unfortunately continuing and provoking

---

1 Historical Museum of Bosnia and Herzegovina (HMBiH, UNS, Box 1, Document 177); Military Archives of Serbia (Arhiv oruzanih snaga Srbije, fond Reich, kutija 40 G, fascikl 3, dokument 25).

retaliation. Our Muslim community, inspired by the spirit of Islamic culture and ethics, condemns any form of disorder. This noble characteristic of Muslims is well known, but misinformation has been being maliciously spread that Muslims are actually responsible for these actions against the Serbs, and all the odium for them is now directed against Muslims and everything is presented as though it were all just a settling of scores between Serbs and Muslims.

Muslims, particularly in our region, now find themselves in great difficulties as a result and abandoned more or less to their own devices, as the defences previously available against the Četniks no longer seem properly effective. Accordingly, if this unrest cannot be fully suppressed by military means, we ask why not combine political and military measures to suppress the disorder and hold everybody guilty of illegal acts before the unrest began accountable and punish them publicly.

We therefore have the honor to ask that you exercise your authority and take the required measures to suppress these disorders and for our protection. Moreover, we ask you to address the Muslims and their problems and afflictions and encourage them in these difficult times, when their eyes are firmly fixed on you. It would be particularly beneficial if you were to come here so that we can inform you personally of these matters and discuss them. If that is not possible, we ask you to confer with us at whatever place is most convenient to you.

In hopeful expectation of your help, we send you our warmest greetings in peace. Tuzla, December 11, 1941.

Twenty illegible signatures

GOSPODINE MINISTRE PREDSJEDNIČE !

    Ponukani teškim kritikama i nemilim pojavama koje se neposredno oko nas odigravaju, uzeli smo za potrebno da se obratimo na Vas, koga smatramo kao pravnog pretstavnika muslimana u Vladi Nezavisne Države Hrvatske i da Vas upoznamo sa stanjem, u kom se nalazimo mi u Tuzli i u tuzlanskom kotaru.

    Pošto se četničko-komunističke akcije sve više i više približuju i samoj Tuzli, a okolna naša muslimanska sela su mnoga već stradala kao: Deveta, Banoviči, Cerik kod Puračiča, selo Gračanica i još druga mjesta. Borbe se vode u blizini Tuzle na Ozrenu, oko Karanovca, tako, da će i sama Tuzla u kojoj je ostalo vrlo malo vojske, naći u ozbiljnoj pogibelji. Znajući što se je odigralo u Koraju, mi strahujemo za naš svijet u ovom našem najjačem muslimanskom kotaru. Od ovih nereda do sada su stradali najviše i gotovo jedino muslimani. A za sve to baš je taj naš svijet kao što i vi znate, najmanje kriv, jer svi oni neredi izgleda da su izazvani ispadima protiv Srba od strane neodgovornih elemenata, a nagalost se ti ispadi protiv njima dešavaju i u najnovije vrijeme, pa to onda izaziva na osvetu. Naš muslimanski svijet inspiriran duhom islamske kulture i etike, osudjuje svaki nered. I ako se zna za ovu lijepu osobinu muslimana, ponamjerno se svuda šire vijesti da su muslimani krivi za mjere protiv Srba, te se sav odijum svaljuje na muslimane i stvari se tako pretstavljaju, kao da je sve ovo razračunavanje izmedju Srba i muslimana.

    Muslimani se stoga nalaze naročito u našim krajevima u teškom položaju, prepušteni gotovo sami sebi, jer izgleda da je i dosadašnja obrana od četnika nije u punoj mjeri uspjela. Prema tome, ako se ovi nemiri ne mogu ugušiti potpuno vojničkih putem, zašto se nebi paralelno sa vojničkim akcijama preuzele i neke političke mjere, za stišavanje nereda na taj način, što se svi krivci za nezakonito čine, koji su ovim nemirima predhodili pozvali na odgovornost i javno kaznili.

    Stoga nam je čast zamoliti Vas, da svojim autoritetom učinite što je potrebno, za štišavanje ovih nereda i za našu zaštitu. Molimo Vas još dalje, a uputite koju riječ muslimanima, da im javno reknete sve što ih boli i ih ohrabrite u ovim teškim vremenima, u kojima su njihovi pogledi u Vas uprti. Naročito bi korisno bilo, kada bi mogli malo medju nas doći, da se o svemu informišemo i porazgovorimo. Pu ako Vam to nije moguće, molili bi Vas, da učinite jednu konferenciju u mjestu, gdje je Vam najzgodnije.

    Ispunjeni nadama u Vašu pomoć, upućujemo Vam svoje mahsuz selame!

    U T u z l i, dne 11. prosinca 1941. god.

Dvadesetdva podpisa nečitljiva.

The Tuzla Resolution of 1941

ZENICA RESOLUTION

The Zenica Resolution, dated May 26, 1942, was signed in Zenica by an informal group of Bosniak citizens of the town and initiated and supported by members of the Islamic Community and El-Hidaje. *It appears to have been addressed to local authorities, calling on them to take further action. There is a transcript in the* Archives of the Islamic Community of Bosnia and Herzegovina *at the* Gazi Husrev-Bey Library.[1]

* * *

The Muslims of Zenica, having convened a meeting over the dispatch of the so-called "Gypsy" Muslims from Travnik to the concentration camps and rumors that the same is to be done with the other so-called "Gypsy" Muslims of Herzeg-Bosna, after thorough consideration of this issue of capital importance for the Islamic community, declare the following:

1. The holy, exalted and legally recognized religion of Islam does not itself recognize the categorization of people by race and class. The only distinctions it acknowledges are of civility and individual virtue, insofar as God, SWT, considers elect those who hold most closely to the precepts of the Faith.

2. The so-called "Gypsy" Muslims are an integral part of the Muslim component of Herzeg-Bosna. They do not differ from other Muslims in any way. They are born and die as Muslims, are entered into the same registers of birth, carry out all the same rituals of Islam, get married with other Muslims, and Muslims have never considered them anything other than Muslims like all the rest. It has never happened in the past that they have been treated in any way differently from the rest. They have always carried out their religious and official duties on an equal basis with all other Muslims and enjoyed all the same rights as all other Muslims at all times, past

---

1   Gazi Husrev-Bey Library, Archives of the Islamic Community of Bosnia and Herzegovina (GHB, ARIZBIH, UM, 1745/42).

and present. All Muslims, without distinction, consider them now, as they always have, to be part of their common body and condemn in the strongest and most strenuous terms possible any separating out or differentiation of these Muslims from the rest. All Muslims want and unanimously seek that these Muslims be accorded the same status and destiny as all the other Muslims in Herzeg-Bosna.

3. The term Gypsy applies properly to the uncivilized nomad (vagrant) without permanent abode, or any degree of civility, who simply wanders from place to place, pursuing a life of theft, and for whom no state or other borders exist.

4. There is an ordinance of the Ministry of the Interior dated August 30, 1941, number 32661/41, that states that the so-called white Gypsy Muslims are not to be touched, because they are considered Aryan. Consequently, none of the measures proclaimed already or to be proclaimed in future regarding gypsies is to be applied to them.

This is why the Muslims of Zenica have decided to forward these conclusions and declarations to the most senior religious authorities, whom they request and urge to do the following:

- To do whatever is required as soon as possible to have the appropriate powers instruct the administrative authorities to ensure that Interior Ministry ordinance no. 32.661/41, dated 30-VIII-1941, is respected and this segment of our Muslim component is protected, like all Muslims with a permanent address and occupation.

- To demand as a matter of urgency that everyone already taken off to the concentration camps be returned to their homes and our Muslim community.

- To request the responsible authorities to hold any bodies or services acting in contravention of said ministerial ordinance of August 30, 1941, number 32661/41, accountable and to punish them accordingly.

In ZENICA, 26 May, 1942.

On behalf of the Muslims of the Zenica district:

Šaćir Konjhodžić, President of the District Court, Abdulah ef. Serdarević, Director of the Madrasah and President of the Waqf and Educational Committee, Mehmedalija Tarabar, landlord, Fadil Imamović, Judge, Ragib Hadžiabdić, Governor of the Prison, Hasib Mujić, Sharia Justice, Midhad Serdarević, Secretary of the Steelworks, Asim ef. Tarabar, jaamat imam, Muhamed Kundalić, Sharia Justice, Dr Hasan Muminagić, Physician, Mensur Serdarević, Manager at the Steelworks, Osman ef. Mutapčić, landlord, Mehmed ef. Čoloman, President of *El-Hidaje,* Teufik Limić, school principal, Husein-beg Kulenović, Treasurer of the Prison, Mustafa Šestić, businessman, Emir Mutapčić, businessman, Salih Mehmedić, businessman, Muhamed Selesković, official, Abdulah Tabaković, craftsman, Safvet Karić, Ahmed Osmanagić, official, Smail Soko, land registrar, Avdaga Hramandić, businessman, Salim Tarabar, landlord, Muhamed Salčinović, businessman, Mustafa Panić, businessman.

Zenički muslimani održali su sastanak povodom upućivanja u sabirne logore muslimana tako zvanih "Cigana" iz Travnika i povodom glasina, da će se isto tako postupiti i sa ostalim muslimanima tako zvanim "Ciganima"-Herceg-Bosne, pa su nakon svestranog proučavanja ovog za islamsku zajednicu vrlo važnog pitanja konstatovali sliježeće:

1/ Sveta, Uzvišena i zakonom priznata vjera Islam ne poznaje podjelu ljudi po rasi i klasi. Jedino priznaje razlikovanje, po uljudbi i pojedinačnoj vrijednosti, pošto su najpribraniji i najplemenitiji kod Boga dž.š. samo oni, koji se najtačnije drže propisa Vjere.

2/ Muslimani t. zvani "Cigani" jesu sastavni dio muslim. elementa u Herceg-Bosni. Oni se ni po čemu ne razlikuju od ostalih muslimana. Rađaju se i umru kao muslimani, vode se u istim matičnim knjigama, izvršavaju sve obrede Islama, žene se i udaju sa ostalim muslimanima i muslimani ih nikada nijesu ni smatrali, da su što drugo nego muslimani kao i ostali. U prošlosti se nije nikada dogodilo, da bi se oni tretirali drukčije. Uvijek su sa ostalim muslimanima jednako izvršavali i vjerske i državljanske dužnosti, a uživali su i ista prava kao i svi muslimani u svim vremenima svoje prošlosti i sadašnjosti. Svi muslimani bez razlike ih i sada kao i uvijek smatraju dijelom svoga vlastitog zajedničkog tijela, te najenergičnije i naješće osuđuju svako izdvajanje i razlikovanje ovih muslimana od ostalih. Svi muslimani hoće i jednodušno traže, da ovi muslimani imaju isti položaj i sudbinu kao i svi ostali muslimani Herceg-Bosne.

3/ Pod pojmom "Ciganin" imade se razumjeti samo necivilizovani nomad /skitnica/, koji nema stalnog nastana, niti određene uljudbi, nego se skita od mjesta do mjesta, provodi lupeški život i za-koga ne postoje nikakve ni državne ni druge granice.

4/ Postoji odredba Ministarstva unutarnjih poslova od 30/8. 1941. broj: 32.661/41, koja određuje, da se u tako zv. "Bijele Cigane" muslimane nema dirati, jer se isti imadu smatrati Arijevcima. Stoga se na iste ne smiju primjenjivati nikakve mjere već određene, ili koje će se u buduće odrediti protiv Cigana.

Prepis ove odredbe se prilaže.

Radi toga su Zenički muslimani odlučili, da ove svoje zaključke i konstatacije upute svojim najvišim vjerskim vlastima, od kojih mole i traže slijedeće:

1/ da se najžurnije učini sve potrebno, da mjerodavni faktori pozovu sve upravne vlasti, da se odredba Ministarstva unutarnjih poslova od 30/VIII. 1941. br. 32.661/41. strogo respektuje i da se ovaj dio našeg muslimanskog elementa kao i svi muslimani, koji imaju svoja stalna boravišta i zanimanja zaštite.

2/ da se najžurnije zatraži da se svi oni, koji su već odvedeni u sabirne logore povrate svojim kućama i našoj muslim. zajednici.

3/ da se zatraži od mjerodavnih faktora, da se one vlasti i organi, koji rade protivno Min. naredbi od 30/VIII. 1941. br. 32.661/41. pozovu na odgovornost i privedu zasluženoj kazni.

U ZENICI, 26 svibnja 1942.

Za muslimane Kotara Zeničkog:

Šaćir Konjhodžić Abdulah Serdarević Mehmedlalja Tarabar
predstojnik kot. suda s.r. direktor medrese i posjednik s.r.
 predsjednik Vak. mear.
 povjerenstva s.r.

Fadil Imamović Ragib Hadžiabdić Hasib Mujić
sudac s.r. upravitelj kaznione s.r. šer. sudac s.r.

The Zenica Resolution of 1942

Midhad Serdarević
tajnik željezare s.r.

Dr. Hasan Muminagić
liječnik s.r.

Mehmed ef. Coloman
posjednik-El-Hidaje s.r.

Mustafa Keatić
trgovac s.r.

Muhamed Selesković
činovnik s.r.

Ahmed Osmanagić
činovnik s.r.

Tarabar Salem
posjednik s.r.

Asim ef. Tarabar
džematski imam s.r.

Mensur Serdarević
činovnik željezare s.r.

Teufik Limić
šk. upravitelj s.r.

Enis Kutapčić
trgovac s.r.

Abdulah Tabaković
obrtnik s.r.

Smail Soko
gruntovničar s.r.

Muhamed Salčinović
trgovac s.r.

Muhamed Fundalić
šer. sudac s.r.

Osman ef. Kutarčić
posjednik s.r.

Kulenović Huseinbeg
blagajnik kaznione s.r.

Salih Mehmedić
trgovac s.r.

Karić Safvet s.r.

Avdaga Haramandić
trgovac s.r.

Mustafa Panjević
trgovac s.r.

The Zenica Resolution of 1942

BOSANSKA DUBICA RESOLUTION

The Bosanska Dubica Resolution, dated January 30, 1942, was signed by an unidentified group of prominent Bosniak citizens of Bosanska Dubica. It appears to be a general statement with no specified addressee, though it does include a list of "demands" or petitions. The only known copy of this resolution is in the Croatian State Archives *and is a transcript.*[1]

* * *

Shouldering with great difficulty the burdens of the ongoing war and exceptional circumstances currently prevailing in Bosnia and Herzegovina, and worried and disturbed by the disloyal and dishonorable deeds of irresponsible and reckless individuals from our town, we, the citizens of Bos[anska] Dubica, deeply outraged and sensible of our responsibility, have passed the following

RESOLUTION

Certain individuals, taking advantage of the revolutionary situation that arose during the first days of the Independent State of Croatia, have managed to impose themselves and usurp the Ustaša administration of our town, and, given their lack of the required reputation or personal and political morality or ability for the task, have recruited both the ignorant and the worst dregs of society into the armed Ustaša organization.

From their very first appearance, these newly minted and self-proclaimed Ustašas, who were previously the adherents of whatever government, current or apparatus was in power in the former Yugoslavia, made

---

1 Croatian State Archives (HDA, *Zbirka mikrofilmova gradiva iz inozemnih arhiva koje se odnosi na Hrvatsku* (ZMGIA-H), HR-HDA-1450, D-2179, MF59, 447. *Rezolucija Bos. Dubičkih Muslimana. Prilog dopisu Zapovjedničtva 3. oružničke pukovnije vojnim i redarstvenim vlastima u Zagrebu*. Datum: 30. siječanj 1942.)

clear how bad things were likely to get and how severe the consequences of their actions would be.

The persecution, looting, and killing of innocent and peaceful townsfolk and villagers of the Orthodox faith started immediately, and in the face of this violence the latter started to take to the woods and take up arms.

This is how the current insupportable and desperate situation arose, in which thousands of our sons, wives, and children are losing their lives, and villages and towns and the fruits of hard labor, sacrifice, and work are being destroyed in barbarous ways across our blood-stained Herceg-Bosna.

Even if the *Poglavnik's* Ordinance has restored normal conditions in the Independent State of Croatia, the members of the Ustaša *Logor* in our town are continuing with their violent methods and are in constant conflict with the district authorities, which, in accordance with the wishes of the majority of the honest, peaceloving, and industrious local citizenry, are attempting to restore order and peace and create trust in the regular authorities of the state.

In spite of this, the members of the Ustaša *Logor* are continuing their violence against the Orthodox population and so profaning the orders of the highest authorities and undermining the moral reputation of the Independent State of Croatia.

We note particularly that during the last [ethnic] cleansing action, and even though calls were distributed to the population to remain peacefully at home, with guarantees for their lives and property, our local Ustašas and others from the various companies that took part in this action most brutally massacred hundreds of children, women, and others, set upon in their own homes. They also plundered over a thousand head of livestock, some of which they slaughtered and distributed amongst the local population and themselves, while the rest was driven off in an unknown direction.

Conscious and honest citizens want order and peace restored, persecution, arson, slaughter and looting stoped, and an end to all violence against Orthodox residents who have remained peacefully living and working in their own homes, regardless of the fact that the Ustaša officials in Bos. Dubica have labeled them enemies of the state.

Our sons and brothers are fighting on the Eastern Front, serving and fighting in the Home Guard, or working in the mines and factories of Germany, while our villages are burning, and our labors and suffering go unseen. We have a moral right to demand our voice be heard. –

We want everyone here to enjoy peace and work and brotherly harmony, we want [a focus on] rebuilding, repairing, and productivity, and we want a bright tomorrow, unburdened by concerns. We want this and we have been waiting for it for a long time.

So, we ask that all Ustaša officials and armed members of the Ustaša *Logor* be relieved of their duties and subjected to the punishment they deserve.

We ask that no Ustaša companies be sent here at all, but only Home Guard companies.

We ask that the veracity of our claims be thoroughly and broadly looked into.

We ask that the petitions in this resolution be given proper consideration, because we do not want the suffer a similar fate to Kulen Vakuf and other places.

Finally, and in front of the entire nation, we reject any and all responsibility!

Followed by the signatures of prominent Dubica Muslims.

The Bosanska Dubica Resolution of 1942

BUGOJNO RESOLUTION

The Bugojno Resolution, dated June 5, 1942, was signed by an informal group of Bosniak citizens of Bugojno and initiated and supported by members of the Islamic Community. The text of the resolution is nearly identical to that of the Zenica Resolution. The original resolution with signatures is in the Archives of the Islamic Community of Bosnia and Herzegovina in the Gazi Husrev-Bey Library.[1]

* * *

The Muslims of Bugojno, having convened a meeting over the dispatch of the so-called "Gypsy" Muslims from Travnik to the concentration camps and rumors that the same is to be done with the other so-called "Gypsy" Muslims of Herzeg-Bosna, after thorough consideration of this issue of capital importance for the Islamic community, declare the following:

1. The holy, exalted and legally recognized religion of Islam does not itself recognize the categorization of people by race and class. The only distinctions it acknowledges are of civility and individual virtue, insofar as God, SWT, considers elect and most noble those who hold most closely to the precepts of the Faith.

2. The so-called "Gypsy" Muslims are an integral part of the Muslim component of Herzeg-Bosna. They do not differ from other Muslims in any way. They are born and die as Muslims, are entered into the same registers of birth, carry out all the same rituals of Islam, get married with other Muslims, and Muslims have never considered them anything other than Muslims like all the rest. They have always carried out their religious and official duties on an equal basis with all other Muslims and enjoyed all the same rights as all other Muslims at all times, past and present. All Muslims, without

---

1   Gazi Husrev-Bey Library, Archives of the Islamic Community of Bosnia and Herzegovina (GHB, ARIZBIH, UM, 1712/42).

distinction, consider them now, as they always have, to be part of their common body and condemn in the strongest and most strenuous terms possible any separating out or differentiation of these Muslims from the rest. All Muslims want and unanimously seek that these Muslims be accorded the same status and destiny as all the other Muslims in Herzeg-Bosna.

3. The term "Gypsies" applies properly to uncivilized nomads (vagrants), without permanent abode or any degree of civility, who simply wander from place to place, pursuing a life of theft, and for whom no state or other borders exist.

4. Existing ordinance no. 32.661/41 of the Ministry of the Interior, dated 30.VIII.1941, stipulates that the so-called "White Gypsy" muslims are not to be touched, because they are to be considered Aryans. As a result, <u>no measures imposed on Gypsies</u> previously or <u>in the future shall apply to them</u>.

A transcript of this provision is attached.

This is why the Muslims of Bugojno have decided to forward these conclusions and declarations to the most senior religious authorities, whom they request and urge to do the following:

1. To do whatever is required as soon as possible to have the appropriate powers instruct the administrative authorities to ensure that Interior Ministry ordinance no. 32.661/41, dated 30-VIII-1941, is respected and this segment of our Muslim component be protected, like all Muslims with a permanent address and occupation.

2. To demand as a matter of urgency that everyone already taken off to the concentration camps be returned to their homes and our Muslim community.

3. To request the responsible authorities to hold any bodies or services acting in contravention of said ministerial ordinance of August 30, 1941, number 32661/41, accountable and to punish them accordingly.

In Bugojno, 5 June, 1942.

For the Muslims of Bugojno district:

Abdulah Mustajbegović, jaamat imam, Hajder Rustempašić, Muharem Krajinić, Sharia Justice, Kasim Terzić, Sharia Justice, Spaho Karadža, Deputy Municipal Mayor, Dervišbey Bušatlija, landlord, Avdo Čizmo, Hasan Alibegović, Ilijas Rustempašić, businessman, Zekir Sulejmanpašić, Jusuf Babić, tailor, Agija Bečirović, Muhamed Bečirović, Dervo Karabeg, Hađo P....., Ibro Karadža, Abdulah A. Karabeg, notary, Salih Šečić, tailor, Rasim Mešić, Hakija Abdalajbegović, Akif Šupić, (illegible), (illegible), Smailbeg Filipović, (illegible), Alija Mlaćo, Sabrija Hadžialić, landlord, Husein (illegible), Redžep Hrgić, teacher, Idrizbey Idrizović, landlord, Mehmed (illegible), shoemaker, Mehmed Hadžibegović, landlord, Muhlisija Kasumović, businessman, Asim Hrgić, metalworker, Muhamed Ćerkez, barber, Nezir Bosto, Ahmed Robović, businessman, Avdo Karadža, tailor, Ibro Ždralović, laborer, Ešref Hadžialić, Zajim Bečirović, laborer, Halil Hamaš...(illegible), laborer, Haki bey Bušatlija, landlord, Mustajbeg (illegible), Muhamed M......(illegible), imam and registrar

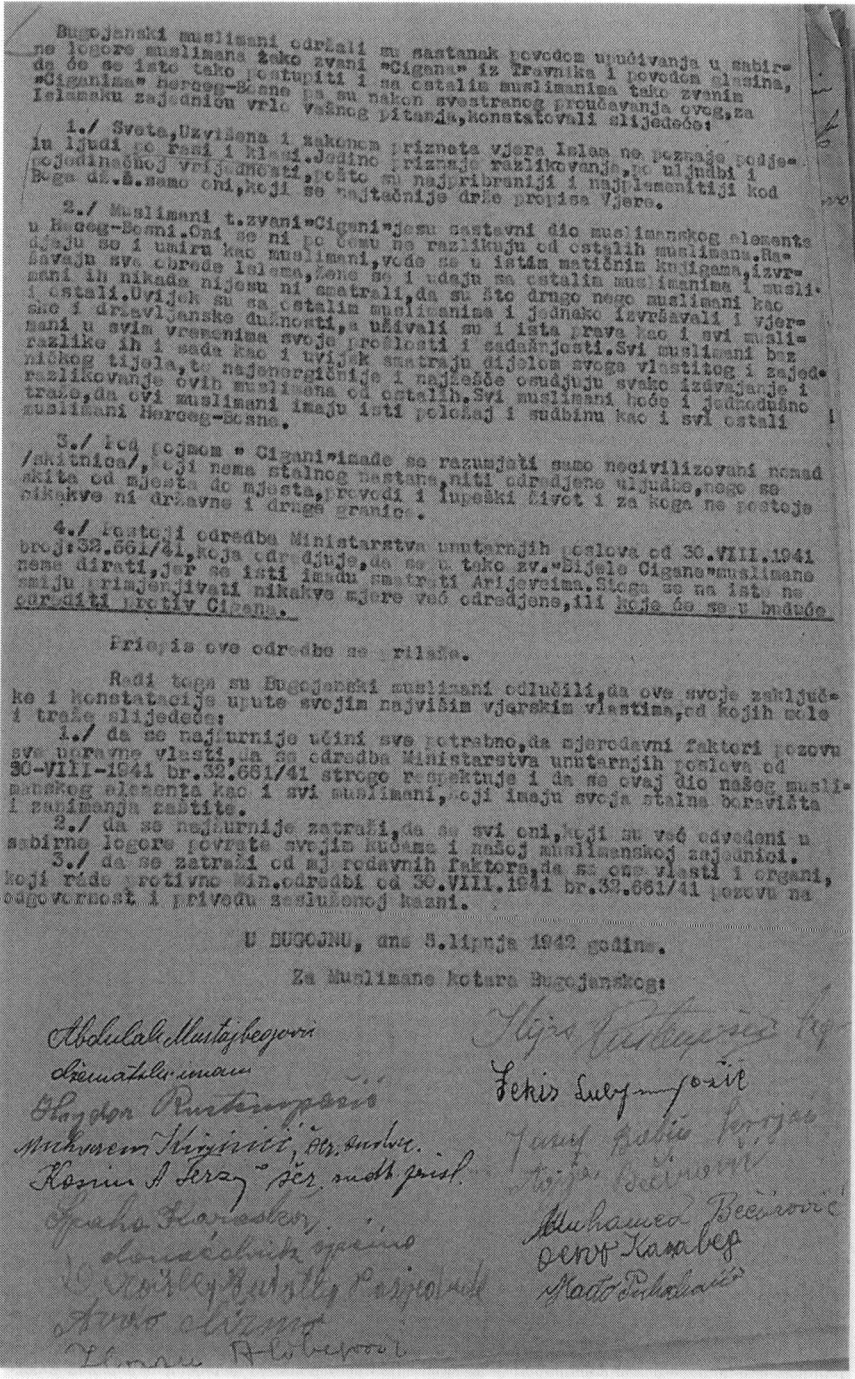

The Bugojno Resolution of 1942

CONTRIBUTORS

Adnan Jahić is Full Professor of Modern History at the Faculty of Philosophy, University of Tuzla, Bosnia and Herzegovina.

Desmond Maurer is Director of the Centre for Historical Studies at International Forum Bosnia, Sarajevo, Bosnia and Herzegovina.

Ermin Sinanović is Executive Director of the Center for Islam in the Contemporary World (CICW) at Shenandoah University, Virginia, USA.

Ferid Dautović is the Director of the Institute for Islamic Tradition of Bosniaks in Sarajevo, Bosnia and Herzegovina.

Hikmet Karčić is Senior Researcher of Genocide Studies at the Institute for Islamic Tradition of Bosniaks in Sarajevo, Bosnia and Herzegovina.

Marko Attila Hoare is Associate Professor and Head of Research at the Department of Political Science and International Relations of the Sarajevo School of Science and Technology, Bosnia and Herzegovina.

Xavier Bougarel is a Researcher at CETOBAC, Centre d'études turques, ottomanes, balkaniques et centrasiatiques, in Paris, France.

INDEX

A
Alajbegović, Mehmed 64
Albania 41–42, 44, 48, 50
Artuković, Andrija 118
Austria-Hungary 40, 42, 44–45, 180
autonomy 7–8, 38, 43, 46, 52, 96, 109, 121, 129–130, 141–142

B
Bajraktarević, Hasan 22, 137, 169–170
Balkan 41, 44–45, 50, 55, 58, 60–61, 99
Bandžović, Safet 5, 9, 15, 60, 103, 105–107, 109, 111–113, 115, 117, 119, 121, 123, 125, 127, 129, 131
Banja Luka 6, 9, 12–16, 21–23, 83, 87–90, 92–93, 95–98, 103, 106, 108, 120, 122–123, 127–128, 130–131, 143, 145, 159, 183, 185, 187–194
Banja Luka 6, 9, 12–16, 21–23, 83, 87–90, 92–93, 95–98, 103, 106, 108, 120, 122–123, 127–128, 130–131, 143, 145, 159, 183, 185, 187–194
Bašić, Salih 160
Belgrade 31, 41, 49–51, 67, 70–71, 77–78, 80, 84, 88, 98, 109, 113–116, 119, 135, 140, 145
Bešlagić, Hilmija 92, 96, 103, 119, 183
Bihać 57, 78, 128, 143
Bijeljina 6, 9, 15–16, 23, 92–93, 104, 120–121, 127, 134–135, 143, 146, 149, 195, 197, 199–200
Bileća 69–70, 72, 111
Bosanska Dubica 6, 9, 15–16, 85–86, 121, 149, 211, 214
Bosanska Krupa 78, 97, 128
Bosnia and Herzegovina 1, 3, 9, 11–12, 16–17, 21–23, 31, 36–40, 42–48, 51, 55, 57, 59–60, 63–64, 67–68, 71, 75, 77, 83, 92, 96, 98, 100–102, 104–106, 108–110, 112, 114, 116–124, 126–142, 144, 146–147, 151–153, 155–156, 158, 160, 162, 164–166, 168, 170, 172, 174, 176, 179–180, 182–184, 186, 188, 190, 192, 194, 196, 198, 200–202, 205–206, 208, 211–212, 214–216, 218

Bougarel, Xavier 5, 9, 16, 25, 133, 135, 137
Bugojno 6, 9, 15, 17, 106, 149, 215–218

C
Cazin 78, 97, 128

Č
Čajniće 117
Čaušević, Džemaludin 67, 75, 80–81, 84, 160, 169
Četnik 53–56, 68–69, 72, 76, 88, 97, 101, 104, 113–115, 120, 124, 139, 146, 201

Ć
Ćemerlić, Asim-beg 106

D
Dobrača, Kasim 19–20, 23, 75–76, 168
Dulić, Tomislav 60, 68, 98–99, 101–102, 135

Đ
Đozo, Husein 137, 169

E
El-Hidaje 6, 8–9, 15, 19–20, 22, 34, 67–68, 74–76, 80, 98, 119, 134–137, 143, 149, 151, 153, 165–166, 168–169, 179, 181, 183, 205, 207

F
Ferdinand, Archduke Franz 44
First World War 43–45
Foča 80, 106, 113, 117, 127
Fočak, Muhamed 19–20, 169–170
Francetić, Jure 71, 121, 127

G

Gajret 96, 180

Gestapo 115

Goražde 105, 117

Greble, Emily 15, 60, 99, 104

H

Habsburg empire 40

Hadžić, Hakija 64, 69, 90, 119, 140, 142, 156, 168, 188, 197

Hadžihasanović, Uzeir-aga 80, 142–143, 146

Hadžijahić, Muhamed 14–15, 64, 75, 94, 104, 123, 131, 170

Handžić, Mehmed 19–20, 67, 75, 80, 119, 136, 169

Hasanbegović, Zlatko 66, 73, 92, 99

Hitler, Adolf 15, 49–50, 54, 59–60, 99, 102, 104

Humo, Avdo 126

I

Islamic Community 16–17, 19, 22–23, 123, 151, 155, 165, 179, 183, 195, 201, 205, 215

Italy 45, 50, 102

J

Jahić, Adnan 5, 9, 17, 63, 65, 67–69, 71, 73, 75–77, 79, 81, 83, 85, 87, 89, 91, 93–95, 97, 99, 101, 109, 160, 189, 198

Jasenovac 7, 13, 51, 57, 59, 127

Jews 7, 12, 15, 21, 31, 51–53, 58–60, 71, 98–99, 104, 107–109, 112–113, 118–119, 122–123, 127–128, 133, 135, 187

K

Karađorđević, King Aleksandar 46, 124

Karađorđević, King Peter II 46, 124

Kingdom of Serbs, Croats, and Slovenes 45, 101

Konjic 87

Kulen Vakuf 75, 86, 91, 97, 117, 186, 213
Kulenović, Džafer 22, 49, 63–67, 72, 89, 93, 119–120, 142–143, 170, 183, 188–189, 201, 207
Kurt, Muhamed 109

M

Merhamet 22
Mešić, Adem-aga 107, 119, 156, 160, 217
Mihajlović, Draža 113
Mostar 6, 9, 12, 14–16, 21, 23, 53, 70–72, 92, 120, 122–124, 126, 131, 134, 143–144, 149, 179, 181–182
Muslim Resolutions 1, 3, 5–6, 8–9, 11–13, 15, 17, 19, 21, 23, 31, 33, 35, 37, 39, 41, 43, 45, 47, 49, 51, 53, 55, 57–59, 61, 63, 65, 67, 69, 71, 73, 75, 77, 79, 81, 83, 85–87, 89, 91, 93–95, 97–147, 149, 152, 156, 158, 160, 162, 164, 166, 168, 170, 172, 174, 176, 180, 182, 184, 186, 188, 190, 192, 194, 196, 198, 200, 202, 206, 208, 212, 214, 216, 218

N

Narodna Uzdanica 22, 80, 195
Nazi Germany 7, 15, 137
Nurkić, Mustafa 22, 188

O

Ottoman 38–43, 58, 60, 100, 134, 138, 195
Ottoman empire 40

P

Pandža, Mehmed 22, 136–137, 169
Partisans 54, 59–60, 76, 81, 109, 112, 116–117, 137, 141
Pašić, Murat-beg 22–23, 93, 109, 121, 135, 168, 181, 197
Pavelić, Ante 7, 19, 50, 64, 66, 94, 103, 107, 124, 127, 130–131, 136, 143
Preporod 105–107, 111, 113, 123, 131
Prijedor 6, 9, 11, 15, 68, 80–85, 87, 97, 120, 127, 131, 135, 143–144, 149, 155–159, 161–164

R

Radić, Stjepan 45, 47
Rahman, Fazlur 29
Reisu-l-ulema 12, 66, 70, 73
Rogatica 106, 108, 110, 117
Roma 7, 17, 31, 33, 51–52, 58, 113, 118, 127, 133, 146

S

Salihagić, Suljaga 22, 90, 92, 96–97, 170, 197
Sandžak 7, 42, 44, 46, 48, 50, 74, 101, 114, 117, 135, 153
Sanski Most 82–83, 97, 128, 159
Sarajevo 3, 6, 8–9, 11–16, 19–23, 44, 60, 64–65, 67–71, 75–76, 78, 80, 86–87, 89, 91–94, 98–99, 104–109, 111, 113, 116–120, 122–124, 126–127, 129–131, 133, 136–137, 140, 142–146, 149, 151, 165, 167–177, 179, 187, 195
Serbia 7, 16, 38–42, 44–45, 48, 50–52, 54–55, 60, 84, 96, 104, 113–115, 130, 135–136, 183, 201
Serbian Orthodox Church 84, 101
Serbs 7, 12, 21, 31–35, 40, 44–47, 52–53, 55–57, 60, 66, 69, 73–74, 76, 81, 83–85, 89, 91–93, 95–96, 98, 101, 103–116, 118–120, 122–124, 126–128, 133–135, 139, 142–145, 157, 165, 179, 186–187, 195–196, 201–202
Skaka, Ahmed 137, 170
Softić, Mustafa 160, 169, 189
Spaho, Fehim 48, 63, 66–68, 70–74, 89, 100, 124, 217
Spaho, Mehmed 48, 63, 66–68, 70–74, 89, 100, 124, 217
Srebrenica 106, 117
Stepinac, Alojize 101
Stolac 72

Š

Šarac, Zaim 76

T

Tanzimat 39

Tito, Josip Broz 35, 48, 137
Travnik 89, 106, 146, 185, 205, 215
Turkey 48, 141
Tuzla 6, 9, 15–16, 69–71, 81, 89, 92–93, 106, 108–109, 120–121, 123, 131, 136, 143, 145, 149, 201–203

U

Ugljen, Asim 73
Ustaša 7–9, 13–14, 16–17, 19, 21, 31, 34–35, 37, 40, 50–54, 56, 59, 63–69, 71, 73–74, 77–78, 80–88, 90, 93–95, 97–99, 102–111, 114, 116, 118–120, 123–124, 126–131, 133–137, 139–144, 146–147, 156–158, 183, 185, 195, 211–213

V

Višegrad 17, 105, 117
Vlasenica 106, 117

Y

Yugoslav Muslim Organization 49, 63, 143
Yugoslavia 7, 12, 19, 31, 37, 39, 47–50, 55, 57–59, 66–67, 76, 81, 85, 88, 96–97, 99–103, 105, 112, 114, 116, 126, 139, 141, 146–147, 180, 211

Z

Zagreb 31, 35, 49, 63–68, 72, 83, 95, 100, 105, 111–112, 117, 121, 129–130, 140, 157, 183
Zenica 6, 9, 15–16, 23, 105, 113, 146, 149, 205–209, 215
Zulfikarpašić, Adil 8, 14, 16, 80, 106, 112, 169, 197

Made in the USA
Columbia, SC
13 July 2021